Design of Experiential Bilingual Teaching for Traditional Chinese Culture

中国传统文化体验式双语教学设计

初清华
孙慧莉 主编

中央编译出版社
Central Compilation & Translation Press

图书在版编目（CIP）数据

中国传统文化体验式双语教学设计：汉文、英文／初清华，孙慧莉主编． —北京：中央编译出版社，2023.11
ISBN 978－7－5117－4526－2

Ⅰ. ①中… Ⅱ. ①初… ②孙… Ⅲ. ①中华文化－文化传播－研究 ②汉语－对外汉语教学－教学研究 Ⅳ. ①G125 ②H195.3

中国国家版本馆 CIP 数据核字（2023）第 191288 号

中国传统文化体验式双语教学设计

责任编辑	郑永杰
执行编辑	周雪凝
责任印制	李　颖
出版发行	中央编译出版社
网　　址	www.cctpcm.com
地　　址	北京市海淀区北四环西路 69 号（100080）
电　　话	（010）55627391（总编室）　　（010）55627311（编辑室）
	（010）55627320（发行部）　　（010）55627377（新技术部）
经　　销	全国新华书店
印　　刷	北京印刷集团有限责任公司印刷一厂
开　　本	710 毫米×1000 毫米　1/16
字　　数	264 千字
印　　张	17.25
版　　次	2023 年 11 月第 1 版
印　　次	2023 年 11 月第 1 次印刷
定　　价	120.00 元

新浪微博：@中央编译出版社　　　微　信：中央编译出版社（ID: cctphome）
淘宝店铺：中央编译出版社直销店（http://shop108367160.taobao.com）　（010）55627331

本社常年法律顾问：北京市吴栾赵阎律师事务所律师　闫军　梁勤
凡有印装质量问题，本社负责调换，电话：（010）55627320

前　言

《中国传统文化体验式双语教学设计》是一本为汉语国际教育专业"传统文化体验与双语传播实践"课程量身打造的教材。

党的十八大以来，以习近平同志为核心的党中央高度重视思想文化建设，明确提出要坚定文化自信，增强文化自觉，"坚定文化自信，是事关国运兴衰、事关文化安全、事关民族精神独立性的大问题"[①]。《中国传统文化体验式双语教学设计》以此为指导，旨在帮助汉语国际教育专业学生掌握中华优秀传统文化的国际表达形式、当代价值和国际影响，掌握相关文化技艺及文化双语教学的步骤和方法，从而提升用英语进行中华优秀传统文化传播的理论和实践水平，助力中华优秀传统文化"走出去"。

一、编写理念

1. 以"建强适应新时代国际传播需要的专门人才队伍"为编写初衷

习近平同志强调，"要全面提升国际传播效能，建强适应新时代国际传播需要的专门人才队伍"[②]。国际中文教育是国家和民族的事业，汉语国际教育专业学生承担着对外传播汉语和中华优秀文化的重任。编写一本翔实、生动的中华优秀传统文化双语教学设计用书，能够夯实汉语国际教育专业学生

[①] 习近平：在中国文联十大、中国作协九大开幕式上的讲话．参见：http://www.xinhuanet.com//politics/2016-11/30/c_1120025319.htm? eqid=fff342320050100a0000000664313536。

[②] 习近平主持中共中央政治局第三十次集体学习并讲话．参见：https://www.gov.cn/xinwen/2021-06/01/content_5614684.htm。

中华优秀传统文化的根基,帮助他们熟悉中华优秀传统文化的国际化表达形式,熟稔中华优秀传统文化的当代价值和国际表征,从而助力海外中华优秀文化教学及传播的顺利开展。

2. 坚持"讲好中国故事,传播好中国声音"

习近平同志强调,"用海外读者乐于接受的方式、易于理解的语言,讲述好中国故事,传播好中国声音"①。故事以其富有吸引力、能够感染人而深受读者欢迎。好的故事,既能"通事",也能"通心"。我们将"用英语讲好中国故事"作为教材编写的基本理念之一:主题文化的起源,统一以精悍、有趣的中华小故事呈现;教案设计中,我们更强调教师变身故事的讲述者和实践者,通过讲好中国故事来增强中华优秀传统文化的感染力,从而实现"向世界阐释推介更多具有中国特色、体现中国精神、蕴藏中国智慧的优秀文化"②。

3. 将"课程思政"贯穿教材编写的始终

教育的根本任务是立德树人,是培养青少年成为担当民族复兴大任的时代新人。中华优秀传统文化是中华民族的精神命脉,中华文化强调"民为邦本""德不孤,必有邻""言必信,行必果",习近平同志认为,这些思想"不论过去还是现在,都有其鲜明的民族特色,都有其永不褪色的时代价值"③。在本书的编写过程中,我们始终秉持"课程思政"理念,将中华优秀传统文化的思想精髓润物无声地融入字里行间:揭示中国人民对幸福、美好生活的向往和追求以及对先进科学技术的孜孜探索等。教材讲稿中还专辟一节,探讨主题文化的当代价值和世界影响力,旨在以跨文化的视角探寻中华优秀传统文化在国际舞台上的表征,从而帮助学生树立文化自信,坚定社会主义核心价值观。我们也希望,当我们的学生真正能够用积淀千年的中华优秀传统文化培根铸魂、启智润心、强健修养、明辨曲直时,也能够自觉于中

---

① 习近平就人民日报海外版创刊 30 周年作出重要批示. 参见:https://www.gov.cn/xinwen/2015-05/21/content_2866369.htm。

② 习近平主持中共中央政治局第三十次集体学习并讲话. 参见:https://www.gov.cn/xinwen/2021-06/01/content_5614684.htm。

③ 习近平在北京大学师生座谈会上的讲话. 参见:https://www.gov.cn/xinwen/2014-05/05/content_2671258.htm?eqid=f3da0a2f0008dc0000000003648a9929。

·前 言·

华文化的对外传播。

二、教材架构

《中国传统文化体验式双语教学设计》全书共十章。第一至五章为传统节日文化双语教学设计，按时间顺序依次为春节文化双语教学设计、元宵节文化双语教学设计、端午节文化双语教学设计、七夕节文化双语教学设计和中秋节文化双语教学设计；第六至十章为民间工艺及技艺双语教学设计，包括中国结文化双语教学设计、泥塑文化双语教学设计、刺绣文化双语教学设计、篆刻文化双语教学设计和中医推拿文化双语教学设计。

每一主题的双语教学设计单元均由双语讲稿和双语教案组成，其中讲稿部分以生动的"中国故事"介绍该文化的起源，同时辅以操作性强、简单有趣、图文并茂的文化体验设计；教案部分详细展示该文化的课堂教学思路和教学步骤。讲稿和教案均由中英文双语撰写。

三、编写特色

1. 以原创双语故事夯实双语教学设计的厚度

本书不仅提供具体的中华文化双语教案，更为重要的是，提供了生动、翔实的中华文化双语讲稿：以"起源—特点—跨文化比较—体验"为线索组织双语讲稿，每一部分都力求资料翔实、文笔生动、图文并茂，这也使得我们的双语讲稿独具特色。我们希望通过具体翔实的原创文稿助力文化教学，从而夯实中华传统文化双语教学设计的厚度。

2. 以跨文化的视角拓宽双语教学设计的广度

与其他介绍中华优秀传统文化的教材不同，本书不但介绍传统文化的历史和特征，还专设章节探讨传统文化的现代表征，如"世界各地的春节文化""中西情人节文化比较"等，以跨文化的视角，摆事实、举案例，从而赋予中华优秀传统文化以当代生命力和当代价值，拓宽中华传统文化双语教学设计的广度。

3. 以文化体验增加双语教学设计的趣味度

本书摆脱了以往文化读物仅对文化做知识性介绍的传统，创造性地加入文化体验教学设计，即配合文化点设计实践操作，如包饺子、制作月饼、教授中医推拿手法等。通过文化体验设计，一方面，提升汉语国际教育专业学生传播中华优秀传统文化的水平和技能；另一方面，帮助对中国文化感兴趣的外国读者，通过参与文化体验，加深对中华文化的体认与感知。

四、结语

中华文化博大精深、源远流长，短短十章篇幅远无法尽数呈现，我们希望以本书的编写为契机，助力今后呈现更多高质量的中华优秀传统文化、革命文化和社会主义先进文化双语教学设计，真正承担起中华文化传播者、践行者的培养重任。后续，本书编写团队还将推出双语教学短视频并通过虚拟仿真技术构建文化体验馆，以更加丰富的资源和手段助推中华优秀文化"走出去"。

使用说明

　　本书适用于汉语国际教育专业"传统文化体验与双语传播实践"课程。本书包含十章,分别是春节文化双语教学设计、元宵节文化双语教学设计、端午节文化双语教学设计、七夕节文化双语教学设计、中秋节文化双语教学设计、中国结文化双语教学设计、泥塑文化双语教学设计、刺绣文化双语教学设计、篆刻文化双语教学设计和中医推拿文化双语教学设计。

　　本书旨在帮助汉语国际教育专业学生掌握以上节日文化和民间工艺及技艺的英语表达方式,培养学生双语传播中华传统文化的能力。双语讲稿部分,汉语国际教育专业学生可以了解该文化的起源、特点,在海外的传播现状以及与海外相似文化的比较。与此同时,讲稿中的文化体验,旨在帮助汉语国际教育专业学生掌握与文化相关的手工及技艺,使未来面向海外受众的中华文化教学更有趣味性。与此同时,双语讲稿内容可在授课时灵活取材。

　　本书的教案以中英双语撰写,按照每课时 40 分钟进行设置,每章文化课预计用时三课时共 120 分钟。第一课时,以文化起源小故事导入新课,并介绍该文化的重要特征,传统节日文化以介绍文化习俗为主,民间工艺及技艺以介绍文化特点为主。第二课时,以中外文化比较或中华传统文化的海外传播为主要内容,在比较中帮助外国受众加深对中华传统文化现代表征的理解。第三课时,为文化体验设计,从文化特点出发,教授外国受众与该文化有关

的手工体验，如包饺子、包粽子、制作月饼、刺绣等。教学过程中可灵活调整时长，如文化体验环节的动手操作相对复杂，则可适当延长体验环节的授课用时，同时压缩文化知识的传授时长。

目 录

第一章　春节文化双语教学设计 ……………………………………… 1
导语 ………………………………………………………………… 2
第一节　春节的习俗：团圆饭、守岁、拜年 ……………………… 2
第二节　世界各地的多元春节：爆竹声中一岁除，春风送暖入屠苏 … 8
第三节　"荠菜中含著齿鲜"：学习包饺子 ……………………… 11
第四节　春节文化双语教案 ……………………………………… 15
讨论与练习 ………………………………………………………… 23

第二章　元宵节文化双语教学设计 ……………………………………… 27
导语 ………………………………………………………………… 28
第一节　元宵节的习俗：舞龙、观灯、吃汤圆 ……………………… 29
第二节　今天的元宵节：龙狮飞舞四大洋，花灯照耀七大洲 ……… 34
第三节　"一碗汤圆情万千"：动手包汤圆 ……………………… 37
第四节　元宵节文化双语教案 ……………………………………… 41
讨论与练习 ………………………………………………………… 50

第三章　端午节文化双语教学设计 ……………………………………… 53
导语 ………………………………………………………………… 54

第一节　端午节的习俗：龙舟、粽子、五彩绳……………………… 54
　　第二节　世界各地的端午节：龙舟驰骋四大洋，粽叶飘香七大洲…… 59
　　第三节　"彩线轻缠红玉臂"：学做五彩绳 ……………………… 62
　　第四节　端午节文化双语教案 …………………………………… 69
　　讨论与练习 ……………………………………………………… 78

第四章　七夕节文化双语教学设计 …………………………… 81
　　导语 ……………………………………………………………… 82
　　第一节　七夕节的习俗：祭月、乞巧、吃巧果……………………… 83
　　第二节　今天的七夕节：两情若是久长时，又岂在朝朝暮暮………… 86
　　第三节　"秾艳尽怜胜彩绘"：动手折纸玫瑰 …………………… 91
　　第四节　七夕节文化双语教案 …………………………………… 99
　　讨论与练习 ……………………………………………………… 108

第五章　中秋节文化双语教学设计 …………………………… 111
　　导语 ……………………………………………………………… 112
　　第一节　中秋节的习俗：饮桂花酒、赏月、吃月饼 ……………… 112
　　第二节　今天的中秋节：佳节共赏天上月，中秋一品人间情 …… 117
　　第三节　"饼有酥与馅"：制作冰皮月饼 ………………………… 120
　　第四节　中秋节文化双语教案 …………………………………… 128
　　讨论与练习 ……………………………………………………… 136

第六章　中国结文化双语教学设计 …………………………… 139
　　导语 ……………………………………………………………… 140
　　第一节　中国结的分类 …………………………………………… 140
　　第二节　中国结的海外传播：托结寓美意 ……………………… 145
　　第三节　"百年有结是同心"：同心结的制作 …………………… 148
　　第四节　中国结文化双语教案 …………………………………… 152

| 讨论与练习 | 160 |

第七章　泥塑文化双语教学设计　　163

导语	164
第一节　泥塑的技法	164
第二节　泥塑与西方雕塑的"和而不同"	167
第三节　"活脱世间泥塑样"：泥塑的体验	172
第四节　泥塑文化双语教案	176
讨论与练习	184

第八章　刺绣文化双语教学设计　　187

导语	188
第一节　四大名绣	188
第二节　刺绣的国际性传播与融合	192
第三节　"古壁丹青色，新花绮绣纹"：苏绣体验	195
第四节　刺绣文化双语教案	203
讨论与练习	211

第九章　篆刻文化双语教学设计　　213

导语	214
第一节　篆刻的分类	215
第二节　"方寸之间，便是天地"：金石文化的传播与交流	220
第三节　"拈笔古心生篆刻"：篆刻体验	223
第四节　篆刻文化双语教案	228
讨论与练习	236

第十章　中医推拿文化双语教学设计　　239

| 导语 | 240 |

第一节　推拿的手法及穴位 …………………………………………… 241
第二节　奥运会上神秘的东方力量：推拿走向世界 ………………… 245
第三节　推拿的体验 …………………………………………………… 248
第四节　中医推拿文化双语教案 ……………………………………… 252
讨论与练习 ……………………………………………………………… 261

后　记 …………………………………………………………………… 264

第一章 春节文化双语教学设计
Chapter Ⅰ Bilingual Teaching Design of the Spring Festival

春节（黄婧瑶 绘）
The Spring Festival（By Huang Jingyao）

中国传统文化体验式双语教学设计

导语
Introduction

从前，凶猛的年兽总是在年末来到村子里伤害村民，直到一位神奇的老爷爷带来了打败年兽的三件法宝——红色、火光和爆竹声。年兽再走进村子，发现村里灯火通明，到处都是红色。门窗上贴着红纸，院子里挂着红灯笼，人们也都穿着红色的衣服，年兽的眼睛被红色刺得睁不开。院子里又传出竹子燃烧的声音，响声震天，年兽被吓得逃走，再也没有来过。从此，人们过上了安宁的生活。

Once upon a time, the ferocious Nian always came to the village at the end of the year to hurt the villagers, until an elderly brought villagers three magic weapons to defeat Nian: red, fire and firecrackers. Nian entered the village and found that the village was brightly lit. There were red papers on the windows and doors, red lanterns hanging in the yard. People were also dressed in red clothes. The sound of bamboo burning in the yard was so loud that the beast was frightened to run away without coming back. From then on, people started to have a peaceful life.

第一节　春节的习俗：团圆饭、守岁、拜年
Section 1　Customs of the Spring Festival: Having a Family Reunion Dinner, Staying up, Sending New Year Wishes

春节历史悠久，是中国民间最隆重的传统节日，传承至今已形成了一些较为固定的习俗。在春节期间，全国各地都会举行丰富多彩的贺岁活动，如买年货、扫房、祭祖、贴对联、吃团圆饭、守岁、拜年、舞狮等。但因为地域文化不同，习俗的内容和形式上存在一些差异。藏族人民会在除夕夜举行盛大的"跳神会"，表示除旧迎新，驱邪降福；壮族人民会在初一清早，去

河边装一壶"新水",期盼新年新气象。

The Spring Festival is the grandest traditional festival among Chinese folk with a long history. Some customs have been established and maintained until today. A variety of activities are held throughout the country to celebrate the Spring Festival, such as New Year shopping, cleaning houses, offering sacrifices to ancestors, pasting red couplets, having a family reunion dinner, staying up until the first day of the new year, sending New Year wishes, watching lion dances and so on. However, people from different regions have different ways of celebration. For example, the Tibetan people will gather for traditional dances on Lunar New Year's Eve to ward off the old, welcome the new, and drive away evil spirits. The Zhuang people will go to the river and fill up a bottle of water in the early morning of the first day of the New Year, expressing their anticipation of a new year.

1. 团圆饭

大年三十晚上的团圆饭是春节的重要习俗之一。团圆饭,是全家人的团圆聚餐,也是一年中最丰盛的一顿饭。中国人从有"年"的概念开始,就有了团圆饭一说。人们通常在农历除夕这一天与家人欢聚一堂、享受美食,一起迎接新年的到来。

传统团圆饭的菜肴蕴含美好的寓意,饱含对未来幸福生活的期待。不过因地域文化不同,团圆饭的菜品也有所差异。在中国南方地区,团圆饭中有两道菜肴必不可少:一是一条头尾完整的鱼,象征年年有余;二是在南方俗称"圆子"的丸子,象征团团圆圆。吃完团圆饭,长辈通常会给晚辈发压岁钱。压岁钱包含了长辈对晚辈平安度岁的祝福,其象征意义远超实际价值。而在北方地区,团圆饭以饺子为主。人们在年三十晚上会提前将饺子包好,待到半夜12点吃,取"新旧交替"之义。又因白面饺子形似银元宝,所以也象征着"新年大发财,元宝滚进来"。此外,人们在包饺子时,还会将花生、红枣、糖、硬币等吉祥的物品放入馅中,表达对新的一年的美好愿望。

1. Family Reunion Dinner

An important custom during the Spring Festival is the family reunion dinner on New Year's Eve, which has a history as long as the Lunar New Year. The family reunion dinner is the biggest feast for the family in the whole year. Family members gather to enjoy delicious food and welcome the New Year.

The food in the family reunion dinner implies best wishes and expectations for a joyful life in the future. However, people from different regions in China enjoy various dishes at the family reunion dinner. In southern China, there are two essential dishes: a fish with a complete head and tail, symbolizing the abundance year after year; balls, commonly known as "yuan-zi" in the south, symbolizing reunion. After the family reunion dinner, the elder usually gives the younger generation the red envelope enclosing money. The red envelope implies the blessings to the younger generation to have a safe year, and its symbolic meaning far exceeds the actual value. In northern China, dumplings are the main dish at the family reunion dinner. People will make dumplings in advance and eat them at midnight of New Year's Eve, symbolizing the old and the new alternation. Dumplings also symbolize "making a fortune in the New Year" as the shape looks like silver. In addition, people put peanuts, jujubes, candies, coins into dumpling fillings to express good wishes for the upcoming year.

2. 守岁

吃团圆饭后，人们通宵不寐、守候新年，这种形式叫作"守岁"。全家人围在火炉旁话家常，一直聊到五更天明，共同期待着新一年的满满幸福。

守岁习俗兴起于西晋，不少文人都创作过有关守岁的诗文。"一夜连双岁，五更分二天。"人们点起蜡烛或油灯，通宵守夜，象征着把一切邪瘟病疫照跑驱走，迎来新一年的吉祥如意。在古代，守岁是为父母或家中老人祈寿的重要方式，因此一般人都会坚持守岁。如今这种习俗仍然普遍，主要表现为一家团聚，通宵守夜，辞旧迎新。一家人围坐在一起享受这团圆的时光，茶点瓜果放满一桌，看春节联欢晚会、打麻将、推牌九等，娱乐活动十分丰富。

2. Staying up

People stay up all night after the family reunion dinner waiting for the New Year. The whole family gathers around the fireplace and chats until dawn to welcome a joyful new year.

Chinese people have been staying up to celebrate the Spring Festival since the Westean Jin Dynasty. Many literati have written poems about staying up. "The old year greets the new year tonight. It is the time to say farewell to the old and welcome the new when the sun rises." People light candles or oil lamps and stay awake all night, driving away all evil plagues and welcoming the auspiciousness of the New Year. In ancient times, staying up was an important way to pray for the longevity of parents or the elderly at home, which was why most people stayed up. This custom still maintains today. The family members reunite and stay up together, enjoying various refreshments and having diverse entertainment activities, such as watching Spring Festival Gala Show, playing mahjong, playing Pai Gow, etc.

3. 拜年

拜年是中国民间的传统习俗,是人们相互表达美好祝愿的一种方式。正月初一,人们开始拜年贺岁。中国人春节拜年大多遵循由内及外、由近及远的原则。初一在家拜祖先、家尊、宗族至亲,初二出门拜姻亲,初三拜其他亲戚与邻里。

在古代,拜年一般是小辈向长辈拜贺新年,包括叩头施礼、祝贺万事如意、问候生活安好等内容。遇到同辈亲友,也要施礼道贺。随着时代的发展,拜年的习俗也日益更新。除了沿袭以往的拜年方式外,又兴起了电话拜年、短信拜年、网络拜年等形式。这些创新不仅是传统习俗的延续,也是现代社会不断发展的产物。

3. Sending New Year Wishes

Another custom during the Spring Festival is sending New Year wishes to each other. People begin to express New Year wishes on the first day of the New Year. Chinese New Year's greetings mostly follow two principles from inside to outside, from near to far. On the first day, people worship their ancestors, the elderly, and close relatives; on the second day, people go out to send congratulations to their in-laws; and on the third day, people visit their other relatives.

In ancient times, the young kowtowed to the elderly to show the New Year greetings, to wish everything goes well and the coming year is full of joy. People also greeted relatives and friends of the same generation. The ways of sending New Year wishes have been changing over time. In addition to the traditional ways of expressing New Year's greetings, some new practices have emerged, such as sending wishes via phone calls, text messages, and the Internet. These innovative forms not only maintain the tradition but also demonstrate the development of modern society.

除了这些众所周知的习俗外，买年货、扫房、贴对联等也是春节必不可少的活动。买年货是将过年期间要用的东西都买齐全。扫房起源于古代人民去除病疫的一种宗教仪式，后演变为对家里的各种物品进行一个全面细致的清洁，寄托了人们除旧迎新的美好愿望。对联是中国特有的文学形式，它对仗工整，简洁精巧，抒发人们对未来最真挚的期盼。家家户户在正月初一前就贴好了春联，带着美好的期待迎接新年。春节期间，全国各地洋溢着热闹喜庆的气氛，这些丰富多彩的贺岁活动凝聚了劳动人民的智慧，反映了广大劳动人民的心声和期盼。

Other essential activities during the Spring Festival include New Year shopping, cleaning houses, pasting red couplets, etc. New Year shopping means that people buy everything they will use for the Spring Festival in advance, such as food and new clothes. Cleaning houses before the New Year originated from a religious ceremony for the ancient people to remove diseases. It later evolved into a comprehensive and meticulous cleaning of all items in the home, expressing farewell to the old year and the good wishes for the New Year. Red couplets are a unique form of literature in China that are neat, concise, and delicate, conveying people's most sincere expectations for the future. Every household pasted couplets before the first day of New Year. All over the country is immersed in a lively and festive atmosphere during the Spring Festival. These various activities embody people's wisdom and reflect their aspirations and expectations.

第一章 春节文化双语教学设计

贴对联（贺艳珠 摄）
Pasting Red Couplets（By He Yanzhu）

买年货（贺艳珠 摄）
New Year Shopping（By He Yanzhu）

第二节 世界各地的多元春节：
爆竹声中一岁除，春风送暖入屠苏

Section 2 Spring Festival Celebration around the World：
With cracker's cracking noise the old year passed away.
The vernal breeze brings us warm wine and warm Spring day

除了中国，世界上还有许多国家庆祝春节，不仅包括受中国文化影响较深的越南、新加坡、韩国等亚洲国家，还包括华人聚集的欧美及大洋洲国家，例如美国、澳大利亚等。

Many countries also celebrate the Spring Festival, including Asian countries in deeply influenced by the Chinese culture, such as Vietnam, Singapore and Republic of Korea, and European and American and Oceanian Countries where Chinese people gather, such as the United States and Australia.

1. 越南

春节是越南最受欢迎、最热闹的全国性传统节日，越南人民庆祝春节的活动形式多样。

逛花市是越南春节的重要习俗之一。越南人最爱的年花有剑兰、大丽菊和桃花。为了将房屋装饰得焕然一新，他们通常会在春节前购买自己喜欢的花卉。粽子是越南春节的必备美食。越南的粽子具有地域性差异。在越南北部，人们通常吃正方形的粽子。而在越南的中部和南部地区，人们吃圆筒形的粽子。除了粽子，人们还会吃象征着幸运的五盆果和金橘。

1. Vietnam

The Spring Festival is not only a traditional festival in Vietnam but also the most popular festival celebrated by the whole country. There are many ways of celebrating the Spring Festival in Vietnam.

Visiting the flower market is one of the important customs. Vietnamese like sword orchids, dahlia and peach blossoms best. They usually buy their favorite flowers before the Spring Festival to decorate the house. People must eat zongzi at the Spring Festival. While people usually eat the zongzi in a square shape called Banh Chung in northern Vietnam and eat the zongzi in a cylindrical shape called Banh Tet in central and southern Vietnam. In addition, people also have a pot of five different types of fruit and eat kumquats, symbolizing good luck.

2. 新加坡

新加坡是一个环境好、景色美的岛国。在新加坡，人口中有近70%是华人，所以在中国春节期间，新加坡也有浓浓的年味。

拜年是当地人最重要的春节习俗。拜年时，人们会在一个漂亮的小纸袋里装进两个代表大吉大利的金橘，为友人送去新春祝福。捞鱼生是新加坡必不可少的特色新春菜肴。它以优质鲜嫩的生鱼片或者鱼条为主要食材，以姜丝、各色蔬果丝和特调酱料为辅，其以配色优美、味道独特给人以视觉和味觉的双重享受。

2. Singapore

Singapore is an island country with good environment and beautiful scenery. Nearly 70% of the people in Singapore are Chinese, so the country is full of festivity during the Spring Festival.

Sending New Year wishes is also the most important custom for the Spring Festival in Singapore. People put two kumquats in a beautiful small paper bag representing good luck and give it to their friends. Yee Sang, also called Prosperity Toss Salad, is an essential dish for the Spring Festival. Its main ingredients are fresh sashimi or fish sticks of high quality, supplemented by shredded ginger, shredded vegetables and fruits, and special sauces. With its colorful look and great taste, Yee Sang is a feast both for sight and taste.

3. 美国

农历新年是美国广为人知的重要节日之一。各地的中国城都会在春节期间举办大游行来庆祝新年。

旧金山唐人街是美国西部最大的唐人街,"花市街会"是旧金山唐人街的传统迎新春活动。在游行队伍中,人们可以欣赏到舞龙、舞狮、杂耍等传统表演。活动现场还设有食品摊位,人们可以品尝到饺子、汤圆等中国美食。

3. The United States

The Spring Festival is one of the well-known festivals in the United States. People have New Year parades in Chinatowns all over the country to celebrate the Spring Festival.

The Chinatown in San Francisco is the largest one in the western United States and its traditional event for the Spring Festival is the Flower Market. People can see dragon dance, lion dance, juggling and other traditional performances in the parade. In addition, there are stalls selling food, where people can taste Chinese delicacies such as dumplings and Tangyuan (glutinous rice balls).

4. 韩国

韩国的春节叫"雪日",意思是美好的开始。韩国的春节日期与中国是一样的,但是在习俗方面存在差异。

中国和韩国春节习俗最大的不同体现在美食方面。中国人春节必备的美食是饺子,而韩国的春节食物叫作"岁餐"。韩国春节代表性的食物是"年糕汤",即用圆圆的米糕片做成的汤。这是因为韩国人喜欢代表纯洁的白色,崇拜象征光明的太阳。并且,韩国春节的重头戏不在除夕而在初一,他们在大年初一这一天不能睡懒觉,要早起祭祀吃"岁餐"。韩国人认为吃太阳形状的白色米糕片意味着纯洁和长寿,饱含着人们对美好未来的无限憧憬。

4. Republic of Korea

The Spring Festival is called "Snow Day" in Republic of Korea, which means a good start. The date of the Spring Festival in Republic of Korea is the same as that in China, but how people celebrate the festival in the two countries is different.

The most significant difference between Chinese and Republic of Korea customs is food. While Chinese people eat dumplings, South Koreans have New Year Meal for the Spring Festival. The representative food of New Year Meal is Tteokguk (rice cake soup). This is because South Koreans like white representing purity and worship the sun, symbolizing light. Moreover, the highlight of the Spring Festival in South Korea is not on New Year's Eve but the first day of New Year. They have to get up early to offer sacrifice to one's ancestors and eat New Year Meal. South Koreans believe that eating white rice cake slices in the shape of the sun means purity and longevity Containing their aspirations and expectations for the future.

现在，越来越多的国家会举办具有中国特色的活动来庆祝中国春节。与此同时，中国传统文化也在不断发展中变得更丰富、更开放，赢得了世界人民的欢迎与喜爱。

Nowadays, more and more countries celebrate the Spring Festival with Chinese cultural activities. In the meantime, Chinese traditional culture, which becomes richer and more open, has been loved and welcomed by people worldwide.

第三节 "荠菜中含著齿鲜"：学习包饺子
Section 3 "The Delicious Shepherd's Purse": Learn to Make Dumplings

1. 材料

白菜、豆腐、食用油、盐、葱、胡椒、饺子皮。

1. Materials

Cabbage, tofu, edible oil, salt, scallion, pepper, dumpling wrappers.

2. 过程

2. Steps

（1）制作饺子馅

（1）Making dumpling fillings

①将白菜冲洗干净。

①Wash the cabbage.

步骤（1）①冲洗白菜（游艺涵 摄）

Step（1）①Wash the Cabbage（By You Yihan）

②白菜帮剁碎，加入少量盐。

②Chop the cabbage and add a little bit of salt.

③10 分钟后，挤出多余水分。

③10 minutes later, squeeze out the excess water of the cabbage.

步骤（1）②剁碎白菜（游艺涵 摄）

Step（1）②Chop the Cabbage（By You Yihan）

④豆腐切碎，放入白菜中，加入食用油、盐、胡椒、葱等调味，顺着一个方向搅拌均匀。

④Chop tofu, and mix with cabbage. Add edible oil, salt, pepper, scallion and other seasonings. Stir them uniformly in one direction.

步骤（1）④搅拌（游艺涵 摄）
Step（1）④Stir（By You Yihan）

（2）包饺子。

（2）Making dumplings.

①取一张饺子皮，在饺子皮的边缘一圈沾一点水，再取适量馅放在饺子皮中间。

①Take a piece of dumpling wrapper, dip a little water around the edge of the wrappers and place an appropriate amount of filling in the middle of the wrapper.

步骤（2）①把白菜馅放在饺子皮上（游艺涵 摄）
Step（2）① Place Filling in the Dumpling Wrapper（By You Yihan）

②对折，将两侧饺子皮的中间捏合。

②Fold in half and pinch both sides of the Dumpling wrapper together.

步骤（2）②对折饺子皮（游艺涵 摄）

Step（2）②Half Folded Dumpling Wrapper（By You Yihan）

③中间右侧部分，用右手的虎口部位将它向中间方向夹紧。

③On the right side, Pinch it towards the middle with the first interdigital space of the right hand.

步骤（2）③捏紧饺子皮（游艺涵 摄）

Step（2）③Pinch the Dumpling Wrapper Tightly（By You Yihan）

④中间左侧部位,用左手的虎口部位将它向中间方向夹紧。

④On the left side, Pinch it towards the middle with the first interdigital space of the left hand.

⑤中间夹紧的部分,再次放在两手的拇指和食指之间捏紧。

⑤Then pinch the middle part of the Dumpling wrapper with your thumb and forefinger.

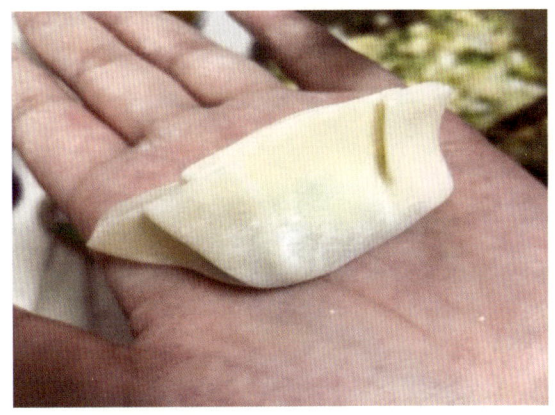

步骤（2）⑤完成（游艺涵 摄）
Step（2）⑤Complete（By You Yihan）

第四节　春节文化双语教案

一、教学对象

对中华文化感兴趣的外国学生。

二、教学内容

1. 中国传统节日春节的起源及风俗；
2. 春节在海内外的体现和表征；
3. 饺子的制作技巧。

三、教学目标

1. 帮助外国学生熟悉中国传统节日之春节文化,并了解春节在海内外的体现和表征;
2. 帮助外国学生掌握春节传统食物饺子的制作;
3. 帮助外国学生理解中国人民自古以来的美好心愿:珍惜亲情、尊老爱幼,对和谐美满家庭的期盼,对未来美好生活的向往以及向着理想目标勇敢奋斗的传统价值观。

四、教学方法

1. 直观法

利用图片、英文视频直观地向学生展示春节的起源及各种风俗活动。

2. 讨论法

通过教师提问、学生自由讨论的方式,请学生交流世界各地的春节。

3. 启发诱导法

启发学生总结对春节内涵的认识,并与本国相关传统文化内涵和价值观进行比较,揭示异同。

4. 对比法

通过介绍不同国家的春节文化,让学生体会到世界各地春节文化的多元性。

5. 演示法

通过演示法,教授饺子的制作方法。

五、课时安排

三课时完成,每课时 40 分钟。
第一课时介绍春节的起源及风俗;
第二课时介绍春节在海内外的体现和表征;
第三课时介绍饺子的制作技巧。

六、教学过程（三课时）

第一课时（40 分钟）：春节的起源及风俗

设计意图：以生动、精练的中华传统小故事开篇介绍春节的起源，力图通过"中国故事"引起学生的兴趣。利用图片、视频、实物等各种丰富手段展示中国人过春节的习俗，帮助学生了解中华民族举国欢庆春节的体现和表征，并揭示其中的深层含义：中国人民对阖家幸福安康的祈盼、对美好生活的不懈追求和努力。

（一）组织教学（约 2 分钟）

教师进入课堂，检查多媒体设备，将教学所用的教案、课件及手工材料准备放置妥当。师生互相问候，教师点名，准备上课。

> T: Good morning, everyone! How are you today? I will start the roll call... Okay, everyone's here. Let's start.

（二）进入新课，介绍春节的起源（10 分钟，内容详见导语）

1. 导入

教师展示中国人过春节的图片，同时板书"春节"二字及拼音；教师领读两遍。

> T: Please look at the photos. Which festival are people celebrating in these photos?

2. 介绍春节的起源：年兽的故事

（1）教师利用图片并结合道具绘声绘色地向学生讲述年兽的故事。

> T: I would like to tell you the story of "Nian" and ask you some follow-up questions after the story.

（2）教师就春节起源故事中的小细节进行提问，考查学生对故事的理解并为后文介绍春节的风俗做准备。

问题：老爷爷告诉大家赶走年兽的三件法宝是什么？（答案：红色、火光和爆竹声）

T: What are the three magic weapons that the elderly told everyone to drive away "Nian"?

（三）介绍春节的主要风俗（约27分钟，内容详见双语讲稿第一节）

1. 导入

（1）教师提问学生，知道哪些过春节的风俗。

T: What are the customs of celebrating the Spring Festival in China?

（2）教师整理学生答案，帮助学生梳理与春节有关的记忆并整合学生知道的春节风俗。

2. 介绍春节主要风俗之一：团圆饭

（1）教师展示中国人吃团圆饭的图片并提问学生。

问题：①照片上有几口人？他们在做什么？（答案：六口人，在干杯）
　　　②桌子上有什么？你吃过哪些？（答案：火锅、螃蟹、羊肉片等）

T: How many people are there in this picture? What are they doing?
T: What are on the table? What have you ever eaten?

（2）教师利用图片介绍团圆饭的菜品，并说明中国南北方团圆饭菜品的差异。

（3）教师总结团圆饭的寓意：一家大小互敬互爱、共叙天伦，围坐餐桌旁是一种幸福的时光。

3. 介绍春节主要风俗之二：守岁

（1）教师展示春晚图片并提问学生。

问题：这些人在做什么？这是什么节目？（答案：春节联欢晚会）

> T: What are these people doing on this picture? What is this show?

（2）教师介绍春节联欢晚会的时长和内容，并通过播放春晚视频引出"守岁"这一主题。

（3）教师介绍"守岁"的寓意：在旧年的最后一天晚上不睡觉，熬夜等待新一年的到来。全家人团聚在一起，通宵守夜，象征着相互陪伴驱散一切邪恶，共同期待新一年美满幸福。

4. 介绍春节主要风俗之三：拜年

（1）教师展示拜年的图片，先请学生仔细观察图片，并回答问题。

问题：①图片中小女孩做出了什么动作？你能模仿一下吗？（答案：作揖）
②老人给小孩子什么东西？（答案：红包）

> T: What does the girl do on this picture?
> T: What does the elderly give to the girl?

（2）教师演示拜年作揖的正确手势，并请学生一同模仿。

男子：右手成拳，左手包住；女子：右手在上，包着左手，不抱拳，只压手。

（3）教师手持实物，向学生展示各类红包；紧接着，设计手机抢红包环节，增加课堂教学的趣味性。

> T: Now, I will show you all kinds of red envelopes.
> T: Next, please enter our Wechat group. I'm going to send a red envelope. Are you ready?

（4）教师总结拜年的寓意：展示中国人尊老爱幼的传统美德，表现人们对新年的美好期待。此外，人们还会带着礼物拜访亲朋好友，体现出中国人对亲情友情的重视。

（四）小结（1分钟）

教师简单回顾春节的起源故事并梳理春节的风俗。

第二课时（40分钟）：世界各地的多元春节

设计意图：通过对其他国家春节习俗的介绍，与我国春节习俗进行比较。引导学生了解中国传统文化节日——春节在国际舞台上的表征和体现，帮助学生更好地体会中国春节文化对全球的影响。

（一）复习回顾（约5分钟）

1. 教师请学生复述年兽的故事。
2. 教师展示图片，提问学生春节有哪些主要风俗。

> T：Let us briefly review the origin of the Spring Festival.
> T：What are the customs of the Spring Festival?

（二）进入新课，介绍世界各地的多元春节（25分钟，内容详见双语讲稿第二节）

1. 导入

教师提问学生，还知道哪些国家过春节。

> T：Which countries celebrate the Spring Festival?

2. 介绍世界各地的多元春节之一：越南

（1）教师通过图片，介绍越南庆祝春节的方式和风俗。
（2）教师提问学生，比较中越两国过春节的风俗有何异同。

> T: What are the similarities and differences between celebrating the Spring Festival in China and Vietnam?

3. 介绍世界各地的多元春节之二：新加坡

（1）教师通过图片，介绍新加坡庆祝春节的方式和风俗。
（2）教师提问学生，比较中新两国过春节的风俗有何异同。

> T: What are the similarities and differences between celebrating the Spring Festival in China and Singapore?

4. 介绍世界各地的多元春节之三：美国

（1）教师通过图片，介绍美国庆祝春节的方式和风俗。
（2）教师提问学生，比较中美两国过春节的风俗有何异同。

> T: What are the similarities and differences between celebrating the Spring Festival in China and the United States?

5. 介绍世界各地的多元春节之四：韩国

（1）教师通过图片，介绍韩国庆祝春节的方式和风俗。
（2）教师提问学生，比较中韩两国过春节的风俗有何异同。

> T: What are the similarities and differences between celebrating the Spring Festival in China and Republic of Korea?

（三）练一练（10分钟，内容详见双语讲稿第二节）

1. 连一连

教师列出越南、新加坡、美国和韩国等国过春节的代表食物或习俗，请学生指出每种食物或习俗分别对应哪个国家。

2. 选一选

教师编写与春节起源和风俗相关的选择题若干，请学生根据教学内容进行选择并订正。

第三课时（40分钟）：学习包饺子

设计意图：通过详细教授包饺子的步骤，帮助学生更好地理解和体会春节文化的内涵和表征。同时鼓励学生包饺子并分享，激发学生热爱中华文化的热情。

（一）导入（2分钟）

教师展示自己包的饺子，并向学生提问。

问题：1. 这是什么？你们吃过吗？

2. 你们想不想自己动手学习包饺子？

> T: What is it? Have you eaten?
> T: Do you want to learn how to make dumplings?

（二）文化体验：教授包饺子（30分钟，内容详见双语讲稿第六节）

1. 教师发放材料并逐一介绍。
2. 教师现场演示并结合动图，教授学生如何包饺子。
3. 教师请学生展示各自成品，并谈谈有什么感想。

（三）本课小结（7分钟）

1. 教师总结中国春节的起源、风俗和世界其他国家人民庆祝春节的风俗。
2. 教师总结世界人民庆祝春节的美好愿望：对未来美好生活的向往、对温暖亲情的期盼和对理想目标的不懈追求。

（四）布置作业（1分钟）

教师请学生课下试着包饺子并与同学和老师分享。

T: Please try to make dumplings after class and share them with your classmates and teachers! That's all for today. See you next time!

七、教学反思

春节是中华民族最负盛名的传统节日，外国学生多有了解，通过本课的讲授，学生可以由表及里更好地理解春节的起源传说以及各种风俗的深层含义，也能更好地理解中华民族的精神价值和精神追求。

教学过程中，教师应力求将传统节日中蕴含的中国精神、中国价值和中国力量及时、有效地穿插在文化知识点的传授过程中，从而培养外国学生从了解到理解再到热爱中华文化的美好情感。此外，体验环节涉及动手包饺子，可考虑在条件允许的情况下选择圆桌教学，从而方便学生分组学习。教授过程中，教师应把注意事项提前交代清楚，以帮助学生提升体验环节的成就感和满足感。

附：辅助教学资源

春晚节目之《中国喜事》视频：https://www.bilibili.com/video/BV1w4411X7iW? share_source＝copy_web。

讨论与练习
Discussion and Practice

1. 讨论

1. Discussion

（1）你们眼里的春节是什么样的？你们家乡或者国家会过春节吗？又是什么样的呢？

（1）In your opinion, what is the Spring Festival? Does your country or hometown celebrate the Spring Festival? If so, what do they do?

（2）如果让你发明一种饺子，说说你的饺子会是什么样子的？（原材料、口味、形状、寓意等）

（2）If you can create a kind of dumplings, what does it look like?（raw materials, flavor, shape and meaning etc）

（3）你认为为什么春节文化能够走出中国，走向世界？

（3）Why do you think people all over the world celebrate the Spring Festival?

（4）对比中国的春节与你们自己国家的新年，你认为它们有什么异同之处？

（4）Comparing the Spring Festival with the New Year celebration in your own country, what are the similarities and differences?

2. 练习

2. Practice

（1）连一连

（1）Matching

| 越南 | A. 花市街会 |
| Vietnam | Flower Market |

| 美国 | B. 年糕汤 |
| The United States | Tteokguk（rice cake soup） |

| 韩国 | C. 粽子 |
| Republic of Korea | Zongzi |

| 新加坡 | D. 捞鱼生 |
| Singapore | Yee Sang |

（2）选一选

（2）Choosing（Select the correct one from the four options）

- 下面哪一个不是中国过年的习俗？（　　）

  Which one of the following is not the custom of the Spring Festival? （　　）

  A. Sending New Year wishes　　　B. Staying up

  C. Having the family reunion dinner　　D. Dragon boat race

- 年兽害怕什么颜色？（　　）

  Which color is Nian afraid of? （　　）

  A. Red　　　B. Green　　　C. Black　　　D. Yellow

- 韩国的春节又叫什么？（　　）

  What is the name of the Spring Festival in Republic of Korea? （　　）

  A. Snow Day　　　　　　B. New Year's Eve

  C. Sun Day　　　　　　D. Nian

- 下面哪种食物寓意着"年年有余"？（　　）

  Which of the following food has the meaning of "the abundance year after year"? （　　）

  A. Chicken　　B. Beef　　C. Fish　　D. Shrimp

答案
Answer

(1)　C　　　　A　　　　B　　　　D

(2)　D　　　　A　　　　A　　　　C

第二章　元宵节文化双语教学设计
Chapter Ⅱ　Bilingual Teaching Design of the Lantern Festival

元宵节（王萱 绘）
The Lantern Festival（By Wang Xuan）

中国传统文化体验式双语教学设计

导语
Introduction

  汉武帝时期，有位善卜卦的能臣名为东方朔。一年冬天，东方朔在御花园中发现一位因过度思念家人而欲自杀的宫女——元宵。东方朔救下元宵并答应设法助她与家人团聚。第二天，东方朔摆出占卜摊，逢人便说正月十五城内必有大火。汉武帝知道后，急忙让他寻求破解之法。东方朔说只需在那天大开城门，让大家拿着红灯笼进城放烟火，假装城里着火就能骗过火神。此外，火神爱吃汤圆，可在城内包汤圆来吸引火神的注意。正月十五，汉武帝命人按东方朔所说大开城门，元宵的家人顺利进城与她团聚。城内也热闹了一夜，平安无事。汉武帝便下令以后每年正月十五全城都挂灯笼、放烟火、包汤圆来供奉火神，消除灾祸。因元宵做的汤圆最好吃，这天也被称为元宵节。

  During the reign of Emperor Wu of the Han Dynasty, there was a minister named Dongfang Shuo, who was also a capable fortune-teller. One day in a snowy winter, Dongfang Shuo saved a maid named Yuan Xiao who wanted to commit suicide in the imperial garden because she desperately missed her family. Dongfang Shuo promised to help her reunite with her family. The next day, he set up a divination stall in the street and told everyone he met that there would be a big fire on the 15th day of the first lunar month. Informed of that, Emperor Wu hurried to ask Dongfang Shuo for a solution. He told the emperor that all they had to do on that day was to keep the city gates widely open, letting everyone bring the red lanterns into the city, and set off fireworks, pretending that the city was already on fire to deceive the God of Fire. Besides, they could also distract the God of Fire with its favorite food Tangyuan (glutinous rice balls). On that day, Emperor Wu did as Dongfang Shuo said, Yuan Xiao's family entered the city and eventually reunited with her. It was such a lively night, and everyone was safe and sound. Ever since then, Emperor Wu made it a tradition to let the whole city hang the lanterns, set off fireworks, and cook

Tangyuan to worship the God of Fire on the 15th day of the first lunar month. Additionally, the maid Yuan Xiao made the most delicious Tangyuan, so this day was also named after her—Yuan Xiao Jie (Lantern Festival).

第一节　元宵节的习俗：舞龙、观灯、吃汤圆
Section 1　Customs of the Lantern Festival: Dragon Dance, Lantern Show, Eating Tangyuan

元宵节是中国的传统节日，历史悠久，习俗丰富。每年正月十五，家家户户齐聚庆祝并举行各式各样的活动。舞龙、观灯、吃汤圆是元宵节最重要的三项民间习俗。中国疆域辽阔，元宵习俗在全国各地不尽相同。正月十五之后人们便要重新开始新一年的生产劳动，故欢庆元宵节蕴含着人们对美好未来的期待。

The Lantern Festival is one of the traditional festivals in China with a long history and various customs. On each 15th day of the first lunar month, every family gathers to celebrate the Lantern Festival. Multiple activities are held, among which watching the dragon dance, lantern show, and eating Tangyuan are the three most important folk customs. However, the customs of the Lantern Festival vary among different areas due to the vast territory of China. After this celebration, people restart their work, thereby the Lantern Festival embodies people's expectations for a better life.

1. 舞龙

舞龙，也称舞龙灯或耍龙灯。在中国古代神话中，龙可呼风唤雨、消灾除疫，是中华民族吉祥的象征。随着历史的发展，舞龙也形成了多种形式，主要有龙灯和布龙。龙灯由竹子扎成龙头、龙身、龙尾，然后在上面糊纸，再涂以颜色，龙身有很多节，每节里面都有灯。布龙则在下方安排舞者手持的木棒。舞布龙时动作复杂，展现出龙雄奇蜿蜒的身姿，且伴有敲锣打鼓，场面热闹非凡。

在中国，春节、元宵节等大型节日庆祝活动中，都会以舞龙来增添节日喜气。海外唐人街的许多华人社区现在仍保留着舞龙传统，常在当地节日庙会中演出。

1. Dragon Dance

Dragon dance is also known as dragon lantern. In Chinese mythology, the dragon has the power of bringing wind and rain, eliminating disasters and epidemics, so the dragon is a symbol of auspiciousness for Chinese people. With the development of history, dragon dance has also formed various types, which mainly include dragon lanterns and cloth dragons. A dragon lantern consists of a dragon head, a dragon body and a dragon tail made of bamboo strips and clothed with colorful paper paste. The dragon body has several sections, and each has a lantern inside. A cloth dragon has wooden sticks held by dragon dancers underneath. Following the beats of gongs and drums, the movements of a cloth dragon dance can be very sophisticated, showing the most virile and agile figure of the dragons. The scene couldn't be livelier.

In China, dragon dance is often performed in many large-scale festival celebrations such as the Spring Festival and the Lantern Festival to add to the festival ambience. Many Chinese communities in overseas Chinatown still retain the tradition of performing dragon dance for the local festivals and temple fairs.

2. 观灯

观灯也叫赏花灯，是元宵节传统习俗之一。节日当天，百姓们挂起灯笼，待月圆之时便出来观赏。这一习俗始于东汉，隋唐时期广泛流传于民间。灯笼种类丰富多样，但大多是由纸、丝绸所制，再以风景、花鸟、人物图案点缀或写上几句吉利话。其中走马灯是一种较为特殊的花灯，一般用纸片剪成马的形状，粘在灯壳里的纸轮上，借由中间火焰的热量推动空气，使灯上的图案转动。此外还有红纱灯、水灯等各具特色的花灯。

花灯不仅可以观赏还能启迪智慧，中国独特的传统民间娱乐活动——猜灯谜就是把谜语写在花灯上，供人们在赏花灯的同时猜谜语，更增添了节日气氛。灯谜谜底常为吉祥祝福的话语，这也体现了劳动人民的智慧和对美好生活的期待。

2. Lantern Show

Lantern show also known as Watching lanterns, is one of the traditional customs of the Lantern Festival. On the day of the Lantern Festival, every household hangs lanterns, and people come out to enjoy the lantern display when the moon is full. This custom originated in Eastern Han Dynasty and was widely spread during Sui and Tang Dynasty. There are various kinds of lanterns, most of which are made of paper and silk, and then embellished with patterns of landscapes, flowers, birds, figures or with a few auspicious words. For instance, a revolving lantern is a special kind of lantern. In this type of lantern, a piece of paper in the shape of running horses is stuck to the paper wheel of a rotatable lamp shell. The heat of the middle flame pushes the air and makes the running horses pattern on the lamp rotate. There are many other distinctive lanterns, such as red yarn lanterns and water lanterns.

In addition, guessing lantern riddles is a unique folk entertainment at the Lantern Festival. Riddles are written on the lanterns, so people can guess the riddles while enjoying the beauty of the lanterns. Answers often contain messages of good fortune, showing people's wisdom and expectations for a better life.

观灯（孙慧莉 摄）
Lantern Show（By Sun Huili）

猜灯谜（耿静茹 绘）
Guessing Lantern Riddles（By Geng Jingru）

3. 吃汤圆

汤圆是元宵节最具代表性的食物，也是中国传统小吃之一。小小的汤圆寄托了古人对未来的期望和对家族团聚的美好祝愿。关于元宵节吃汤圆的最早记载见于宋朝，汤圆的外皮是用糯米粉制作而成，内馅有芝麻、玫瑰、果仁、豆沙等多种。汤圆包好后放进开水里煮五分钟，口感香甜柔软，令人回味无穷。由于做法不同，北方的汤圆叫作元宵，是将馅料放在糯米面中滚成圆球制作而成。

地区不同，汤圆里的馅料也不同，有甜有咸。中国苏州地区有肉汤圆和荠菜汤圆，浙江宁波地区则喜食黑芝麻汤圆。随着时代的发展，越来越多的新式汤圆不断出现，如水果汤圆、巧克力汤圆等。但最传统、最受欢迎的依然是芝麻汤圆和豆沙汤圆。汤圆象征着合家团聚，表达了人们对和谐圆满的向往。

3. Eating Tangyuan

Tangyuan is the most representative food of the Lantern Festival and a famous traditional snack in China. This small round ballon trusts the expectations to the future and the most beautiful wishes for family reunions. The earliest record of eating Tangyuan during the Lantern Festival was found in Song Dynasty. The wrapper is made of glutinous rice flour, and the fillings are usually sesame, roses, nuts or sweet adzuki beans. Put Tangyuan in boiling water and cook for five minutes. No one could easily forget this perfect mixture of sweet and soft taste. In Northern China, Tangyuan is also called Yuanxiao due to a different way of making. Yuanxiao is made by rolling the filling in glutinous rice flour.

Different regions may have different fillings for their Tangyuan, sweet or salty. In Suzhou, people eat meat Tangyuan and shepherd's purse Tangyuan, while in Ningbo, people prefer sesame flavor. With the development of the times, more and more new flavors of Tangyuan have been appeared constantly, such as fruit flavor, chocolate flavor and so on. However, the most traditional and popular flavors are still sesame flavor and sweet adzuki beans flavor. For Chinese people, Tangyuan symbolizes reunion and completion.

汤圆（曾可欣 摄）
Tangyuan（By Zeng Kexin）

此外，元宵节的传统习俗还有舞狮子。舞狮子和舞龙一样，在中国都是吉祥的象征。舞狮表演一般需要两个演员，一人舞狮头，一人舞狮尾。在中国，每到元宵节，不仅可以看到舞龙、舞狮、赏花灯、猜灯谜等热闹场面，还能品尝到美味的汤圆。从这些习俗中我们能看出中国人对家庭团聚、吉祥如意的追求。

The lion dance is also included in the traditional customs of the Lantern Festival. Similar to the dragon dance, the lion dance is a symbol of good fortune. Lion dance usually consists of two actors, one wearing a special lion headgear, the other holding the tail. During every Lantern Festival in China, you can see the lively scene such as lion dance, dragon dance, lantern show, lantern riddles and so on, and taste the most delicious Tangyuan. All these traditions have shown Chinese people's earnest pursuit of the family reunions and great desire for auspiciousness.

第二节　今天的元宵节：
龙狮飞舞四大洋，花灯照耀七大洲
Section 2　Today's Lantern Festival：Dragon and Lion Dance across Four Oceans, Colorful Lanterns Shine over Seven Continents

由于海外华人逐渐增多，世界上越来越多的国家对中国文化产生了兴趣。元宵节文化对中国的邻国也产生了深远影响，如新加坡、马来西亚、日本、韩国等。传统元宵节与当地文化融合后，形成了多元的元宵节文化。现在，不仅是中国，世界上很多地方都会举办灯会和其他活动来欢度元宵节。

More and more countries are gaining interest in Chinese culture as more Chinese people choose to live abroad. From a historical perspective, the Lantern Festival culture has a huge influence on neighboring countries of China, such as Singapore, Malaysia, Japan, Republic of Korea, etc. Therefore, a more diverse Lantern Festival culture was formed after integrating with the local culture. Nowadays, many places in the world are holding Lantern Shows as well as other activities to celebrate the Lantern Festival.

1. 新加坡

在东南亚，来自中国南部的华人比例很大，因此元宵节传承了中国南方地区的习俗。新加坡部分地区还会在元宵节举办"踩街"活动，活动上有精彩的武术、舞狮和"南音"表演。这一活动常在天福宫外的直落亚逸街举行，沿街还设有出售中国特色小吃饮品的商铺，天福宫内也会举办相关的双语展览和猜灯谜活动，供家长和孩子一同参观体验，场面十分壮观。

1. Singapore

In Southeast Asia, most of the Chinese immigrants are from southern China, so its local Lantern Festival has inherited the customs of southern China. Some parts of Singapore will also hold "Street-Strolling" activity during the Lantern Festival, in which many people can enjoy wonderful martial arts, the lion dance and "Nanyin" performances. These special activities are usually held on Telok Ayer Street outside the Thian Hock Keng Temple. Chinese snacks and drinks are also sold along the street. Thian Hock Keng Temple would also hold Lantern Festival relevant bilingual exhibitions and Lantern Riddles guessing event. Parents and their children can join together, the scene is very spectacular.

2. 马来西亚

马来西亚的元宵节习俗——"抛柑接蕉"十分浪漫。单身男女在元宵夜齐聚河岸，将自己的姓名和联系方式写于柑橘或香蕉上，女生抛柑橘，男生扔香蕉。如果看到喜欢的人就打捞起对方扔的水果以取得联系，缔结一段好姻缘。因"橘"的谐音是"吉"，所以柑橘在马来西亚代表吉祥，蕴含着大吉大利之意。

2. Malaysia

In Malaysia, they have a romantic custom of the Lantern Festival: "Throw away and Pick up Oranges and Bananas". According to this unique custom, single men and women will gather on the river banks on the night of the Lantern Festival and throw the oranges and bananas which wrote their names or telephone numbers into the river. Girls will throw the oranges, while boys will throw the bananas. If one feel saffection for someone in this activity, they could pick the fruit he or she threw to keep in contact with its owner. Notably, orange presents the good fortune in Malaysia due to its similar sound to "luck" in Chinese.

3. 日本

日本的元宵节在公历一月十五日，也叫小正月，这一天主妇可以休息。早上人们会吃小豆粥，希望能消除灾祸。当地中华街会举办赏灯活动，街头还会有一些舞龙舞狮和传统舞蹈表演。最与众不同的庆祝活动便是火祭，人们用火来驱赶疾病和不幸。当火烧完的时候，新年庆典活动也就结束了。

3. Japan

In Japan, the Lantern Festival is also called the First Full Moon Festival, falling on the 15th of the first month of a year in the Gregorian calendar. On this day, housewives could have a rest. Besides, Adzuki bean porridge is the traditional food that people would eat in the morning, with the hope to eliminate the disaster. Lantern exhibitions, Dragon Dance and Lion Dance will also be held along the streets. Later on that day, the unique celebration—fire offering, is held in the hope of kicking diseases and misfortunes away. The New Year celebration also ends when the fire dies out.

4. 韩国

在韩国，元宵节这一天不吃元宵而吃一种红豆、小米、糙米、黑豆和糯米做成的五谷饭与各式各样的坚果，还会喝"耳明酒"，以祈祷新的一年不患疾病。烟火、花灯和街头表演同样必不可少。农村地区最典型的习俗就是烧月亮屋，将松树的树干搭成圆锥形屋架，挂上写着新年愿望的纸条，圆月升起后，将月亮屋用手中的火把点燃，默念心中的愿望。火堆点燃后，围在火堆旁唱歌跳舞，来驱赶鬼怪与疾病。

4. Republic of Korea

In Republic of Korea, instead of Eating Tangyuan, every family will cook five-grain rice made with five ingredients, including adzuki beans, millet, coarse rice, black beans and glutinous rice. Moreover, they also eat all kinds of nuts and drink special alcohol called "Guibargi Wine", hoping for a happy and healthy new year. Fireworks, Lantern Shows and street performances are also indispensable. The most traditional custom in rural areas is to burn the moon house. The trunk of the pine tree is built into a conical roof frame, and the paper with the New Year's wishes is hung on it. After the full moon rises, the moon house is lit with the torch in the hand, and the wishes in the heart are silently read. When the fire is lit, they sing and dance around it to drive away ghosts and diseases.

5. 西方国家

在美国、波兰、意大利、乌克兰、英国等欧美国家和地区，元宵节最初是由华人带去的，他们在当地举办庆祝活动，后来当地民众也逐渐参与其中。庆祝方式虽以赏灯为主，但与中国传统花灯不同，这些彩灯别具一格，融入了当地特色。如今，新西兰最大的城市奥克兰已经成功举办了数十场元宵庆祝活动。除了灯会外，当地海外华人还会举办舞龙舞狮表演，吸引路人驻足观看。西方国家的部分地区也通过放孔明灯来庆祝元宵节：人们聚集在广场上，将自己的心愿写在孔明灯上，一起倒数，同时放飞孔明灯。

5. Western Countries

In countries like America, Poland, Italy, Ukraine and UK, the Lantern Festival was first brought and celebrated by Chinese immigrants. Then it appeals to more locals to join in. The major celebration activity is the lantern show. Unlike traditional Chinese lanterns, these lanterns bring more local elements into their characteristics. Nowadays, Auckland, the largest city in New Zealand, has successfully hosted dozens of Lantern Festival shows. Apart from the lantern shows, local Chinese communities often hold dragon or lion dance performances in the street, attracting passerby to stop to appreciate. Some parts of western Countries also celebrate the Lantern Festival by launching sky lanterns. People gather in the square, and they will let go of their sky lanterns which wrote their wishes when the countdown ends.

第三节 "一碗汤圆情万千"：动手包汤圆
Section 3 "A Bowl of Tangyuan Includes a Various Kinds of Feelings": Learn to Make Tangyuan

1. 材料

芝麻粉、白糖、香油、糯米粉、温水。

1. Materials

Sesame powder, sugar, sesame oil, glutinous rice flour, warmwater.

2. 步骤

2. Steps

（1）制作馅料：将芝麻粉倒入碗中，加入白糖和香油混合，搅拌均匀。

（1）Make the fillings：Mix sesame powder with sugar and sesame oil. Stir the paste until it is mixed well.

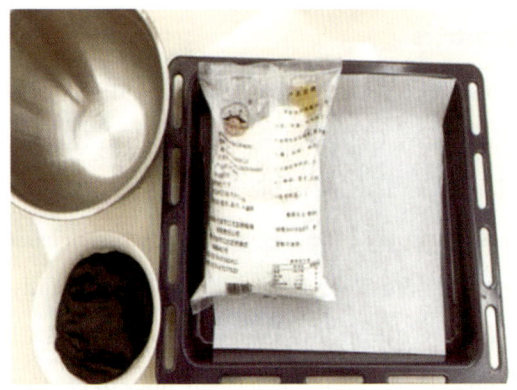

步骤（1）把芝麻粉与白糖、香油混合（曾可欣 摄）
Step（1）Mix Sesame Powder with Sugar and Sesame Oil（By Zeng Kexin）

（2）制作外皮：糯米粉加水，揉成面团。

（2）Make the skin：Add a moderate amount of water to the glutinous rice flour and blend it until it turns into a smooth dough.

步骤（2）糯米粉加水，揉成面团（曾可欣 摄）
Step（2）Add Some Water to the Glutinous Rice Flour and Turns it into a Smooth Dough（By Zeng Kexin）

（3）从面团中拿出一小团用手掌压扁，并将馅料放进去。

（3）Get a small piece of dough and press it with your palm. Then put some fillings in it.

步骤（3）将馅料放进小面团（曾可欣 摄）
Step（3）Put the Fillings in Your Dough（By Zeng Kexin）

（4）用面皮将馅料包裹好，然后在掌心轻轻揉搓，直到变成表面光滑的小球。

（4）Wrap the fillings with the skin and gently knead it in your palm until it becomes a smooth ball.

步骤（4）揉成表面光滑的小球（曾可欣 摄）
Step（4）Knead it Until it Becomes A Smooth Ball（By Zeng Kexin）

（5）把元宵放进煮沸的水中，在锅里搅动一下防止粘锅。煮 5 分钟直到元宵漂浮在表面上。

（5）Boil some water and put Tangyuan in when it is boiled. Move them around so they won't stick together. Cook for 5 minutes until they float.

步骤（5）煮熟汤圆（曾可欣 摄）
Step（5）Cook Tangyuan（By Zeng Kexin）

（6）用碗和汤勺盛起来，品尝汤圆。

（6）Take Tangyuan out of the pot and taste them.

步骤（6）品尝汤圆（孙慧莉 摄）
Step（6）Taste Tangyuan（By Sun Huili）

第四节　元宵节文化双语教案

一、教学对象

对中华文化感兴趣的外国学生。

二、教学内容

1. 中国传统节日元宵节的起源及风俗；
2. 元宵节在海内外的体现和表征；
3. 元宵的制作方法。

三、教学目标

1. 帮助外国学生熟悉中国传统节日元宵节文化，并了解元宵节在海内外的体现和表征；
2. 帮助外国学生掌握元宵节传统食物汤圆的制作方法；
3. 帮助外国学生理解中国人民自古以来的美好心愿：对幸福安宁生活的向往、对和谐美满家庭的期盼、对健康强健身体的追求以及与此有关的温情、崇尚、健康与和谐的传统价值观。

四、教学方法

1. 图片、视频法

利用图片、英文视频向学生展示元宵节的起源及各种风俗活动。

2. 演示法

通过演示法，教授汤圆的制作方法。

3. 互动法

通过教师提问、学生回答的方式，加强师生的互动以达到文化的交流。

4. 引导法

引导学生自己总结对元宵节的认识，并加深对对元宵节文化内涵的思考。

5. 练习法

通过一些简单练习，加深学生对元宵节内容的记忆。

6. 启发联想法

启发学生对元宵节中蕴含的价值观进行思考，联想与本国相关传统文化内涵和价值观进行比较，揭示异同。

五、课时安排

三课时完成，每课时 40 分钟。
第一课时介绍元宵节的起源及风俗；
第二课时介绍元宵节在海内外的体现和表征；
第三课时介绍元宵的制作方法。

六、教学过程（三课时）

第一课时（40 分钟）：元宵节的起源和风俗

设计意图：以生动、精练的中华传统小故事开篇介绍元宵节的起源，力图通过"中国故事"引起学生的兴趣。利用图片、视频、实物等各种丰富手段展示中国人过元宵节的习俗，帮助学生了解元宵节，并揭示其中的深层含义：中国人民对阖家幸福安康的祈盼、对美好生活的不懈追求和努力。

（一）组织教学（约 2 分钟）

教师进入课堂，检查多媒体设备，将教学所用的教案、课件及手工材料准备放置妥当。师生互相问候，教师点名，准备上课。

> T: Good morning, everyone! How are you today? Let's start the roll call first... Okay, everyone's here. Classes begin.

（二）进入新课，介绍元宵节的起源（10分钟，内容详见双语讲稿导语）

1. 导入

教师展示中国人过元宵节的图片，同时板书"元宵"二字及拼音；教师领读两遍。

> T: Please look at the photos. Can you guess what festival the Chinese celebrate?

2. 介绍元宵节的起源：东方朔与"元宵"的故事

（1）教师利用图片，以角色扮演的方式绘声绘色地向学生讲述东方朔与"元宵"的故事。

> T: Now, let me tell you the story of Dongfang Shuo and Yuan Xiao. Please listen carefully. After telling the story, I have a few questions for you.

（2）教师就元宵节起源故事中的小细节进行提问，考查学生对故事的理解并为后文介绍元宵节的风俗做准备。

问题：①东方朔建议十五晚上在城内做什么吃可吸引火神的注意？（答案：汤圆）

②东方朔还建议十五晚上臣民一起做什么？（答案：挂灯、满城点鞭炮、放烟火）

> T: What did Dongfang Shuo suggest to cook in the city that could attract the attention of the God of Fire? on the 15th night?

（三）介绍元宵节的主要风俗（约27分钟，内容详见双语讲稿第一节）

1. 导入

（1）教师提问学生，知道哪些过元宵节的风俗。

> T: What are the customs of Chinese people celebrating the Lantern Festival?

（2）教师整理学生答案，帮助学生梳理与元宵节有关的记忆并整合学生知道的元宵节风俗。

2. 介绍元宵节主要风俗之一：舞龙

（1）教师播放元宵节舞龙视频，并提问学生。

问题：①视频中的人在做什么？（答案：舞龙）

②你知道龙代表着什么吗？（答案：中华民族吉祥的象征）

> T: What are the people doing in the picture?
> T: Do you know what dragon represents in China?

（2）教师总结舞龙的寓意：龙可以呼风唤雨、消灾除疫。我国自古即以农业立国，风调雨顺对于生产生活具有极为重要的意义，古人希望得到龙的庇佑，由此形成了元宵节舞龙、观灯的习俗。

3. 介绍元宵节主要风俗之二：观灯

（1）教师展示花灯和猜灯谜图片并向学生解释字条上的文字。

（2）教师利用图片介绍灯笼和灯谜的由来，同时展示不同样式的灯笼；紧接着，教师出示课前制作好的英文灯谜，邀请学生参与有奖猜灯谜活动，以此增加课堂教学的趣味性。

（3）教师介绍猜灯谜的内涵：灯谜可以增添节日气氛，还展现了古代劳动人民的智慧和美好愿望。

4. 介绍元宵节主要风俗之三：吃汤圆

（1）教师展示汤圆的图片，请学生猜一猜是什么。

问题：图片中的食物是什么？你吃过吗？（答案：汤圆）

> T：What is the food in the picture? Have you eaten?

（2）教师播放包汤圆的小视频，同时介绍汤圆的馅料和口味，并请学生回答问题。

问题：如果让你制作汤圆，你会放什么馅料？（无固定答案）

> T：Do you prefer sweet Tangyuan or salty Tangyuan? If you were asked to make Tangyuan, what fillings would you put?

（3）教师总结吃汤圆的寓意：在元宵节吃汤圆不仅是一种好兆头，而且也希望家人平安、团圆。

（四）小结（1分钟）

教师简单回顾元宵节的起源故事并梳理元宵节的风俗。

第二课时(40 分钟):世界各地的多元元宵节

设计意图:通过对其他国家元宵节习俗的介绍,与我国元宵节习俗进行比较。引导学生了解中国传统文化节日——元宵节在国际舞台上的体现,帮助学生更好地体会中国元宵节文化对全球的影响。

(一)复习回顾(约 5 分钟)

1. 教师请学生复述东方朔和"元宵"的故事。
2. 教师展示图片,提问学生元宵节有哪些主要的风俗。

> T: Let us briefly review the origin of the Lantern Festival.
> T: Do you know the main customs of the Lantern Festival?

(二)进入新课,介绍世界各地的多样元宵节(25 分钟,内容详见双语讲稿第二节)

1. 导入

教师提问学生,还知道哪些国家过元宵节。

> T: Which other countries do you know celebrate the Lantern Festival?

2. 介绍世界各地的多元元宵节之一:新加坡

(1)教师展示世界地图,指出新加坡的地理位置。
(2)教师播放视频,向学生介绍新加坡元宵节"踩街"风俗。

> T: What are the similarities and differences between Chinese and Singaporeans celebrating the Lantern Festival?

3. 介绍世界各地的多元元宵节之二：马来西亚

（1）教师展示世界地图，指出马来西亚的地理位置。

（2）教师展示图片，介绍马来西亚浪漫的"抛柑接蕉"习俗。

> T：Look at this picture. What are these people doing?

4. 介绍世界各地的多元元宵节之三：日韩

（1）教师展示世界地图，指出日本和韩国的地理位置。

（2）教师展示日本火祭图片和韩国烧月亮屋图片，分别介绍日本和韩国庆祝元宵节的方式和风俗。

5. 介绍世界各地的多元元宵节之四：西方国家

（1）教师展示世界地图，指出西方国家的大致范围。

（2）教师展示新西兰舞龙舞狮图片，介绍一些西方国家庆祝元宵节的方式和风俗。

6. 元宵节习俗比较

教师提问学生，比较中国和以上国家或地区在欢度元宵节时有何相同或相异的习俗。

> T：What are the similarities and differences between Chinese and other countries in celebrating the Lantern Festival?

（三）练一练（10分钟，内容详见双语讲稿第四节）

1. 连一连

教师列出中国、日本、新加坡和马来西亚等国的元宵节习俗，请学生指出每个国家分别对应哪个习俗。

2. 选一选

教师编写与元宵节相关的选择题若干，请学生根据教学内容进行选择并订正。

第三课时（40分钟）：学习包汤圆

设计意图：通过详细教授包汤圆的步骤，帮助学生更好地理解和体会元宵节文化的内涵和表征。同时鼓励学生包汤圆并分享，激发学生对中华文化的热情。

（一）导入（2分钟）

教师展示自己包的汤圆，并向学生提问。

问题：你们想不想自己动手学学包汤圆？

> T: Do you want to learn how to make Tangyuan?

（二）文化体验：教授包汤圆（30分钟，内容详见双语讲稿第三节）

1. 教师发放材料并逐一介绍。
2. 教师现场演示并结合动图，教授学生如何包汤圆。
3. 教师请学生展示各自成品，并谈谈有什么感想。

（三）本课小结（7分钟）

1. 教师总结中国元宵节的起源、风俗和世界其他国家人民庆祝元宵节的风俗。
2. 教师总结世界人民庆祝元宵节的美好愿望：对家庭团圆的期盼、对幸福安宁生活的向往。

（四）布置作业（1分钟）

教师请学生课下试着包汤圆并与同学和老师分享。

> T: Please try to make Tangyuan after class and share them with our classmates and teachers! Class is over, see you next time!

七、教学反思

元宵节又叫上元节,至今已有千年历史。时间为每年的农历正月十五,它紧随春节之后,是一年中第一个月圆之夜,同时也标志着春节庆典的结束。元宵节素有舞狮、猜谜和吃汤圆的习俗,过了这一天人们就要进入新一年的生产劳动中,所以他们在元宵节这一天欢庆,蕴含着人们对家人团聚以及对未来生活的美好期待。

由于元宵节紧承春节,教师在教学时,可以结合春节的相关习俗进行比较教学,以帮助学生从时间、内容上进行区分。由于猜灯谜是元宵节的重要风俗之一,教师可以充分利用这一风俗开展游戏教学,一方面帮助学生理解元宵节的特有习俗,另一方面活跃课堂气氛、增加课堂教学的趣味性。

此外,文化体验环节涉及动手包汤圆,可考虑在条件允许的情况下圆桌教学,从而方便学生分组学习。教授过程中,教师应把注意事项提前交代清楚,如糯米粉与水的比例问题等。在满足安全条件的前提下,教师可准备煮锅,待学生包好汤圆后现场煮熟,满足学生品尝美食的愿望,以帮助学生提升体验环节的成就感和满足感。

除了包汤圆外,还可以教授学生利用彩纸制作各种灯笼,手工灯笼的制作也不失为元宵节文化体验教学的重要参考项目。

附:辅助教学资源

1. B站英文UP主"叫我蹇就好"的包汤圆视频(英语口语):https://b23.tv/u6MDnV。

2. B站英文UP主"StormSue"[元宵节传说(英文版)—哔哩哔哩]:https://b23.tv/f7Rf4T。

3. B站UP主"背包旅神"的闹元宵视频:https://b23.tv/Nvjoix。

讨论与练习
Discussion and Practice

1. 讨论

1. Discussion

（1）你更喜欢甜汤圆还是咸汤圆？如果让你发明一种汤圆，说说你的汤圆会是什么样的？（原材料、口味、寓意等）

（1）Do you like sweet or salty Tangyuan? What would you Tangyuan look like if you were asked to invent a new kind？（Desribe its material, flavor, the meaning, etc.）

（2）你们最喜欢元宵节的哪一个习俗？你们国家或者家乡庆祝元宵节吗？它又是什么样的？

（2）What is your favorite Lantern Festival custom? Does your country or hometown celebrate the Lantern Festival? And what's that like?

（3）你的国家或者家乡有没有类似"抛柑接蕉"这样的浪漫习俗？是什么样的？

（3）Is there any romantic custom like "throwing away and picking up oranges and bananas" in your country or hometown? And what's that like?

（4）对比中国的元宵节与你们国家的传统节日，有什么相同或不同之处？

（4）Comparing the Lantern Festival of China with the traditional festivals in your own country, what do these traditional festivals have in similarities or differences in your opinion?

2. 练习

2. Practice

（1）连一连

（1）Matching

马来西亚　　　　　　　　A. 踩街
Malaysia　　　　　　　　　Street-strolling

新加坡　　　　　　　　　B. 火祭
Singapore　　　　　　　　 Fire offering

中国　　　　　　　　　　C. 抛柑接蕉
China　　　　　　　　　　Throw away and Pick up Oranges and Bananas

日本　　　　　　　　　　D. 舞龙
Japan　　　　　　　　　　Dragon Dance

（2）选一选

(2) Choosing (Select the Correct one from the four options)

- 咸汤圆的馅料应该是以下哪一种？（　　）

  Which should be the filling of salty Tangyuan? （　　）

  A. peanuts　　　　　　　　　　B. beef

  C. sweet adzuki beans　　　　　　D. chestnuts

- 汤圆又叫作什么？（　　）

  What Tangyuan can also be called? （　　）

  A. lantern　　　B. Yuanxiao　　　C. dumpling　　　D. bao zi

- 哪个城市已经举办了数十场元宵灯会了？（　　）

  Which city has held dozens of the Lantern Festival? （　　）

  A. Tokyo　　　B. Sidney　　　C. Paris　　　D. Auckland

- 元宵节的结束意味着什么？（　　）

  What does the end of the Lantern Festival mean? （　　）

  A. The start of Spring Festival　　　B. The end of the Spring Festival

  C. The start of the Dragon Boat Festival　　D. The end of the Dragon Boat Festival

答案
Answer

(1) C   A   D   B

(2) B   B   D   B

第三章　端午节文化双语教学设计
Chapter Ⅲ　Bilingual Teaching Design of the Dragon Boat Festival

端午节（王萱 绘）
the Dragon Boat Festival（By Wang Xuan）

中国传统文化体验式双语教学设计

导语
Introduction

  屈原，爱国爱民，对楚国贡献良多。公元前278年，秦军打败毫无反手之力的楚军，占领了楚国国都。屈原得知故土失守，悲痛欲绝。他走到汨罗江边，闭上双眼，回忆着楚国昔日的国泰民安，再反观今日的国破家亡，唏嘘不已，抱石跳江结束了自己短暂的一生。屈原投江自尽后，人们想要找到他的尸体，却失败了。于是楚国人民划着船把自己家里的食物投到江里让鱼虾去吃，从而避免屈原的尸体被鱼虾吃掉。人们采取这种方式一方面是为了保护英雄遗骨，另一方面也寄托着人们珍惜生命、爱好和平的心愿。

  Qu Yuan, a patriotic poet who loved his people, made a significant contribution to the ancient state of Chu. In 278 B.C., the army of Qin conquered the capital of Chu after Chu's fiasco. When Qu Yuan heard this news, he was smitten with mourn. Qu Yuan couldn't stop his tear with peaceful and prosperous Chu flash backs. Country defeated and home lost, he decided to jump into the Miluo River with a rook and end his life. After his suicide, the people of Chu rowed their boats and put food into the river to avoid fish and shrimps eating Qu Yuan's body. People doing this also conveyed their wishes to cherish life and peace.

第一节　端午节的习俗：龙舟、粽子、五彩绳
Section 1　Customs of the Dragon Boat Festival：Dragon Boat, Zongzi, Five-color Silk Thread

  每年农历五月初五是端午节。端午节的习俗体现在日常生活的方方面面。在穿戴方面，主要有戴五彩绳、佩香囊等习俗；在吃喝方面，主要有吃粽子、吃鸡鸭鹅蛋、喝雄黄酒等习俗；在住的方面，主要是挂艾草菖蒲、熏苍术等习俗；在行方面，主要是赛龙舟。除此以外，人们还会在端午节进行拜神祭

祖、用雄黄酒画"王"字、采草药、放纸鸢等活动。

Dragon Boat Festival is on the fifth day of the fifth lunar month every year. To celebrate the Dragon Boat Festival, Chinese people have a set of customs in different aspects of life. In terms of wearing, they wear the Five-color Silk Thread and scented pouch; in terms of eating, Zongzi, chicken, duck and goose eggs, realgar wine are specific food for festival; in terms of living, people smoke atractylodes and hang mugwort or calamus outside of the outer door of their houses; and in terms of transportation, they hold dragon boat races. Besides, Chinese people worship gods and ancestors, use realgar wine to draw the Chinese character "wang" (king), collect herbs and fly paper kites and so on.

拜神祭祖（赵银莹 摄）
Worship to Gods and Ancestors
（By Zhao Yinying）

放纸鸢（张嘉妤 摄）
Fly Paper Kites（By Zhang Jiayu）

1. 龙舟

龙舟，源于龙图腾祭祀，后来逐渐成为一项闻名海外的传统民间水上体育项目。龙舟，即龙形的船，船身绘有各式各样与龙相关的图画或图腾。受地域影响，不同地区的龙舟制作方法和比赛规则有所不同，颇有趣味。例如广东人在造龙舟时会选一些有寓意的数字，例如船长——33.88米，也就是"生生猛猛"的意思。

龙舟赛具有功利性、纪念性和竞技性三个特点。功利性是指原始时期的先民会在江水里争相竞渡、寻觅食物。纪念性是指龙舟竞渡是为纪念屈原而闻名于世。竞技性则是现代龙舟赛最显著的特点，源于1976年香港龙舟邀请赛。随着时代的发展，赛龙舟也逐渐变成了一项国际性的群体活动，甚至在奥运赛场上也能看到它的身影。2021 年 8 月 3 日，中国龙舟作为表演队伍，在东京奥运会皮划艇的比赛场崭露头角，开始了中国龙舟的奥运之旅，以另一种方式展示着中华传统文化的璀璨辉煌。

1. Dragon Boat

The dragon boat was derived from the dragon totem worship. Later, it gradually became one of the traditional water sports renowned both in China and other countries. As the name implies, the dragon boat is a boat in the shape of a dragon, where there are pictures or totems of dragons painted. Interestingly, influenced by geography, different regions in China have diverse ways to make dragon boats and various rules to hold races. For example, when people make dragon boats in Guangdong Province, they prefer to choose some meaningful numbers such as 33.88 meters, which means "lively and energetic".

The dragon boat race has three characteristics: utilitarian, commemorative, and competitive. The utilitarian comes from the ancestors conducted the race to contend for food. The comemorative refers to the dragon boat race is famous in honor of Qu Yuan. However, originating from the Hong Kong Invitational Dragon Boat Race in 1976, the dragon boat race in modern times is competitive and has become an international group activity. On 3rd August 2021, the Chinese dragon boat team presented at a kayak final at Tokyo 2020 Olympics as a performance team, which was a special way to showcase Chinese traditional culture to the world.

2. 粽子

粽子，源于古代竹筒装米。相传，为了避免江中的鱼虾啃食屈原的尸体，人们便会将粽子投入江中以引诱鱼虾。粽子主要是由粽叶、糯米以及不同的馅料组成，形状各异，香飘十里。粽子形状没有南方和北方之分，五湖四海皆以三棱锥为主，少数也有柱体的，如浙江湖州的"枕头粽"。而由于饮食习惯的不同，粽子口味具有鲜明的地域性特点，南方大多数是馅料为五花肉和绿豆的咸粽子，北方则大多数是馅料为红枣和豆沙的甜粽子。

如今，人们并不仅仅只在端午食粽，粽子早已成为一道传统特色小吃，深受国内外食客的青睐。近年来，粽子更是出口美国、德国、澳大利亚等十多个国家和地区，出口量连年居高不下，粽香越飘越远。

2. Zongzi

Zongzi, a variation of the ancient bamboo rice, was initially thrown into the river to prevent fish and shrimp from eating Qu Yuan's body. Zongzi is mainly made up of reed leaves, glutinous rice, and different fillings; it has a slightly sweet aroma when cooked. Zongzi can be made into different shapes, but there is no apparent difference in the shape of Zongzi between the northern part and the southern part. Zongzi mainly looks like a triangular pyramid; sometimes, it can be cylindrical too, such as the "pillow zongzi" in Huzhou, Zhejiang province. Considering different eating habits, the flavors of Zongzi are pretty distinctive. Salty zongzi with pork belly and green beans is mainly seen in the south, while sweet zongzi with red jujube and bean paste is mainly seen in the north.

Nowadays, Zongzi is not only the special food for the Dragon Boat Festival, but a traditional snack welcomed by people domestically and abroad. Zongzi has been exported to more than ten countries and regions like America, Germany, and Australia in recent years. The export of Zongzi has been increasing year by year, the fragrance of Zongzi has been drifting further and further.

粽叶和糯米（张嘉妤 摄）
Reed Leaves and Glutinous Rice（By Zhang Jiayu）

3. 五彩绳

五彩绳,也叫五彩丝、五色丝等,源自我国古代传统的五行观。它是一种用白、红、黑、黄、绿五种颜色的粗丝线搓成的彩色线绳。这五种颜色与五行,即金、火、水、土、木一一对应,各有其意,意蕴着和谐与生生不息。

在古代,农历五月被叫作"毒月",是一个代表着灾祸的月份。人们认为五彩绳可以保护小孩子,可以给小孩子带来一年的好运气。因此每逢端午,长辈们将早早编好的五彩绳戴在孩子们的手腕、脚腕和脖子上,希望可以驱灾避祸,祈福纳吉。五彩绳的佩戴也颇多讲究,表现为"男左女右",且须在日出之前进行佩戴。后来,五彩绳随着节日内涵的丰富不断创新,最典型的便是五彩网兜。

3. Five-color Silk Thread

The five-color silk thread is interwoven by thick silk threads in white, red, black, yellow and green. These five colors are related to an ancient Chinese view of the Five Elements: metal, fire, water, earth, and wood. They all have their meanings, implying harmony and prosperity.

In the past, the fifth lunar month was known as the "poisonous month". May is a month representing misfortune. It is believed that the five-color silk thread can protect the children and bring them good luck for the whole year. Therefore, adults will put the five-color silk thread they made in advance on children's wrists, ankles,

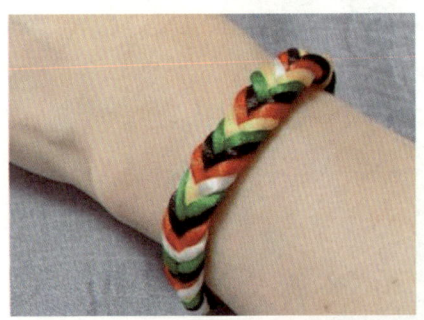

戴在手腕上的五彩绳(张嘉妤 摄)
Five-color Silk Thread on the Ankle
(By Zhang Jiayu)

五彩网兜(张嘉妤 摄)
Five-color Net Pocket
(By Zhang Jiayu)

and necks at the Dragon Boat Festival, hoping that children can be happy and safe. However, the five-color silk thread has to be put on boys' left hands and girls' right hands before sunrise. Later, the five-color silk thread is constantly innovated with the development of the festival—the five-color net pocket is the most representative one.

端午节的众多风俗中，无论是哪一种风俗习惯，都反映了中国人民自古以来简单美好的愿望：对健康强健身体的追求，对幸福安宁生活的向往，对和谐美满家庭的期盼。

All the customs reflect Chinese people's simple but best wishes: the pursuit of good health, joyful and peaceful lives and harmonious families.

第二节 世界各地的端午节：
龙舟驰骋四大洋，粽叶飘香七大洲
Section 2 Dragon Boat Festival Around the World:
Dragon Boat Sails across the Four Oceans,
Zongzi's Fragrance Lingers on the Seven Continents

端午节，作为中国的传统节日之一，深受中国人民的喜爱。随着世界文化的融合与发展，端午节及其文化也渐渐被传播到海外，并有了创新与发展。

The Dragon Boat Festival, one of the traditional festivals in China, is dearly loved by Chinese people. With the integration and development of cultures around the world, the Dragon Boat Festival and its customs have been gradually known and celebrated by people in other countries and have been innovated and improved.

1. 越南

作为邻国的越南是中国端午文化的青睐者之一。随着时代的发展，越南在继承中国端午节传统的基础上，创新了一系列端午美食，粽子尤为突出。

越南粽子是越南人在农历新年和端午节必不可少的传统美食。与中国的三棱锥形粽子不同，越南粽子分圆筒形和方形两种。他们在农历新年吃的粽子多为圆形，又叫"年粽"，一般用来祭拜天地神明和祖先，端午节吃的粽子则是方形粽。越南民族认为，圆形的粽子代表天，方形的代表地，合起来象征着天地合一，万事顺利；那么食粽则蕴含着对新一年风调雨顺、五谷丰登的祈盼。与中国相同的是，粽子在越南也有甜咸之分，端午节吃的方形粽便是馅料为肉和胡椒粉的咸粽子。但越南人通常选择用芭蕉叶来包粽子，极富越南地方特色。

1. Vietnam

Vietnam, a neighbor of China, favors the culture of the Dragon Boat Festival and has innovated some food for the Festival, among which Zongzi is the most successful one.

Vietnamese must eat zongzi during the Lunar New Year and the Dragon Boat Festival. Unlike the Chinese Zongzi in the shape of a triangular pyramid, Vietnamese Zongzi can be cylindrical or square. Zongzi eaten during the Lunar New Year are cylindrical ones, also called "Nian Zong", usually used to worship gods and ancestors. Square zongzi is usually eaten during the Dragon Boat Festival. Vietnamese hold the view that the cylindrical shape represents the sky and that the square is the earth; these two types of Zongzi together represent the oneness of the sky and the earth and mean that everything goes well. Eating Zongzi stands for the wishes of the smooth and plentiful proceeding year. Vietnamese Zongzi shares some features with Chinese Zongzi—Vietnamese Zongzi can also be salty or sweet. For example, square Zongzi for the Dragon Boat Festival is filled with meet and pepper. However, Vietnamese use Japanese banana leaves to wrap Zongzi instead of reed leaves, which shows their local style.

2. 韩国

春节、寒食、端午和中秋是韩国四大传统节日。江陵端午祭是韩国著名的端午庆祝活动，原是祈祝丰收的庆典，但深受中国端午文化的影响。

江陵端午祭庆祝活动从农历四月初五开始，直到农历五月初七。祭祀活动主要有舞蹈表演、萨满祭祀、民间艺术展示等形式。"车轮饼"是韩国人江陵端午祭必吃的美食，它主要由小米、粟米等淀粉和香菜、葱粒等制成。人们还会把新鲜的艾草嫩叶捣碎之后，再和米粉揉制在一起，做成车轮的形状，制成"车轮饼"。"车轮饼"象征着生机与活力。

2. Republic of Korea

The Spring Festival, Hansik Festival, Dragon Boat Festival, and Mid-Autumn Festival are four traditional Republic of Korea festivals. Gangneung Danoje Festival is a famous activity for celebrating Dragon Boat Festival in Republic of Korea. It was a celebration for praying for a good harvest but was deeply influenced by the Dragon Boat Festival in China.

Gangneung Danoje Festival starts from 5th April to 7th May in the Lunar calendar. Ritual activities contain dance performances, Shaman sacrifice, folk loric art performances, etc. People must eat the "wheel cake" during Gangneung Danoje Festival. The cake is made of millet or corn starch, coriander and sliced shallot. People will also crush the fresh leaves of wormwood, merge them with rice flour, and then shape it like a wheel. The "wheel cake" represents vitality and energy.

3. 德国

除了粽子，龙舟也划向了世界，深受世界各国人民的喜爱。这一项充满趣味性和竞争性的比赛在美国、德国、英国、俄罗斯等国家非常流行。

其中，赛龙舟的习俗在德国落地生根已经有30多年了。1989年，赛龙舟传到德国，德国人在汉堡举行了首届"龙舟节"。1991年之后，龙舟赛改在德国法兰克福举行。德国杜伊斯堡的趣味龙舟赛曾因为其规模之盛大而被收进了吉尼斯世界纪录。龙舟赛当天，人们会摩拳擦掌，精心打扮一番；同时，人们还可以在比赛间隙欣赏中国功夫的表演。

3. Germany

The dragon boat race also presents itself to the world and is loved by people from different countries. This interesting and competitive race is famous in countries like the America, Germany, the UK and Russia.

Germany has had the dragon boat race for more than 30 years since 1989 when the first dragon boat festival was hosted in Hamburg. From 1991, the venue for the dragon boat festival was changed to Frankfurt. The dragon boat race in Duisburg has entered the Guinness Book of World Records for its large scale. On race day, people dress themselves up and look forward to the competitive boat race. People also can watch Chinese kungfu during the interval of the boat races.

如今，粽子和赛龙舟似乎格外"出圈"。一方面，是因为粽子美味，龙舟娱乐性强；另一方面，则是因为它们代表着全世界人民共同的美好愿望——和谐、健康与幸福。

Nowadays, Zongzi and the dragon boat race seem extremely popular. For one thing, Zongzi is delicious, and the dragon boat race riches in entertaining; for another thing, they both represent the best wishes of people around the world——harmony, health and happiness.

第三节 "彩线轻缠红玉臂"：学做五彩绳
Section 3 "Five-color Silk Thread Wrap Charming Arms": Learn to Make the Five-color Silk Thread

1. 材料

五根相同长度和特定颜色的绳子（白、绿、黑、红、黄）、一把剪刀、一个夹子。

1. Materials

Fivesilk threads of the same length and specific color (white, green, black, red and yellow), a pair of scissors, a clip.

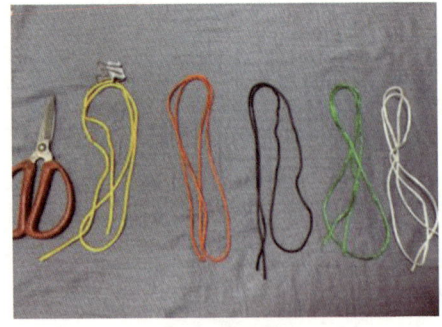

材料（张嘉妤 摄）
Materials (By Zhang Jiayu)

2. 步骤
2. Steps

（1）将五根绳子对折。

（1）Fold the five silk threads in half.

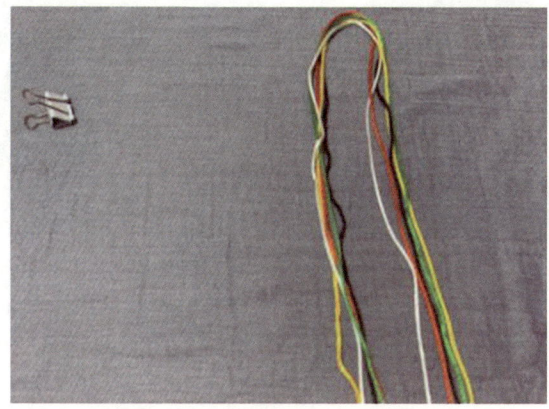

步骤（1）对折绳子（张嘉妤 摄）
Step（1）Fold the Threads in Half（By Zhang Jiayu）

（2）左手固定绳子，右手搓动两根绳子。

（2）Fix the silk thread with the left hand and rub two silk threads with the right hand.

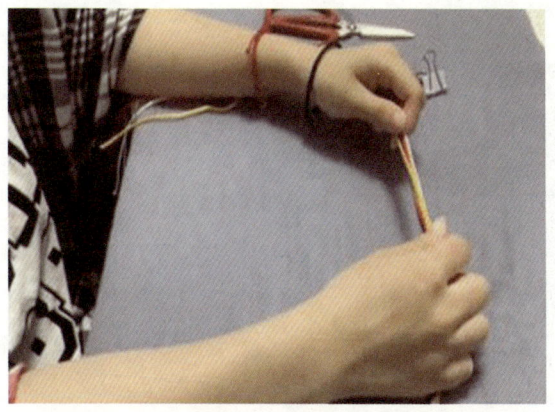

步骤（2）左手固定，右手搓动（张嘉妤 摄）
Step（2）Fix the Threads with the Left Hand and Rub Them with the Right Hand（By Zhang Jiayu）

（3）用手指将绳子轻轻一顶，形成两股拧结。

(3) Gently push silk threads with your fingers to form a double twist.

步骤（3）①不断搓动（张嘉妤 摄）

Step（3）①Rub the Threads

（By Zhang Jiayu）

步骤（3）②拧结（张嘉妤 摄）

Step（3）②Form a Double Twist

（By Zhang Jiayu）

（4）制作蛇结。

(4) Make snake knots.

①先将左边的线绕一圈，放在右边线下。

①Wrap the left silk thread around first and then put them under the right silk thread.

步骤（4）①绕线（张嘉妤 摄）

Step（4）①Wrap the Thread（By Zhang Jiayu）

②右边的线先绕食指一圈,再压到另一端的线的下面。

②Wrap the right side of the silk thread around the index finger, first and then press to the other end of the silk thread below.

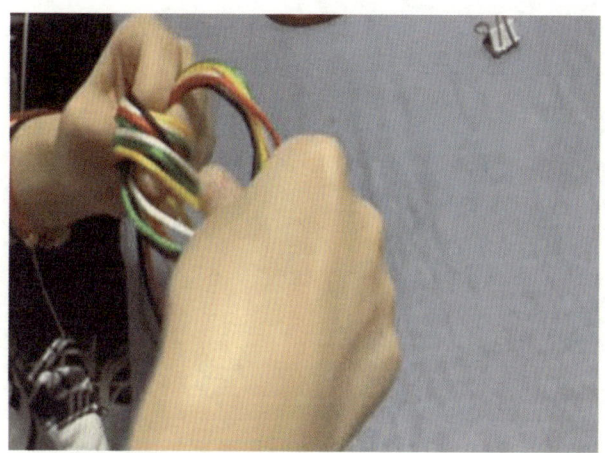

步骤(4) ②绕线(张嘉好 摄)
Step (4) ②Wind the Thread (By Zhang Jiayu)

③串线并拉紧。

③String and tighten.

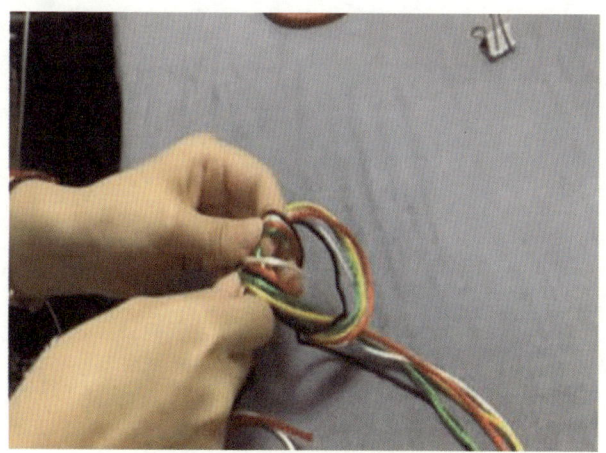

步骤(4) ③穿线并拉紧(张嘉好 摄)
Step (4) ③String and Tighten (By Zhang Jiayu)

④效果图如下。

④The rendering is as follows.

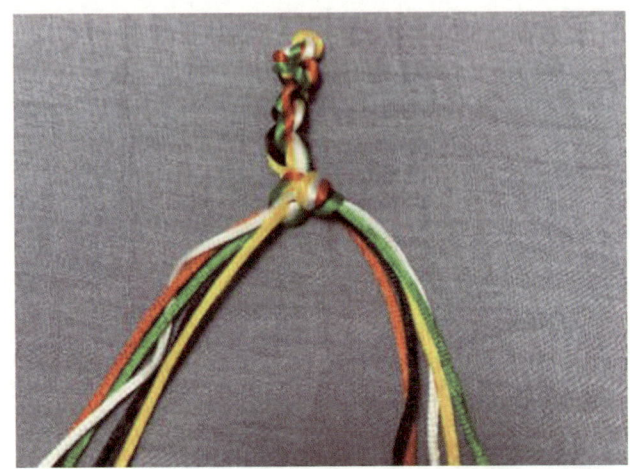

步骤（4）④效果图（张嘉妤 摄）
Step（4）④The rendering（By Zhang Jiayu）

（5）用夹子固定。

（5）Secure with clips.

步骤（5）固定（张嘉妤 摄）
Step（5）Secure（By Zhang Jiayu）

（6）编织。先将右边的红绳拉至左边再把左边的红绳拉至右边，其他颜色的绳子按照上面步骤重复。

（6）Knitting. First, pull the red silk thread on the right to the left, and then pull the red silk thread on the left to the right. Repeat the above steps for the silk thread of other colors.

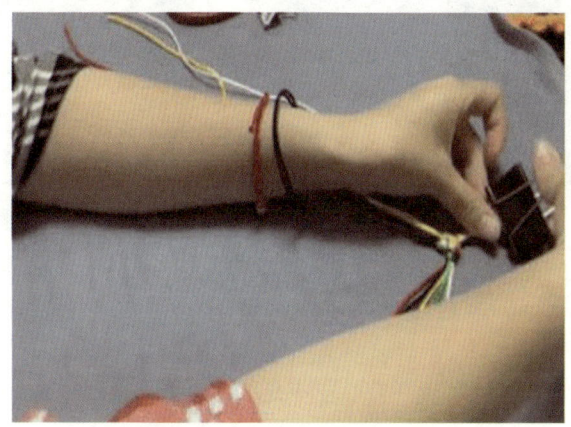

步骤（6）编织（张嘉妤 摄）
Step（6）Knit（By Zhang Jiayu）

（7）交叉后把绳子拉紧。

（7）Tighten the silk threads after crossing.

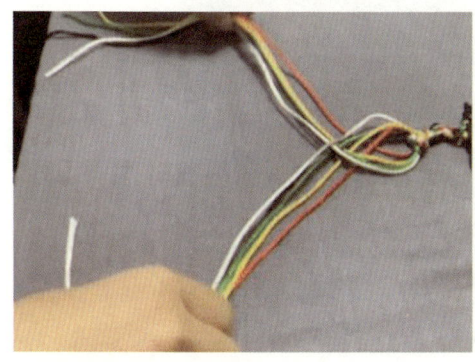 

步骤（7）①交叉（张嘉妤 摄）　　步骤（7）②拉紧（张嘉妤 摄）
Step（7）①Cross（By Zhang Jiayu）　　Step（7）②Tighten（By Zhang Jiayu）

（8）重复步骤（4）。再编一个蛇结。

（8）Repeat step（4）. Make another snake knot.

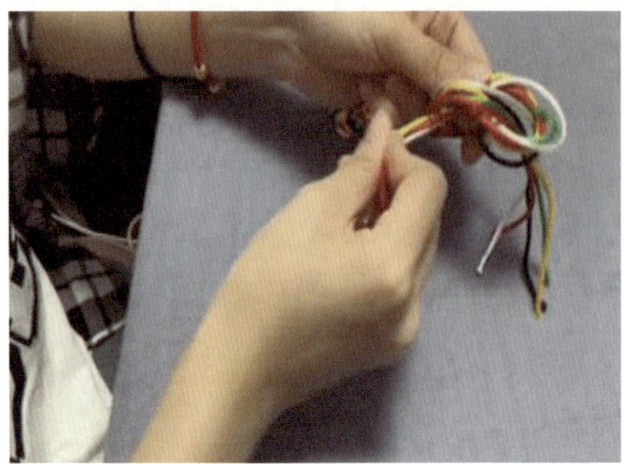

步骤（8）重复编蛇结（张嘉妤 摄）
Step（8）Repeat to Make Another Snake Knot（By Zhang Jiayu）

（9）剪去除红色以外的其他线。

（9）Cut off other silk threads except for the red one.

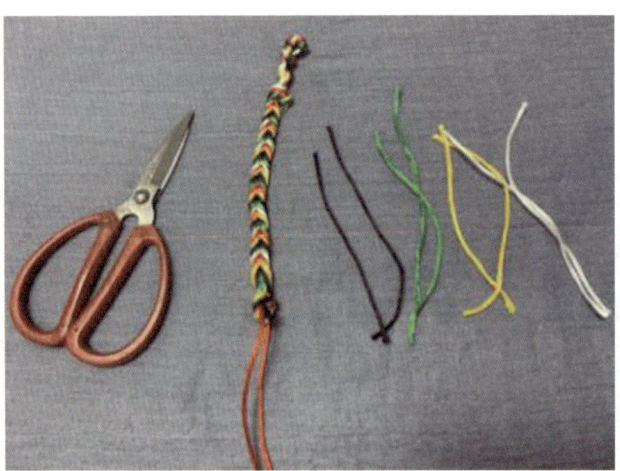

步骤（9）修剪多余的彩线（张嘉妤 摄）
Step（9）Cut off Other Threads Expect for the Red One（By Zhang Jiayu）

（10）在尾部穿上饰品并打结。

（10）Put ornaments on the tail and tie a knot.

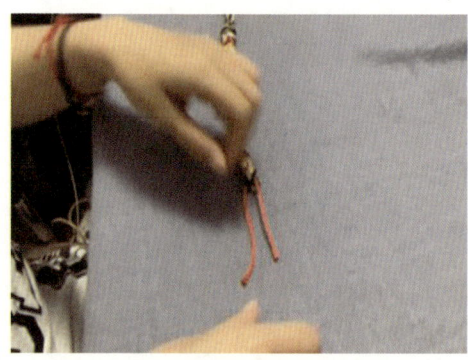

步骤（10）①装上饰品（张嘉妤 摄）
Step（10）①Put Ornaments
（By Zhang Jiayu）

步骤（10）②打结（张嘉妤 摄）
Step（10）②Tie a Knot
（By Zhang Jiayu）

（11）将五彩绳的两端串在一起。制作完成！

（11）String the two ends of the five-color silk thread together. Complete!

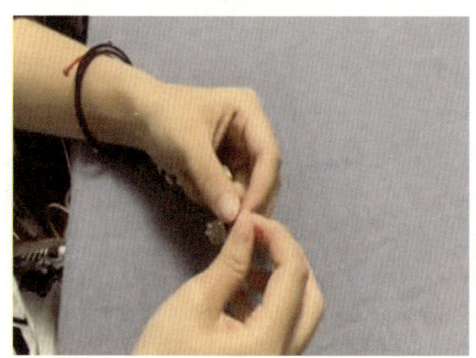

步骤（11）①两端衔接（张嘉妤 摄）
Step（11）①String the Two Ends
（By Zhang Jiayu）

步骤（11）②完成（张嘉妤 摄）
Step（11）②Complete
（By Zhang Jiayu）

第四节　端午节文化双语教案

一、教学对象

对中华文化感兴趣的外国学生。

二、教学内容

1. 中国传统节日端午节的起源及风俗；
2. 端午节在海内外的体现和表征；
3. 五彩绳的制作技巧。

三、教学目标

1. 帮助外国学生熟悉中国传统节日之端午节文化，并了解端午节在海内外的体现和表征；
2. 帮助外国学生掌握端午节传统手工五彩绳的制作；
3. 帮助外国学生理解中国人民自古以来的美好心愿：对幸福安宁生活的向往，对和谐美满家庭的期盼，对健康强健身体的追求以及与此有关的温情、健康与和谐的传统价值观。

四、教学方法

1. 图片、视频法

利用图片、英文视频向学生展示端午节的起源及各种风俗活动。

2. 演示法

通过演示法，教授五彩绳的制作方法。

3. 互动法

通过教师提问、学生回答的方式，请学生介绍各自国家端午节文化的相关表征。

4. 启发诱导法

启发学生总结对端午节内涵的认识，并与本国相关传统文化内涵和价值观进行比较，揭示异同。

五、课时安排

三课时完成，每课时 40 分钟。

第一课时介绍端午节的起源及风俗；

第二课时介绍端午节在海内外的体现和表征；

第三课时介绍五彩绳的制作技巧。

六、教学过程（三课时）

第一课时（40分钟）：端午节的起源和风俗

设计意图：以生动、精练的屈原投江历史故事开篇介绍端午节的起源，力图通过"中国故事"引起学生的兴趣。利用图片、视频、实物等各种丰富手段展示中国人过端午节的习俗，帮助学生了解端午节的表征，并揭示其中的深层含义：中国人民自古以来对幸福安宁生活的向往，对和谐美满家庭的期盼、对健康强健身体的追求以及与此有关的温情、健康与和谐的传统价值观。

（一）组织教学（约2分钟）

教师进入课堂，检查多媒体设备，将教学所用的教案、课件及手工材料准备放置妥当。师生互相问候，教师点名，准备上课。

> T: Good morning, everyone! How are you today? Let's start the roll call first... Okay, everyone's here. Let's start our lesson.

（二）进入新课，介绍端午节的起源（10分钟，内容详见双语讲稿导语）

1. 导入

（1）教师展示3张食物的图片，请学生分别辨识，并猜一猜哪一种是端午节的特色食品，以此引入端午节主题，同时回顾复习春节和元宵节特色食物。

问题：这些是什么节日的特色食物？你猜哪一种是今天我们要讲的端午节吃的食物？（答案：饺子—春节；汤圆—元宵节；粽子—端午节）

> T: Do you remember these food? Guess what kind of food you will eat at the Dragon Boat Festival.

（2）教师板书"端午"二字及拼音并领读两遍，教师向学生说明端午节的时间。

2. 介绍端午节的起源：屈原投江的故事

（1）教师利用图片，以角色扮演的方式绘声绘色地向学生讲述屈原投江的悲壮故事。

（2）教师就端午节起源故事中的小细节进行提问，考查学生对故事的理解并为后文介绍端午节的风俗做准备。

> T: Now, let me tell you the story of Qu Yuan. Please listen carefully. After telling the story, I have a few questions for you.

问题：①屈原是战国时期哪个国家的人？（答案：楚国）

②屈原投的什么江？他为什么投江？（答案：汨罗江；不想亲眼看到自己深深爱恋的国家被毁灭，以身殉国）

③屈原投江后，百姓为什么把自己家里的食物投进江里？（答案：不忍心看到屈原的尸体被鱼虾吃掉）

> T: Which country is Qu Yuan from?
> T: In which river did Qu Yuan commit suicide? Why did he commit suicide?
> T: After Qu Yuan died, why did the people throw food into the river?

（3）教师总结屈原投江的故事，指出屈原崇高的爱国品质、百姓对屈原的崇拜以及对和谐幸福生活的追求。

（三）介绍端午节的主要风俗（约27分钟，内容详见双语讲稿第一节）

1. 导入

（1）教师就屈原投江的故事再次设计问题提问学生。

问题：在屈原投江的故事中，老师讲到哪些端午节的习俗？（答案：包粽子、赛龙舟）

> T: In the story of Qu Yuan, what customs of the Dragon Boat Festival did I talk about?

（2）教师整理学生答案，帮助学生整合与端午节有关的风俗。

2. 介绍端午节主要风俗之二：包粽子

（1）教师展示粽子食材的照片，并就内容提问学生。

问题：①你知道这些食材是什么吗？（答案：粽叶和糯米）
②为什么粽子要用粽叶包裹着？（答案：一方面，为了不让鱼虾吃到；另一方面，粽叶的香气也可以使粽子更加美味）

> T: Do you know what these ingredients are?
> T: Why are Zongzi wrapped in reed leaves?

（2）教师结合图片介绍粽子的不同口味、馅料和外形，同时简单说明造成这些差异的地域原因。

3. 介绍端午节主要风俗之一：赛龙舟

（1）教师播放赛龙舟的视频，帮助学生感受端午节赛龙舟的热烈气氛。

（2）教师利用图片讲解龙舟的特殊长度及意义。

（3）教师总结赛龙舟的寓意：既强身健体，也表现出对图腾龙的崇拜以及对祖先的尊重。

4. 介绍端午节主要风俗之三：五彩绳

（1）教师展示自己编的五彩绳，并请学生回答问题。

戴在手腕上的五彩绳

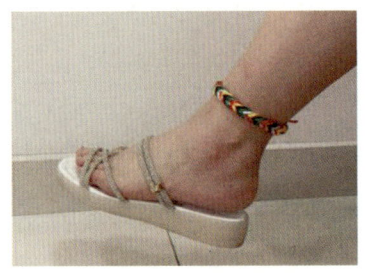
戴在脚腕上的五彩绳

问题：①五彩绳有哪五种颜色？（答案：白、红、黑、黄、绿）

②你们猜，端午节为什么要佩戴五彩绳呢？（答案：保护小孩子，给小孩子带来一年的好运气）

> T: What are the five colors of the five-color silk thread?
> T: Why do people wear the five-color silk thread on the Dragon Boat Festival?

（2）教师结合图片讲解五彩绳的佩戴学问，并邀请学生一起佩戴。

戴在男生左手的五彩绳

戴在女生右手的五彩绳

（四）小结（1 分钟）

教师简单回顾端午节的起源故事并梳理端午节的风俗。

第二课时（40 分钟）：世界各地的多元端午节

设计意图：通过对海外其他国家端午节习俗的介绍与比较，引导学生了解中国传统文化节日——端午节在国际舞台上的表现，帮助学生更好地体会中国端午节文化对全球的影响。

（一）复习回顾（约 5 分钟）

1. 教师请学生复述端午节起源——屈原投江的故事。
2. 教师展示图片，提问学生端午节有哪些主要的风俗。

> T: Let us briefly review the origin of the Dragon Boat Festival.
> T: Please look at these pictures. What are the customs of the Dragon Boat Festival?

（二）进入新课，介绍世界各地的多元端午节（25 分钟，内容详见双语讲稿第二节）

1. 导入

教师提问学生，还知道哪些国家过端午节。

> T: Which countries celebrate the Dragon Boat Festival?

2. 介绍具有特色的龙舟赛：德国的"龙舟热"

（1）教师展示世界地图，指出德国的地理位置。

（2）教师播放视频及图片，向学生介绍德国赛龙舟的历史及特点。

（3）教师总结海外"龙舟热"的原因：人民对强健体魄的渴望、对团队协作的热衷。

3. 介绍世界各地的粽子：越南和韩国的"粽子"

（1）教师展示世界地图，指出越南和韩国的地理位置。

（2）教师展示以上两国的"粽子"，请学生分别描述一下每种"粽子"的特点并猜一猜它们分别来自哪个国家。

（3）教师分别介绍越南和韩国庆祝端午节时的特色"粽子"，从材料、形状、做法等角度分别与我国的粽子进行比较。

（三）练一练（10分钟，内容详见双语讲稿第四节）

1. 连一连

教师列出中国、越南、韩国和德国的端午习俗，请学生指出每个习俗分别对应哪个国家。

2. 选一选

教师编写与端午节起源和风俗相关的选择题若干，请学生根据教学内容进行选择并订正。

第三课时（40分钟）：学习五彩绳的编织

设计意图：通过详细教授五彩绳的编织步骤，帮助学生更好地理解和体会端午节文化的内涵和表征。同时鼓励学生编织五彩绳并分享，激发学生热爱中华文化的热情。

（一）导入（2分钟）

教师展示编织的五彩绳，并向学生提问。

五彩绳

问题：这个五彩绳好看吗？你们想不想学习怎么制作？

> T: Does this five-color silk thread look good? Do you want to study how to make it?

（二）文化体验：教授五彩绳的编织（30分钟，内容详见双语讲稿第三节）

1. 教师发放材料并逐一介绍材料。
2. 教师现场演示并结合图片，教授学生如何编织五彩绳。
3. 教师请学生展示各自成品，并谈谈有什么感想。

（三）本课小结（7分钟）

1. 教师总结中国端午节的起源、风俗和世界其他国家人民庆祝端午节的风俗。
2. 教师总结世界人民庆祝端午节或举行赛龙舟比赛的美好愿望：对和谐、健康、幸福生活的追求和向往。

（四）布置作业（1分钟）

教师请学生课下试着编一个五彩绳并把它送给你喜欢的人。

> T: Please try to make a five-color silk thread after class and give it to the person you like! Class is over, see you next time!

七、教学反思

端午节是中国四大传统节日之一，是为了纪念战国时期楚国伟大的诗人、政治家屈原。端午节与春节、元宵节一样，对中国周边国家产生了深远的影响，越南、韩国以及其他国家都会在端午节这一天举行活动。赛龙舟是端午节活动的重要组成部分，尽管西方国家并没有过端午节的习俗，但美国、德国很多城市都有专业的赛龙舟队伍，并定期举行比赛，吸引了不少民众积极

参与。

端午节的教学应围绕屈原投江而进行,无论是屈原投江的原因还是流传至今的各种习俗,都应该在交代清楚屈原投江故事的前提下,运用启发式教学的方法引导学生进行理解,帮助学生从认识屈原的人格、精神品质开始过渡到对各种习俗中人与自然的和谐统一的认知。

此外,本节课的文化体验环节设计了五彩绳的编织教学,如果条件允许,教师也可以组织学生学习包粽子。当粽叶飘香、龙舟赛起时,道一声"端午安康",寄托对生活的无限美好祈愿。

附:辅助教学资源

抖音英文包粽子视频:https://v.douyin.com/eov2tdV/。

讨论与练习
Discussion and Practice

1. 讨论

1. Discussion

(1)你们眼里的龙舟是什么样的?你们家乡或者国家有龙舟赛吗?又是什么样的?

(1)What do the dragon boats look like? Does your country or hometown have dragon boat races? If your country or hometown has, please describe it.

(2)如果让你发明一种粽子,说说你的粽子会是什么样子的?(原材料、口味、形状、寓意等)

(2)If you can create one kind of Zongzi, how will you make it?(Describe it from the raw moterial, flavor, shape, meaning etc.)

(3)你认为为什么粽子和龙舟能够走出中国,走向世界?

(3)Why do you think Zongzi and dragon boats can be famous in other countries?

（4）对比中国的端午节与你们自己国家的传统节日，你认为传统节日有什么相同之处？

(4) Comparing the Dragon Boat Festival in China with the traditional festivals in your own country, what do you think the traditional festivals have in common?

2. 练习

2. Practice

（1）连一连

(1) Matching

| 韩国 | A. 年粽 |
| South Korea | Nian Zong |

| 越南 | B. 五彩绳 |
| Vietnam | Five-color silk thread |

| 中国 | C. 龙舟赛 |
| China | Dragon boat race |

| 德国 | D. 车轮饼 |
| Germany | Wheel Cakes |

（2）选一选

(2) Choosing (Select the correct one from the four options)

- 咸粽子的馅料应该是以下哪一种？（　　）

Which should be the filling of salty zongzi? (　　)

A. salt egg yolk　　B. red jujube　　C. bean paste　　D. chestnuts

- 五彩绳不可以戴在哪个部位？（　　）

Where can't wear the five-coloured silk thread? (　　)

A. neck　　B. wrist　　C. ankle　　D. waist

- 哪个国家会举办一年一度的"龙舟节"？（   ）

  Which country holds the annual Dragon Boat Festival? （   ）

  A. Japan   B. America   C. Germany   D. Canada

- 中国广东省的龙舟有着特殊的长度，它长为多少米？（   ）

  The dragon boat in Guangdong Province of China has a certain length, so how long is it? （   ）

  A. 33.33   B. 33.66   C. 33.99   D. 33.88

答案
Answer

(1) D   A   B   C

(2) A   D   C   D

第四章　七夕节文化双语教学设计
Chapter IV　Bilingual Teaching Design of Qixi Festival

七夕节（王萱 摄）
The Qixi Festival (By Wang Xuan)

中国传统文化体验式双语教学设计

导语
Introduction

相传，织女是天上的神仙，牛郎则是人间的凡人，他无父无母，和一头神仙化作的老牛相依为命。牛郎对偷偷下凡洗澡的织女一见钟情，老牛告诉牛郎只要偷走织女的衣裳，织女不能飞回天庭，便会成为他的妻子。于是牛郎偷偷藏起了织女的衣裳，织女在寻找衣服的时候爱上了牛郎。二人情投意合，在人间过上了男耕女织的幸福生活。过了几年，老牛久病不治。临死之前，它告诉牛郎剥下自己有神力的牛皮，今后会大有用处。好景不长，王母娘娘在得知自己的女儿与凡人成亲后勃然大怒，从人间带走了织女。凡人牛郎无计可施，这时他突然想起了老牛的忠告，急忙拿出牛皮并坐在上面。牛郎紧追不舍，就在快追上的时候，王母娘娘用发簪划出一片星河拦住了他。织女和牛郎因分隔两地而痛哭不已，喜鹊们被他们的深情感动，搭了一座鹊桥。王母娘娘无奈，只好允许织女和牛郎每年农历七月初七在鹊桥上相会一次。这便是一年一度的七夕节的由来。

It is said that Weaver Girl was a fairy in heaven, while Cowherd was a mortal in the human world. He was an orphan and depended on an old cow transformed by an immortal. Weaver Girl sneaked out from heaven and came to take a bath. Cowherd fell in love with her at the first sight. The old cow told Cowherd that the Weaver Girl wouldn't fly back to heaven and would become his wife if he stole her clothes. Therefore, Cowherd secretly hid Weaver Girl's clothes. Weaver Girl fell in love with Cowherd when looking for clothes. After that, they lived together and enjoyed a happy life. After a few years, the old cow died of a long-term illness. Before he died, he told the Cowherd to peel off his magical cowhide, which would be of great benefit in the future. Unfortunately, the Queen Mother from heaven flew into a rage when she heard that her daughter was married to a man. The Queen Mother came and took Weaver Girl back to heaven. The ordinary cowherd had nothing to do. At this time, he suddenly remembered the advice of the old cow, hurriedly took out the cowhide and sat on it. Cowherd was trying to catch them, but the Queen Mother drew the galaxy with a hairpin to stop him. Weaver Girl and Cowherd cried mournfully because they were separated from each other. Magpies were moved by their love and built a magpie bridge. The Queen Mother had no choice but to allow the Weaver Girl and the Cowherd to meet on the magpie bridge on the seventh day of July in the lunar calendar every year. This is the origin of the Qixi Festival.

第一节 七夕节的习俗：祭月、乞巧、吃巧果
Section 1 Customs of the Qixi Festival: Offer Sacrifices to the Moon, Beg for Dexterity, and Eat Qiaoguo

七夕节从西汉开始普及，鼎盛于宋代。在七夕节这一天，人们通常会祭月、乞巧和吃巧果。许多地区的年轻姑娘还喜欢用树的液浆兑水洗头发，用花草染指甲也是大多数女子与儿童的庆祝方式。因为有情男女总在七夕夜晚对着天上的织女祈求，期望自己可以获得美满的姻缘，所以，七夕节又被称为"中国情人节"。

The Qixi Festival got popular in the Western Han Dynasty and flourished in the Song Dynasty. At the Qixi Festival, people usually offer sacrifices to the moon, beg for dexterity and eat Qiaoguo. Young girls in many areas also like to wash their hair with the liquid pulp of trees mixed with water. Dyeing nails with flowers and plants is also a way to celebrate the Qixi Festival for most women and children. Because affectionate men and women always pray to the weaver girl in the sky on Qixi night, hoping that they can get a happy marriage. Therefore, the Qixi Festival is also known as "Chinese Valentine's Day".

1. 祭月

祭月主要有两种形式，一种是拜织女，一般由女性祭拜；另一种是拜魁星，一般由男性祭拜。

织女是爱情的象征。在进行拜织女仪式前,女孩子们会提前斋戒一天。到主持仪式的人家里后,她们先在案前焚香礼拜,接着围坐在桌前,默念自己的愿望。不同地方拜织女的形式也各不相同。在中国福建,人们相伴来到七娘妈(织女)庙,供奉花果、脂粉、牲礼等。

魁星在中国古代是掌管文章兴衰的神,在文人学子心中具有至高无上的地位。"拜魁星"一般有三个步骤。祭拜前,学子要先糊一个右手拿着笔的纸人魁星,并将其放在案台上。祭拜时,学子鸣炮焚香礼拜。祭拜后,大家坐在一起享用美食。

1. Offer Sacrifices to the Moon

There are two main forms of offering sacrifices to the moon. One is women worshipping Weaver Girl, the other is men worshipping Kuixing.

Weaver Girl symbolizes love. Before the worship ceremony, the girls often fast one day in advance to bathe. When everyone arrived at the home of the host, the girls first burned incense before the table, then sat around the table, reciting their wishes towards Weaver Girl. Different places worship Weaver Girl in different forms. In Fujian Province, people usually worship at the Qiniangma (Weaver Girl) temple with flowers and fruits, rouge, domestic animals, etc.

Kuixing was the God judging if articles were good in ancient China, so he was the most important God for scholars. "Worship Kuixing" generally includes three steps. Students should first make a paper figure Kuixing with a pen in his right hand, and put it on the table before the worship. Then, students set fireworks, burn incense and worship Kuixing. After the worship, students sit together and enjoy delicious food.

2. 乞巧

"乞巧"是女子之间相互比赛手艺的一个民俗。"乞巧"的形式多种多样,如穿针乞巧、对月穿针等。

第一种形式是穿针乞巧,又叫"赛巧"。她们用事先准备好的相等数量的针线进行比赛,谁穿得越快,谁乞到的巧越多,那么这个人便是得巧者。穿得慢的称为"输巧","输巧"的人要将自己事先准备好的奖品送给得巧者。女孩子们也会互相赠送准备好的礼品，表达深厚的友情。乞巧的第二种形式是"对月穿针"。七夕傍晚，乞巧祭拜结束后，女子将准备好的五彩丝线和七根银针拿出来，互相比试穿针技艺，谁先把七根针穿完，就预示着将来她能成为巧手女。

2. Begging for Dexterity

"Qiqiao"（beg for dexterity）is a folk custom of women competing with each other. There are many forms of "Qiqiao", such as threading the needle race and threading seven needles in the moonlight, etc.

The first form of Qiqiao is the threading the needle race, girls compete and thread an equal number of needles prepared in advance. The fastest and most skillful girl is the one who have successfully begged for dexterity. Those who thread slower are called "qiao-losers" and should give their prepared prizes to the fastest girl. Girls will also give each other prepared gifts to express deep friendship. The second form of Qiqiao is threading seven needles in the moonlight. On the evening of Qixi Festival, girls take out the prepared colorful silk thread and seven silver needles after the worship. Girls compare their needle threading skills. Whoever successfully threads the seven needles first will become a skillful woman in the future.

3. 吃巧果

在七夕节，人们乞巧时的代表性食物是巧果。"巧"和"桥"同音，人们认为七夕吃巧果可以帮助牛郎织女在鹊桥上相会。

巧果，又叫"乞巧果子"，是中国的传统美食之一。巧果形状各异，可以用"七曲八弯"来形容。虽然巧果主要由简单的油、面、糖、蜜制成，但是人们总是可以凭借巧手将巧果捏得令人垂涎三尺，例如可以在白面团里加入青汁粉、南瓜和紫薯等食材，将白色巧果创新成五颜六色的"新品种"。七夕晚上，人们将巧果放在庭院的桌子上，祭月结束后，人们往往会聚在一起品尝巧果。然而随着时间的推移，巧果逐渐由各种糕点取代。

3. Eat Qiaoguo

At the Qixi Festival, Qiaoguo is the representative food when people beg for dexterity. "Qiao" is homonymous with "bridge", and "guo" means fruits. People think that eating Qiaoguo at the Qixi Festival can help Cowherd and Weaver Girl meet on the bridge.

Qiaoguo, also known as "Qiqiao guozi", is one of the traditional delicacies in China. Qiaoguo varies in shapes, which people describe as "multiple bends". Although Qiaoguo is mainly made of oil, flour, sugar and honey, people can always make it delicious with their skillful hands. For example, barley leaves powder, pumpkin, purple potato and other ingredients can be added to the white dough to innovate the white fruit into a colorful "new variety". On the evening of the Qixi Festival, people put Qiaoguo on the table in the courtyard. After the worship, people often get together to eat Qiaoguo. However, Qiaoguo was gradually replaced by other cakes with the time.

第二节　今天的七夕节：
两情若是久长时，又岂在朝朝暮暮
Section 2　Today's Qixi Festival：
If Love between Both Sides Can Last for Aye,
Why Need They Stay Together Night and Day?[①]

七夕节，又被称为"中国情人节"。随着时代的发展，情人节日益受到年轻一代的喜爱，七夕节也因为和情人节相似的文化内涵——对甜蜜爱情的追求而逐渐被年轻人所关注。与此同时，中国的七夕节文化也慢慢走出国门，与越南、日本、韩国等国的民族文化融合发展，开辟了新的天地。

The Qixi Festival is also known as "Chinese Valentine's Day". Valentine's Day and the Qixi Festival have a similar cultural connotation — the pursuit of sweet love, so the Qixi Festival attract the attention of the younger generation. At the same

---

① 许渊冲译。

time, China's Qixi Festival culture is slowly going abroad, integrating with the native cultures of Japan, Republic of Korea, Vietnam and other countries, attaining a wider development.

1. 越南

越南人庆祝七夕节的方式和中国有异曲同工之妙。越南华人祭月所用的贡品主要是菱角、金钱饼、花生等,其中还包含极具代表性的"禾秧"和"七姐盘"。

与中国不同的是,越南的七夕节还是祭奠死者的日子。在这一天,人们通常会在门口放上美味的食物,以便死者的灵魂能够吃饱喝足、毫无牵挂地离开。越南人认为虽然七夕是情人节,但是在七月结婚便会和牛郎织女一样相隔两地。所以,他们通常不会选择在七月举办婚礼。

1. Vietnam

The way Vietnamese celebrate Qixi Festival is similar to that of in China. Vietnamese Chinese sacrifice to the moon with water chestnut, cakes, peanuts, etc. They also use rice seedling which represents Cowherd's good harvest and a plate containing thread, needles, and cosmetics.

Unlike China, the Qixi Festival in Vietnam is also a day to show respect to the departed. On this day, people usually put delicious food at the door so that the soul of the departed can be full and leave without concern. Vietnamese believe that although Qixi Festival is Valentine's day, a couple getting married on this day will be separated the same as Cowherd and Weaver Girl. Therefore, they usually don't choose to hold their wedding in lunar seventh month.

2. 日本

日本七夕节称"Tanabata",与中国不同的是,日本七夕节的日期是阳历7月7日。七夕节的习俗继承了乞巧的形式,但是其中的内涵却发生了巨大变化。中国的七夕多是年轻男女的节日,而日本的七夕是男女老少都会庆祝的祈愿节。

每年七夕节,日本的男女老少便会聚集在一起准备新鲜的树枝,并将这些树枝别在大门或者玄关处。人们还会用各式各样的"短册",也就是五颜六色的纸条来装饰树枝。这些纸条并不仅仅起装饰作用,人们还会将自己的愿望写在"短册"上,祈祷自己的愿望能够尽快实现。日本还会举办"七夕祭",人们常常会穿着华丽的服装,跟着花车开始热闹的游行,极富民族特色。

2. Japan

The Qixi Festival is called Tanabata in Japan and falls on the seventh day of July in the Gregorian calendar differing from that of in China. The custom of the Qixi Festival inherits the form of begging for dexterity, but its connotation has changed greatly. The Qixi Festival in China is a festival mainly for the young while it is a prayer festival celebrated by men, women, old and young in Japan.

At the Japanese Qixi Festival, men, women, the old and the young gather together to prepare fresh branches and pin them at the gate or porch. In addition, people will decorate branches with all kinds of colorful paper strips. People also write their wishes on the paper strips to pray for their wishes to come true. In addition, "Qixi Festival Celebration" is usually held, where people wear gorgeous cultural clothing and join a lively parade with floats.

3. 韩国

祭祀是韩国必不可少的庆七夕活动,主要有集体祭祀和家庭祭祀两种,这是韩国人独特的庆祝形式。此时祭祀的目的不再是乞巧,而是为了祈求平安。祭祀前,妇女会在案台上放上干净的井水以便祭祀的时候使用。

由于中国和韩国同处东亚文化圈,中韩两国的七夕节习俗也有相同之处。和中国一样,韩国七夕节最具代表性的习俗是祭月。七夕早上,韩国的妇女们将黄瓜、香瓜、花生等贡品放在案台上,祈求自己能和织女一样获得灵巧的双手。除了祭月外,韩国人还会在七夕这天晒书曝衣,各家各户的庭院都铺满了拿出来晒的衣服和书籍。

3. Republic of Korea

On Qixi Festival day, South Koreans will also hold sacrificial activities, mainly including collective sacrifice and family sacrifice. This is a unique form of celebration for South Koreans. At this time, the purpose of sacrifice is no longer to beg for dexterity, but to pray for safety. Women put clean well water on the table for sacrifice before the activity.

As China and Republic of Korea are located in the East Asian cultural circle, the customs of the Qixi Festival in China and Republic of Korea also have similarities. The most representative folk custom of South Korean Qixi Festival, like China, is to offer sacrifices to the moon. On the morning of the Qixi Festival, South Korean women put tributes, such as cucumbers, cantaloupes, peanuts and other foods on the table, praying that they could get dexterous hands like Weaver Girl. Additionally, South Koreans also dry books and clothes on Qixi Festival, and the courtyards of each family are covered with clothes and books.

西方国家一般不庆祝七夕节，而是庆祝情人节。情人节，又称"圣瓦伦丁节"，是欧美各国青年人最喜爱的节日之一。西方情人节和中国七夕节都体现了年轻男女对忠贞爱情的向往，但是由于中西方人性格的差异，庆祝方式大相径庭。

Western countries generally don't celebrate the Qixi Festival, but celebrate Valentine's day. Valentine's day, also known as "Saint Valentine's Day", is one of the favorite festivals for young people in western countries. Both Western Valentine's day and the Qixi Festival reflect the yearning of young men and women for loyal love, but due to the differences between Chinese and Western personalities, the celebration methods are very different.

4. 法国

爱墙，法国浪漫的代表物。在情人节这一天，成千上万的情侣们来到写满了"我爱你"的爱墙前互相拥抱，互诉衷肠。

法国最令情人向往之地非情人小镇莫属。情人小镇从1965年开始举办情人节活动，每年都有来自全国各地的情侣到情人小镇参加庆祝活动，情侣们还可以在情人小镇的情人花园一起种下属于自己的爱情之树。如果在情人节这一天年轻男女遇到了自己的心仪之人，他们便可以拿走街头玫瑰应急箱里的玫瑰花去表达爱意。街头玫瑰应急箱的设置不仅给一见钟情的男女提供了表达爱意的机会，而且还让巴黎的街道洋溢着浪漫与幸福。

4. France

Love wall（French：Le mur des je t'aime），the representative of French romance. On Valentine's day，thousands of lovers come to the love wall which full of "I love you" to hug and tell each other their hearts.

The most desirable town in France for lovers is Saint Valentin. Saint Valentin started to have Valentine's Day activities in 1965. Every year，lovers from all over the country come to Saint Valentin to participate in celebrations and plant their own love tree in the lover's garden of Saint Valentin. If young men and women meet their loved one on this day，they can get the roses from the emergency box to express their love. The setting of rose emergency box on the street provides an opportunity for men and women to express their love to the one they fall in love with at first sight，and also makes Paris full of romance and happiness.

5. 美国

在美国，无论老少，几乎所有夫妻或者情侣都会庆祝情人节。美国人认为，情人节是所有相爱的男女必须共同庆祝的一个节日。

鲜花和巧克力是美国情人节的经典礼物，选择隆重过节的情侣或夫妻还会提前在餐厅订好位置，用浪漫的烛光晚餐来庆祝节日。并且，已有子女的父母也需要给自己的孩子准备好鲜花和巧克力，给予他们最诚挚的祝福，希望自己的孩子能在将来获得忠贞的爱情。小朋友也会带上糖果和心形的贴纸去学校，到了学校后，大家互相赠送礼物，互道祝福。情人节在美国是全员参与的重要节日。

5. The United States

In the United States，almost all couples，no matter what they ages are，celebrate Valentine's day. Americans believe that Valentine's Day is a festival that all loving men and women must celebrate together.

Flowers and chocolates are the classic gifts of Valentine's day in the United States. Couples who choose to celebrate the festival well will also book a place in the restaurant in advance and celebrate the festival with a romantic candlelight dinner for two. Moreover, parents with children also need to prepare flowers and chocolates for their children, giving them the most sincere wishes, and hoping that their children can get loyal love in the future. Children will also bring candy and heart-shaped stickers to school. When they arrive at school, they will exchange gifts and blessings. Valentine's Day is an important festival for all people in the United States.

玫瑰花(黄婧瑶 摄)
Roses(By Huang Jingyao)

第三节 "秾艳尽怜胜彩绘":动手折纸玫瑰
Section 3 "Delicate Colors of Roses are Better than Color Painting": Learn to Make Paper Roses

1. 材料

三张彩纸、胶棒。

1. Materials

Three pieces of colored paper, a glue stick.

2. 注意事项

如果你有任何问题，请举手提问。

2. Attention

If you have any questions, please raise your hand.

3. 步骤

3. Steps

（1）拿出一张准备好的正方形彩纸，对折 3 次。将折好的彩纸展开，顺时针旋转 90°，再重复对折 3 次，并展开。

（1）Fold a square colored paper in half three times. Unfold the colored paper and rotate it clockwise by 90°. Fold it in half for three times and unfold it.

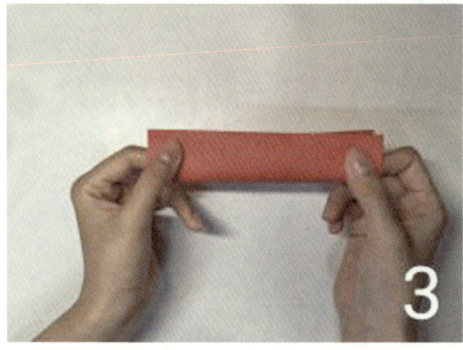
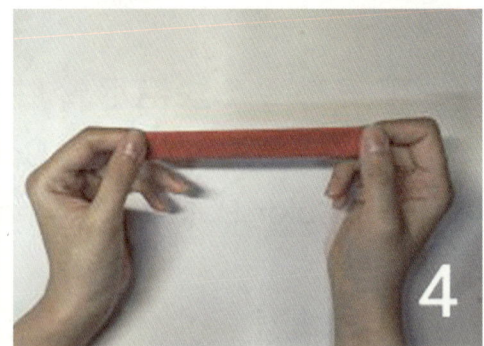

步骤（1）对折（王萱 摄）

Step（1）Fold in Half（By Wang Xuan）

（2）沿着彩纸的两条对角线对折两次，展开。在每个角的两个格子处向内折叠，重复4次。沿着其中一条对角线再次对折，再将长边对折，使得①②两点重合，展开；沿着另一条对角线重复以上步骤。

（2）Fold the colored paper twice along the two diagonals and unfold. Fold inward at the two squares of each corner and repeat 4 times. Fold in half again along one of the diagonals, and fold the long side in half to make sure that ① and ② overlap before unfolding it. Repeat the above steps along the other diagonal.

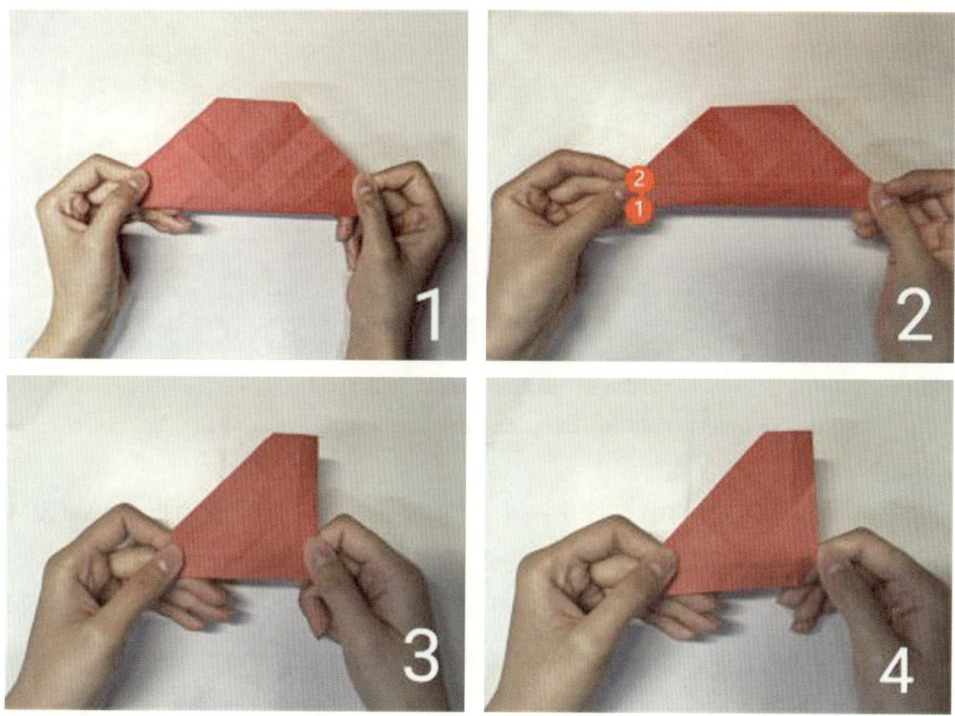

步骤（2）沿着对角线对折（王萱 摄）
Step（2）**Fold Diagonally**（By Wang Xuan）

（3）在角的两个格子处向内折叠，展开。用手指抵住彩纸中央，沿着折线将其整理好，展开如图2所示。沿着四个角的折线进行折叠，如图3所示。

（3）Fold inward at the two corners and unfold. Press your finger against the center of the colored paper, arrange it along the fold line, and unfold it, as shown in Picture 2. Fold along the crease of the four corners, as shown in Picture 3.

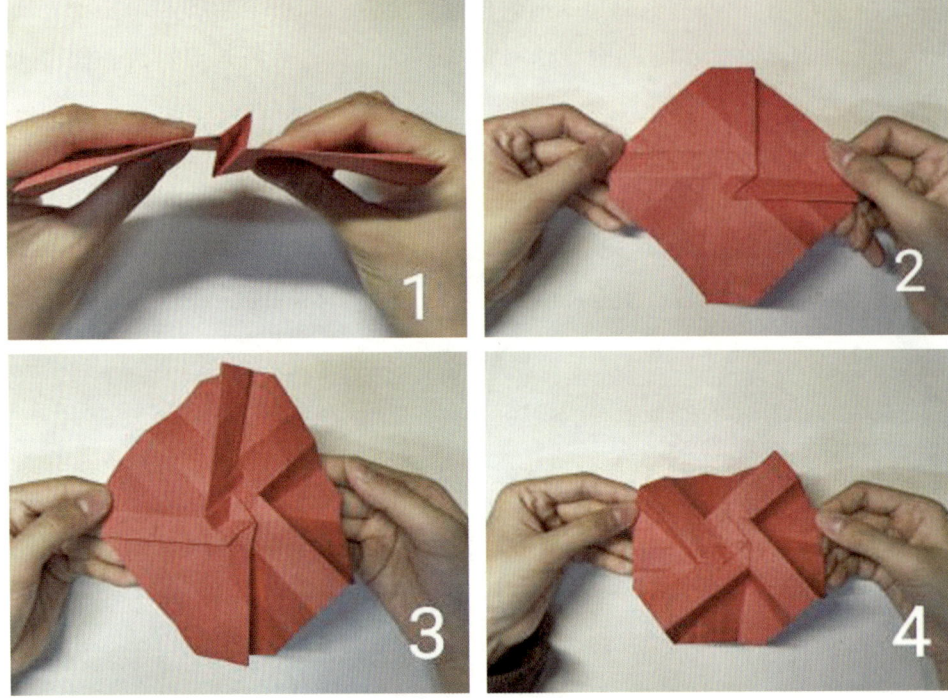

步骤（3）沿着折线对折（王萱 摄）
Step（3） Fold in Half along the Crease（By Wang Xuan）

（4）在彩纸四边的中点折出一个三角形，并沿着折线继续折叠，重复4次。如图3所示一个压一个地固定花瓣。

（4）Fold a triangle at the midpoint of one side of the colored paper, and fold in half along the crease. Repeating this step for the rest three sides of the colored paper（see Picture 3）. Fix the petals one by one.

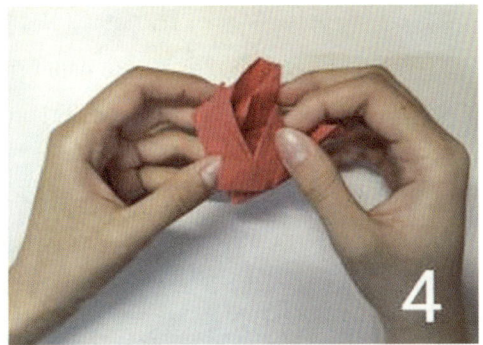

步骤（4）折出玫瑰花的模样（王萱 摄）
Step（4）Fold into the Shape of a Rose Flower（By Wang Xuan）

（5）调整花瓣，整理花朵。

（5）Adjust the petals and tidy the flowers.

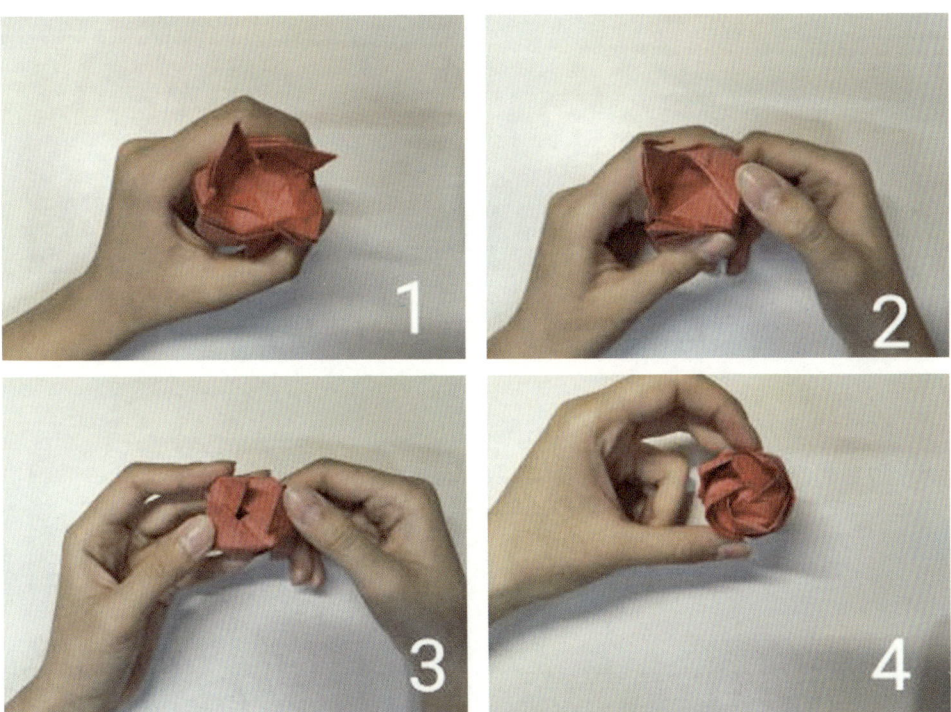

步骤（5）整理（王萱 摄）
Step（5）Tidy（By Wang Xuan）

（6）先折出"米"字折痕，再沿着折线向内折叠。

(6) Fold a piece of green paper in half lengthwise and unfold it. Fold the paper in half crosswise and unfold it. Fold the paper diagonally and unfold it, and repeat this step for the other two corners. Fold inward along the creases.

步骤（6）折"米"字（王萱 摄）
Step (6) Fold out the "米" (By Wang Xuan)

（7）沿着折线进行折叠，如图所示。

(7) Fold along creases, as shown in picture.

· 第四章　七夕节文化双语教学设计 ·

步骤（7）折叠（王萱 摄）
Step（7）Fold（By Wang Xuan）

步骤（7）折叠并翻转（王萱 摄）
Step（7）Fold and Flip（By Wang Xuan）

（8）用彩纸制作根茎。

（8）Roll another piece of colored paper to make a stem.

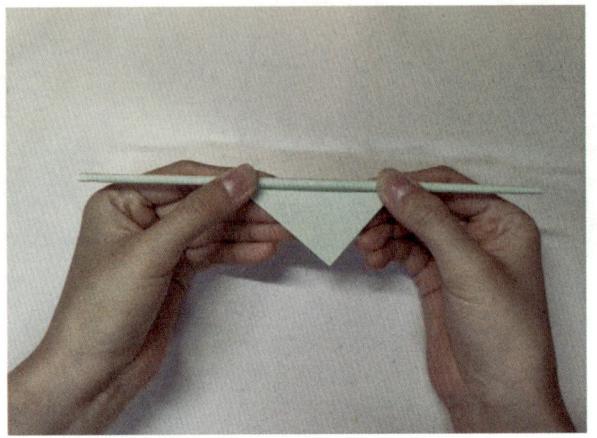

步骤（8）制作根茎（王萱 摄）
Step（8）Make a Stem（By Wang Xuan）

（9）用胶棒在彩纸的一个角涂上胶水，并固定。

（9）Use the glue stick to the corner onto the paper roll.

步骤（9）粘贴（王萱 摄）
Step（9）Paste（By Wang Xuan）

（10）组装花朵、枝叶和根茎。

（10）Assemble paper flowers, leaves and the stem.

步骤（10）组装（王萱 摄）
Step（10）Assemble（By Wang Xuan）

（11）完成！

（11）Complete！

步骤（11）完成（王萱 摄）
Step（11）Complete（By Wang Xuan）

第四节　七夕节文化双语教案

一、教学对象

对中华文化感兴趣的外国学生。

二、教学内容

1. 中国传统民间节日七夕节的起源及风俗；
2. 七夕节在海内外的体现和表征；
3. 西方情人节的体现和表征；
4. 玫瑰花的制作技巧。

三、教学目标

1. 帮助外国学生熟悉中国传统民间节日之七夕节文化；
2. 了解七夕节在我国邻国，如日本、越南和韩国等的体现和表征；
3. 比较我国七夕节与西方情人节的异同；
4. 帮助外国学生掌握七夕节玫瑰花的制作；
5. 帮助外国学生理解中西方由于性格的差异对爱情的追求方式有所不同：我国人民因为内敛的性格，对待爱情的方式是含蓄的；西方人民因为外向的性格，对待爱情的方式是主动的。

四、教学方法

1. 图片、视频法

利用图片、英文视频向学生展示七夕节的起源及各种风俗活动。

2. 演示法

通过演示法，教授玫瑰花的制作方法。

3. 互动法

通过教师提问、学生回答的方式，请学生介绍各自国家的七夕节/情人节的相关表征。

4. 讨论法

四人为一小组，讨论中国七夕节和西方情人节的不同。

5. 启发诱导法

启发学生总结对七夕节内涵的认识，并与本国相关传统文化内涵和价值观进行比较,揭示异同。

五、课时安排

三课时完成,每课时40分钟。
第一课时介绍七夕节的起源及风俗;
第二课时介绍七夕节在海外的流传和西方情人节的习俗;
第三课时介绍纸玫瑰花的制作技巧。

六、教学过程(三课时)

第一课时(40分钟):七夕节的起源和风俗

设计意图:以生动、精练的牛郎织女中华传统小故事开篇介绍七夕节的起源,力图通过"中国故事"引起学生的兴趣。利用图片、视频、实物等各种丰富手段展示中国人过七夕节的习俗,帮助学生了解七夕节的表征,并揭示其中的深层含义:中国人民祈求美好爱情,期待和谐幸福。

(一)组织教学(约2分钟)

教师进入课堂,检查多媒体设备,将教学所用的教案、课件及手工材料准备放置妥当。师生互相问候,教师点名,准备上课。

> T: Good morning, everyone! How are you today? Let's start the roll call first... Okay, everyone's here. Class begins.

(二)进入新课,介绍七夕节的起源(10分钟,内容详见双语讲稿导语)

1. 导入

(1)教师询问学生,在自己国家有没有跟爱情相关的节日,以此引入七夕节主题。

中国传统文化体验式双语教学设计

> T: Do you have any festivals related to love in your country? Please share this festival with us.

（2）教师板书"七夕"二字及拼音并领读两遍，教师向学生说明七夕节的时间及"七"在汉语中的意义。

2. 介绍七夕节的起源：牛郎织女的故事

（1）教师利用图片，以角色扮演的方式绘声绘色地向学生讲述牛郎和织女的故事。

> T: Now, let me tell you the story of Cowherd and Weaver Girl. Please listen carefully. After telling the story, I have a few questions for you.

（2）教师就七夕节起源故事中的小细节进行提问，考查学生对故事的理解并为后文介绍七夕节的风俗做准备。

问题：①织女是谁的女儿？（答案：王母娘娘）
②每年七月初七，牛郎和织女在谁搭起的桥上相会？这座桥叫什么桥？（答案：喜鹊，鹊桥）

> T: Whose daughter is Weaver Girl?
> T: On the seventh day of the seventh lunar month every year, who sets up a bridge for Cowherd and Weaver Girl to meet? What's the name of this bridge?

（三）介绍七夕节的主要风俗（约27分钟，内容详见双语讲稿第一节）

1. 导入

（1）教师提问学生，知道哪些过七夕节的风俗。

> T: What are the customs of Chinese people celebrating the Qixi Festival?

（2）教师整理学生答案，帮助学生梳理与七夕节有关的记忆并整合学生知道的七夕节风俗。

2. 介绍七夕节主要风俗之一：祭月

（1）教师展示三张都包含月亮的图片，请学生发现其中的共同点，引出"祭月"主题。

问题：你能发现这三张图片中的共同点吗？（答案：月亮）

T: Please look at the three pictures. Can you find something in common?

（2）教师利用图片解释祭月的两种形式：拜织女和拜魁星。

（3）教师总结祭月的寓意：古人对月亮的尊敬和对团圆、圆满的期待与追求。

3. 介绍七夕节主要风俗之二：乞巧

（1）教师展示穿针的图片，并现场演示穿针，请学生回答自己在做什么。

T: Please look at the picture and tell me what am I doing?

（2）教师结合织女的职业，运用启发式教学帮助学生理解七夕节穿针乞巧的原因。

（3）教师设计穿针比赛，邀请学生参与有奖穿针活动，以此增加课堂教学的趣味性。

（4）教师介绍穿针乞巧的内涵：古代女子对巧手的追求和期待。

4. 介绍七夕节主要风俗之三：吃巧果

（1）教师展示巧果的图片，请学生猜一猜是什么。

问题：图片中的食物是什么？你吃过吗？（答案：巧果）

T: What is the food in the picture? Have you had it?

（2）教师请学生品尝巧果，并介绍巧果的来历以及制作材料。

（3）教师总结吃巧果的寓意：古代女子对美好姻缘的期许和追求。

（四）小结（1分钟）

教师简单回顾七夕节的起源故事并简单梳理七夕节的风俗。

第二课时（40分钟）：世界各地的多元爱情节日

设计意图：通过对周边国家七夕节习俗以及西方情人节的介绍与比较，帮助学生更好地理解世界各地爱情节日的异同，以及世界人民对美好爱情的期盼和幸福生活的追求。

（一）复习回顾（约5分钟）

1. 教师请学生复述牛郎和织女的故事。
2. 教师展示图片，提问学生七夕节有哪些主要的风俗。

> T：Let us briefly review the origin of the Qixi Festival.

（二）进入新课，介绍世界各地的多元爱情节日（25分钟，内容详见双语讲稿第二节）

1. 导入

教师提问学生，还知道哪些国家过七夕节或者类似的爱情节日。

> T：Which countries do you know celebrating the Qixi Festival?

2. 介绍世界各地的多元爱情节日之一：越南七夕节

（1）教师展示世界地图，指出越南的地理位置。

（2）教师播放视频，向学生介绍七夕节祭月的风俗。

（3）教师提问学生，比较中越两国过七夕节的风俗有何异同。

> T: What are the similarities and differences between China and Vietnam in celebrating the Qixi Festival?

3. 介绍世界各地的多元爱情节日之二：日本七夕节

（1）教师展示世界地图，指出日本的地理位置。

（2）教师展示各式各样的"短册"图片，介绍日本七夕节的乞巧习俗，并从参与者、内容和内涵等方面说明日本七夕节的不同之处。

4. 介绍世界各地的多元爱情节日之三：韩国七夕节

（1）教师展示世界地图，指出韩国的地理位置。

（2）教师播放视频，向学生介绍七夕节拜织女、晒书曝衣的风俗。

（3）教师提问学生，比较中韩两国过七夕节的风俗有何异同。

> T: What are the similarities and differences between Chinese and South Korean celebrating the Qixi Festival?

5. 介绍世界各地的多元爱情节日之四：法国情人节

（1）教师展示世界地图，指出法国的地理位置。

（2）教师介绍法国巴黎街头的玫瑰应急箱以及情人小镇的特色活动，帮助学生了解法国情人节的特色。

6. 介绍世界各地的多元爱情节日之五：美国情人节

（1）教师展示世界地图，指出美国的地理位置。

（2）教师展示美国情人节的礼物，并从参与者、礼物、内涵等角度说明美国情人节的特色之处。

（三）练一练（10分钟，内容详见双语讲稿第四节）

1. 连一连

教师列出中国、越南、日本和法国等国的七夕习俗，请学生指出每个习俗分别对应哪个国家。

2. 选一选

教师编写与七夕节起源和风俗相关的选择题若干，请学生根据教学内容进行选择并订正。

第三课时（40分钟）：学习制作纸玫瑰花

设计意图：通过详细教授制作玫瑰花的步骤，帮助学生更好地理解和体会七夕节文化的内涵和表征。同时鼓励学生折玫瑰花并分享，激发学生热爱中华文化的热情。

（一）导入（2分钟）

教师展示自己折的纸玫瑰花，并向学生提问。

问题：你们知道这是什么吗？它的用处是什么？（答案：玫瑰，表达爱意等）

> T: Do you know what this is? What do people use it for?

（二）文化体验：教授制作纸玫瑰花（30分钟，内容详见双语讲稿第三节）

1. 教师发放材料并逐一介绍。

2. 教师现场演示并结合动图，教授学生如何折纸玫瑰花。

3. 教师请学生展示各自成品，并谈谈有什么感想。

（三）本课小结（7分钟）

1. 教师总结中国七夕节的起源、风俗和世界其他国家人民庆祝七夕节的风俗。

2. 教师总结世界人民庆祝爱情节日的美好愿望：年轻男女对忠贞爱情的向往，具有祈求美好爱情、期待和谐幸福的含义。

（四）布置作业（1分钟）

教师请学生课下试着折一朵纸玫瑰花并把它送给你喜欢的人。

> T: Please try to make one rose after class and give them to the person you like! Class is over, see you next time!

七、教学反思

风靡世界的情人节展示了西方爱情文化的独特之处，殊不知，中国也有这样的爱情节日——七夕节。中国的七夕节不但有一个关于爱情的美丽传说，更蕴含着内容丰富的多重意义，如祭月、乞巧等。

不同文化背景下的爱情节日，无论是参与对象还是内容形式等，都大相径庭，但是对于美好爱情和幸福生活的追求是全世界人民的共同意愿，因此在教学中，应突出中外爱情节日的比较：既有对中国与周边国家七夕节的比较，也有中国七夕节与西方情人节的比较，在比较中揭示异同，在比较中展示中华传统节日的内涵和意蕴。

"赠人玫瑰，手有余香"，体验折纸玫瑰的各个环节，既是一次七夕节的文化体验，又是一次手工大比拼。当学生手捧七彩纸玫瑰时，一定会感慨自己具备了成为能工巧匠的潜质，也希望学生们把自己的劳动成果赠予自己所爱的人，让中国的七夕节文化得以传播。

附：**辅助教学资源**

牛郎织女的故事：https：//haokan.baidu.com/v?pd=wisenatural&vid=6622706756659885104

讨论与练习
Discussion and Practice

1. 讨论

1. Discussion

（1）你们有没有听过关于爱情的故事呢，能和大家分享一下吗？

（1）Have you ever heard a love story? Can you share it with us?

（2）你们更喜欢中国七夕节的哪一个习俗，为什么？

（2）Which one of the customs of the Qixi Festival do you like most and why?

（3）西方情人节也是象征爱情的节日，你认同吗？

（3）Western Valentine's Day is also a festival symbolizing love. Do you agree?

（4）大家是否会庆祝情人节，怎么庆祝呢？

（4）Do you celebrate Valentine's day? How do you celebrate it?

（5）对比七夕节和情人节，你认为两者有何异同？

（5）What are the similarities and differences between the Qixi Festival and Valentine's day?

2. 练习

2. Practice

（1）连一连

（1）Matching

中国 China	A. 七姐盘 A plate containing thread, needles, and cosmetics
法国 France	B. 祭月 Offer sacrifices to the moon
日本 Japan	C. 七夕祭 Qixi Festival Celebration
越南 Vietnam	D. 情人小镇 Saint Valentin

(2) 选一选

(2) Choosing (Select the correct one from the four options)

- 越南与下列中国哪个省份交界？（　　）

  Which province of China borders Vietnam？（　　）

  A. Jiangsu　　　B. Guangxi　　　C. Shandong　　　D. Guangdong

- 哪个选项与乞巧无关？（　　）

  Which optionis not related to Begging for Dexterity？（　　）

  A. Qiaoguo　　　　　　　　　　　　　　　　B. Douqiao

  C. Threading seven needles in the moonlight　　D. Qiao-losers

- 哪个国家有"爱墙"？（　　）

  Which country has Love Wall（French：Le mur des je t'aime）？（　　）

  A. Japan　　　B. America　　　C. France　　　D. Canada

- 以下哪个是中国七夕节的传统习俗？（　　）

  Which one is the traditional custom of the Qixi Festival in China？（　　）

  A. Eating steamed cakes

  B. Pinning fresh branches at the gate or porch

  C. Emergency Boxes of Rose

D. Worshipping Weaver Girl

答案
Answer

(1) B   D   C   A

(2) B   A   C   D

第五章　中秋节文化双语教学设计
Chapter V　Bilingual Teaching Design of Mid-Autumn Festival

中秋节（王萱 绘）
The Mid-Autumn Festival（By Wang Xuan）

导语
Introduction

很久以前，天上突然同时出现了十个太阳，火热的阳光晒干了河水，晒死了庄稼，老百姓没有水喝也没有粮食吃，难以生存。英勇的后羿用神弓射下其中九个太阳，解救了大家。许多人纷纷拜他为师，心术不正的逢蒙也混了进来。后羿偶然得到一颗仙药，并将其交予妻子嫦娥保管。农历八月十五这天，逢蒙持刀闯入后羿家中，威胁嫦娥交出仙药。善良的嫦娥情急之下吞食仙药，随后便飞向月亮，变成了神仙。此后，每年的这一天，百姓们都会祭拜月亮，感念嫦娥，祈求团圆。这就是中秋节的由来。

A long time ago, ten suns suddenly appeared in the sky at the same time. Rivers and lakes dried up, while plants and crops withered. With no water to drink and no food to eat, people couldn't survive. A brave man named Hou Yi shot down nine of the ten suns with a magic bow and saved people. Many people became his apprentices, including Pang Meng, a man who had evil intention. Hou Yi got an elixir by accident and gave it to his wife Chang'e for safe keeping. On the 15th day of the eighth lunar month, Pang Meng broke into Hou Yi's house with a sword and threatened Chang'e to hand over the elixir. In desperation, Chang'e swallowed it. In no time, she transformed into an immortal, flying towards the moon. Since then, on this day people worshiped the moon to appreciate Chang'e and pray for reunion. This is the origin of the Mid-Autumn Festival.

第一节 中秋节的习俗：饮桂花酒、赏月、吃月饼
Section 1 Customs of the Mid-Autumn Festival: Drinking Osmanthus Wine, Appreciating the Moon, Eating Moon Cakes

中秋节作为中国的一个传统节日，其风俗习惯丰富多彩、经久不衰。

自古以来，中秋节就有饮桂花酒、赏月、吃月饼等习俗。每逢中秋，亲朋好友都会互赠月饼以表祝福。到了晚上，全家欢聚一堂。吃完团圆饭后，大家一边分享美味的月饼，一边赏月闲谈。家家户户都洋溢着团圆和睦的气氛。

As a traditional festival in China, the Mid-Autumn Festival has a variety of enduring customs. Since ancient times, people have been admiring and worshiping the full moon by drinking osmanthus wine, appreciating the moon, eating moon cakes and so on. Every year at the Mid-Autumn Festival, friends and relatives always give moon cakes to each other to express their best wishes. In the evening, all families gather together and have a family reunion dinner. After dinner, they will share the delicious moon cakes, appreciate the full moon and chat together. Everywhere is immersed in an atmosphere of harmony and happiness.

1. 饮桂花酒

饮桂花酒是中秋节的众多习俗之一。中秋正值桂花盛开时节，民间盛行采摘桂花，酿制成桂花酒。传说中，好心的酿酒娘子救下吴刚大仙变成的老人后，天上飘下一个装着桂花种子的黄布袋，从此人间才有了桂花酒。桂花酒色泽浅黄，芳香馥郁，有开胃健脾之功效，且老少皆宜，是亲朋团聚时的必备佳酿。

饮桂花酒习俗传承至今，仍深受人们喜爱。与此同时，还出现了许多桂花美食，如桂花蜜、桂花鸭、桂花藕等。这些桂花美食，通常是中秋佳节餐桌上不可或缺的美味。中秋阖家团圆之际，人们品尝桂花美酒美食，互相分享节日祝福。

1. Drinking Osmanthus Wine

Drinking osmanthus wine is one of the many customs of the Mid-Autumn Festival. Osmanthus flowers are in full bloom at the Mid-Autumn Festival so it is popular among the people to pick the osmanthus flowers and make osmanthus wine. According to legend, after a female winemaker saved an old man changed by the immortal Wu Gang, a yellow cloth bag came from the sky with a lot of osmanthus seeds inside. Since then, there has been osmanthus wine in the world. Osmanthus wine, with yellow and fragrant light, is a great appetizer for all ages. It is also the best drink for family and friend reunions.

This custom is still popular until now. Meanwhile, more osmanthus delicacies appeared, such as osmanthus honey, osmanthus duck, osmanthus lotus root and so on. These osmanthus delicacies are often presented on people's dinner tables during the Mid-Autumn Festival. Families taste osmanthus wine and eat osmanthus food, sharing blessings with each other.

2. 赏月

古代，人们通过祭拜月亮上的嫦娥以祈求平安幸福。魏晋时期，随着人们对天体有了更理性的认识，赏月传统开始形成，其盛于唐宋并变得更加欢娱。

中秋佳节，人们在独自赏月之时，不免会想到远在异乡的亲人。许多古人的诗中也会借赏月来表达相思和渴望团圆的情感。苏轼《水调歌头》说道："人有悲欢离合，月有阴晴圆缺，此事古难全。但愿人长久，千里共婵娟。"苏轼将月亮的圆缺与人生的离合相比，表达人间的离别是难免的，即使相隔千万里也还是能够通过同一轮月亮遥寄相思。这让读到这首诗的人都对未来充满希望。现在，随着时代的发展，人们可以用手机拍下中秋佳节的圆月，并通过电话或微信视频等多种方式，表达对远方家人的思念。

2. Appreciating the Moon

Ancient Chinese people worshipped Chang'e in the moon to pray for peace and happiness. In the Wei and Jin Dynasties, people had a more rational understanding of the moon, and started to appreciate the moon. This activity flourished in the Tang and Song Dynastiesand became more entertaining.

At the Mid-Autumn Festival, when people are admiring the full moon alone, they may inevitably think of their families and relatives far away. Many ancient poems also express the feelings of lovesickness and desire for reunion by describing the moon. Su Shi *Prelude to Water Melody* said that "Men have sorrow and joy; they part or meet again. The moon is bright or dim and she may wax or wane. There has been nothing perfect since the olden days. So let us wish that man will live long as he can! Though miles apart, we'll share the beauty she displays". Su Shi compared the wane and wax of the moon with the separation and reunions of life. It means departure is inevitable. Even though being thousands of miles apart, they can enjoy the same moon and share an expression of missing their loved ones. This poem gives the reader expectations for the future.

With the development of science and technology, people can also take pictures of the moon at the Mid-Autumn Festival by mobile phone and express their missing for their family members far away through phone calls, WeChat video and so on.

3. 吃月饼

月饼是中秋节的特色美食，有十分悠久的历史。古时，月饼是祭拜月神的贡品，唐朝开始才形成中秋节吃月饼的习俗；明清时期，中秋节吃月饼发展成为普遍的风俗。时至今日，月饼的种类越来越多，而且大多具有地方特色，其中最有名的主要有三种：第一种是广式月饼，饼皮图案精美，口感酥软，是现在中秋节最常见的月饼；第二种是京式月饼，饼皮没有图案，皮馅制作精细繁杂，是北方月饼的主要代表；第三种则是苏式月饼，饼皮酥松，多为肉馅，盛行于江浙一带。

随着文化融合的发展以及与时俱进的追求，许多风格独特的新式月饼广受人们青睐，如法式月饼、冰皮月饼和冰淇淋月饼等。除此之外，水果月饼、海鲜月饼、火腿月饼等特殊口味的月饼也层出不穷。月饼外形圆润，寓意团圆美好，寄托了人们祈望全家团圆的美好愿望，也表达了对亲朋好友的思念之情。在中秋节，人们把月饼赠送给亲朋好友，寓意着将美好祝福送给他人。

3. Eating Moon Cakes

Moon cakes are the special food of the Mid-Autumn Festival, which have a long history. In ancient times, moon cakes were offered as tribulation to the moon god during the Mid-Autumn Festival. The custom of eating moon cakes during the Mid-Autumn Festival began to form in the Tang Dynasty. By the Ming and Qing Dynasties, it had become a common custom to eat moon cakes at the Mid-Autumn Festival. Until now, there are more and more kinds of moon cakes. Many of them have local characteristics. Three kinds of moon cakes are the most famous. The first kind is the Cantonese-style moon cake, with delicate designs and tender taste. It is one of the most well-known kinds. The second kind is the Beijing-style moon cake, which does not have patterns on the skin, but its skins and fillings are exquisitely made. This type is the main representative of moon cakes in northern China. The third kind is the Suzhou-style moon cake, with crispy skin and meat fillings, which is popular in Jiangsu and Zhejiang areas.

With cultural convergence and the advancement of the times, many innovative moon cakes are favored by more and more people, such as French moon cakes, ice skin moon cakes, ice cream moon cakes, etc. In addition, there are many special flavors of the moon cakes, such as fruit moon cakes, seafood moon cakes, ham moon cakes and so on. The shape of a mooncake is round, meaning reunion and happiness. It reflects people's good wishes for family reunion and sentiment of missing for relatives and friends. At the Mid-Autumn Festival, people also give moon cakes to their friends and relatives, which means giving good wishes to others.

除了以上常见的三种中秋节风俗之外，中国南方地区依然保留着拜月的习俗。人们在院子里设香案台，摆上月饼、水果等贡品，全家依次祭拜月神，祈求平安。中秋也是玩花灯的节日，不同地方的花灯各不相同，但都没有元宵节一样的大型灯会。中秋节的风俗多种多样，都蕴含着人们对家庭团圆、生活幸福的美好期望。

In addition to the three common Mid-Autumn Festival customs mentioned above, worshipping the moon is still popular in China's southern region. On the evening of the Mid-Autumn Festival, an incense table is set up in the courtyard and tributes such as moon cakes and fruits are placed on the table. The whole family worship the moon to pray for safety. The Mid-Autumn Festival is also the day to play with lanterns. Different places have different lanterns, but there is no large-scale lantern fair like the Lantern Festival. The diverse customs of the Mid-Autumn Festival are all based on people's good expectations for family reunions and happy life.

第二节 今天的中秋节：
佳节共赏天上月，中秋一品人间情
Section 2　Today's Mid-Autumn Festival：
Appreciating the Full Moon during the Festival, Sharing the Same Feelings in the World

受中华文化影响，中秋节也成为中国周边国家和地区的传统节日。在与当地文化交流与融合的过程中，中秋节演变成为各具地区特色的节日。

Influenced by the Chinese culture, the Mid-Autumn Festival has also become a traditional festival in some other countries and regions around China. In the process of cultural exchange and integration with the local people, the Mid-Autumn Festival has evolved into a festival with its own regional characteristics.

1. 越南

在越南，中秋节被称为"望月节"，也是越南儿童的节日。"阿贵"的传说口耳相传，他因为误用污水浇灌仙树而被带上月宫，是越南的"嫦娥"。中秋节的晚上，孩子们最喜欢手提鲤鱼灯出游，这是因为传说有人用纸制的鲤鱼灯压制住了害人的鲤鱼精，因此孩子们在中秋之夜会提着鲤鱼灯，既有祈求平安之意，也预示着他们能够取得成功。有些地方还会有舞狮表演。到了晚上，全家欢聚一堂，在欣赏月亮的同时品尝美味的月饼与水果。

1. Vietnam

In Vietnam, the Mid-Autumn Festival is called Tết Trung Thu and it is also a festival for Vietnamese children. The legend of "Cuôi" has been passed down orally. He was taken to the moon palace for watering the fairy tree with the misuse of sewage. So in Vietnam, Cuôi is like Chang'e in Chinese legend. On the evening of the Mid-Autumn Festival, children like to travel with carp lanterns. This is because it is said that someone in ancient times made a carp lantern with paper and succeeded in suppressing a carp monster who always harmed people. So at the evening of the

Mid-Autumn Festival, children go out with carp lanterns everywhere. This not only means praying for peace, but also indicates that the children could achieve success. There are also lion dances in some places. At night, the whole families gather together, appreciating the moon and tasting delicious moon cakes and fruits.

2. 泰国

在泰国，中秋节又被称为"祈月节"。人们在这天参拜月亮，互相祝福。供桌上会放着中国民间传说中的"八洞神仙"，摆满寿桃、月饼之类的美食。传说中，中秋祈月，八仙会带着寿桃到月宫给观音祝寿，神仙们就会赐福人间。泰国还有榴莲味的特色月饼。柚子是泰国人在中秋节必吃的当季水果，柚子又大又圆，象征"团圆"。

2. Thailand

In Thailand, the Mid-Autumn Festival is also called the "Moon-Praying Festival". On this day, people worship the moon and bless each other. On the table, there will be the "Eight Immortals" of Chinese folklore. Longevity peach buns, moon cakes and other delicacies will also be presented on the table. According to Thai legend, when people were praying to the moon at the Mid-Autumn Festival, the Eight Immortals would take the longevity peach buns to the Palace in the Moon to celebrate Guanyin's birthday with good wishes blessing the world. Thailand also has durian-flavored moon cakes. Grapefruit is the season fruit Thais must eat at the Mid-Autumn Festival. It is big and round, as a symbol of reunion.

3. 韩国

在韩国，中秋节是一年中的三大节日之一，韩语称为"秋夕"，人们有三天假期庆祝佳节。节前人们会利用周末扫坟祭祖。秋夕当天，全家人穿着传统服饰出游，到景福宫等地进行踢毽子、打陀螺等各种民俗活动。韩国独特的中秋食物是松饼。松饼形如半月，用米粉制成，内馅是豆沙、枣泥等，放在铺满松针的蒸屉上蒸熟，象征收获。

3. Republic of Korea

In Republic of Korea, the Mid-Autumn Festival is one of the three major festivals of the year, which is called "Chuseok" in Korean. People have a three-day holiday to celebrate the festival. Before the festival, South Korean people will pay respects to their ancestors at weekends. On the festival day, the whole family dress the traditional clothes and travel to places like Gyeongbokgung Palace. They can kick shuttlecocks, play the spinning top and experience many other folk activities. South Korea's unique Mid-Autumn Festival food is Songpyeon. Songpyeon is shaped like a half moon, made of rice flour and filled with bean paste, jujube mud, etc. They are steamed on a steamer covered with pine needles, symbolizing harvest.

4. 日本

在日本，中秋节被称为"十五夜"，也叫"芋名月"。日本人在这一天同样有赏月的习俗，在日语里称为"月见"，赏月时吃的不是月饼，而是江米团子，又叫作"月见团子"。由于这个时期正是收获的季节，为了表达对大自然的感谢，日本人会举行各种庆祝活动。一些寺院和神社还会举办专门的赏月会，人们穿上富有民族特色的服装，抬着神龛到庙里进香。

4. Japan

In Japan, the Mid-Autumn Festival is known as "Jugoya", also known as "Moon-viewing Festival". The Japanese also have the custom of appreciating the moon on this day, known as "Tsukimi". Japanese people do not eat moon cakes, but glutinous rice dumplings, also called "Tsukimidango" when appreciating the moon. Since this period is the harvest season, the Japanese hold various celebrations to express their gratitude to nature. Some monasteries and shrines also have special activities to enjoy the moon. People put on ethnic costumes and carry shrines to the temple to offer incense.

随着时代的发展和华侨文化的影响，中秋节在东南亚、东亚和欧美一些国家也逐渐流行。海外华人华侨齐聚一堂，邀请当地居民，热闹过中秋。同时许多国家也融入自身特色，举办各式活动，欢庆中秋团圆。

With the development of the times and the influence of overseas Chinese culture, the Mid-Autumn Festival has gradually become popular in Southeast Asia, East Asia and some countries in Europe and America. Overseas Chinese people gather together and invite local residents to celebrate the Mid-Autumn Festival. At the same time, many countries integrate their characteristics to hold various activities to celebrate the Mid-Autumn Festival reunion.

第三节 "饼有酥与饴":制作冰皮月饼
Section 3 "Small Cakes are Filled with Malt Sugar and Ghee": Learn to Make Ice Skin Moon Cakes

1. 材料

预拌粉100g、草莓粉20g、熟食粉20g、豆沙馅料100g、模具1个、大碗1只、筷子1双、一次性手套1双。

1. Materials

Premixed flour 100g, strawberry powder 20g, cooked powder 20g, bean paste filling 100g, an embossing mold, a large bowl, a pair of chopsticks and a pair of disposable gloves.

准备材料(乔龙妍 摄)
Materials(By Qiao Longyan)

2. 步骤

2. Steps

（1）将冰皮月饼预拌粉和草莓粉倒入碗中。

(1) Pour premixed flour and strawberry powder into a bowl.

步骤（1）倒粉（乔龙妍 摄）
Step（1）Pour Powder（By Qiao Longyan）

（2）加入开水，开水和预拌粉的比例为1∶1。

(2) Add boiling water as much as the premixed flour.

步骤（2）加入开水（乔龙妍 摄）
Step（2）Add Boiling Water（By Qiao Longyan）

（3）用筷子搅拌。

（3）Stir with your chopsticks.

步骤（3）搅拌（乔龙妍 摄）
Step（3）Stir（By Qiao Longyan）

（4）稍冷却后揉成团。

（4）Knead it into a ball after cooling.

步骤（4）揉面（乔龙妍 摄）
Step（4）Knead（By Qiao Longyan）

（5）将饼皮分成25g一个。

（5）Divide the crust into pieces with each 25g.

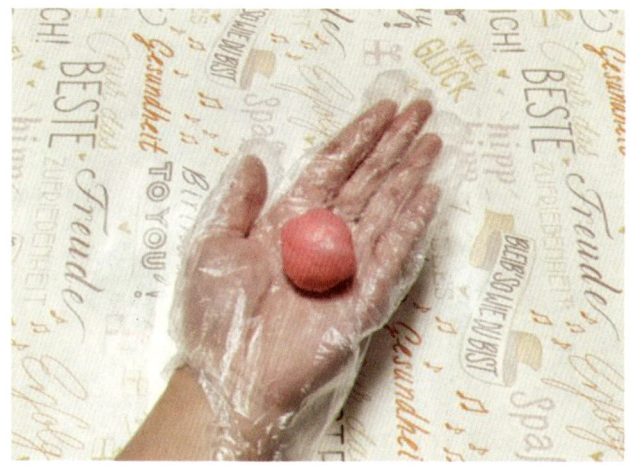

步骤（5）分冰皮（乔龙妍 摄）
Step（5）**Divide the Crust**（By Qiao Longyan）

（6）将馅料分成25g一个。

（6）Divide the filling into pieces with each 25g.

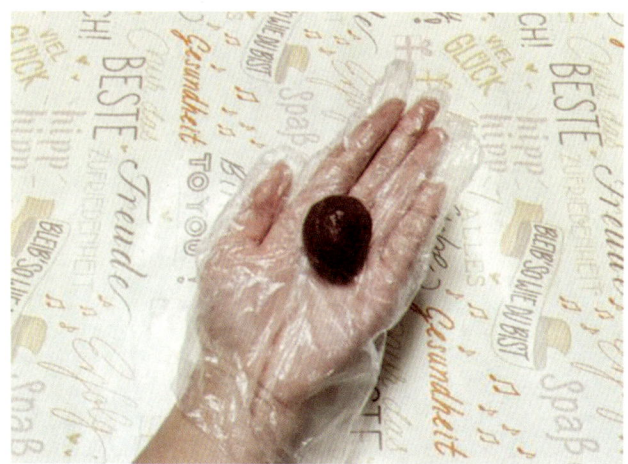

步骤（6）①分馅（乔龙妍 摄）
Step（6）①**Divide the Filling**（By Qiao Longyan）

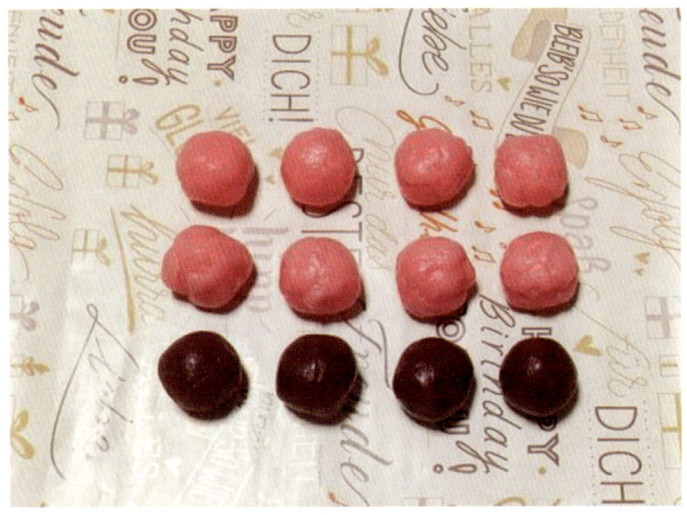

步骤（6）②完成分剂（乔龙妍 摄）
Step（6）②Complete the Division（By Qiao Longyan）

（7）取一个饼皮压扁包住馅料并揉圆。

（7）Press a piece of crust to wrap the filling and roll it to a ball.

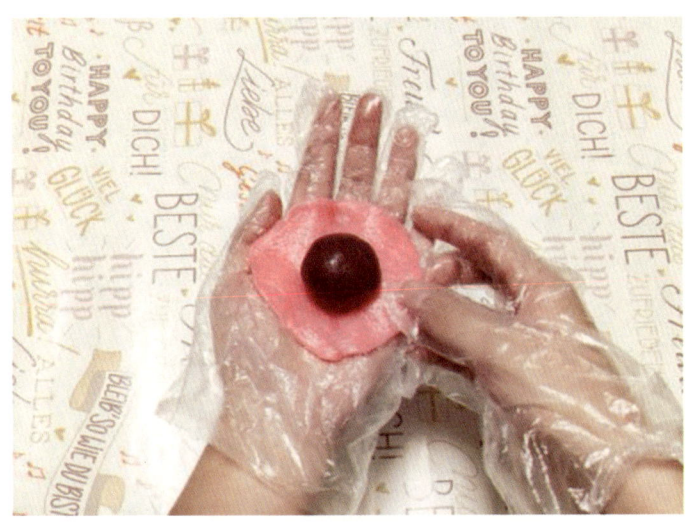

步骤（7）①包馅（乔龙妍 摄）
Step（7）①Wrap the Filling（By Qiao Longyan）

·第五章　中秋节文化双语教学设计·

步骤（7）②收口搓圆（乔龙妍 摄）
Step（7）②Close the Wrap（By Qiao Longyan）

（8）将圆团和模具都粘上熟食粉。

（8）Touch both the ball and the mold with cooked powder.

步骤（8）粘熟食粉（乔龙妍 摄）
Step（8）Touch the Cooked Powder（By Qiao Longyan）

（9）将圆团放入模具。

（9）Place the ball into the mold.

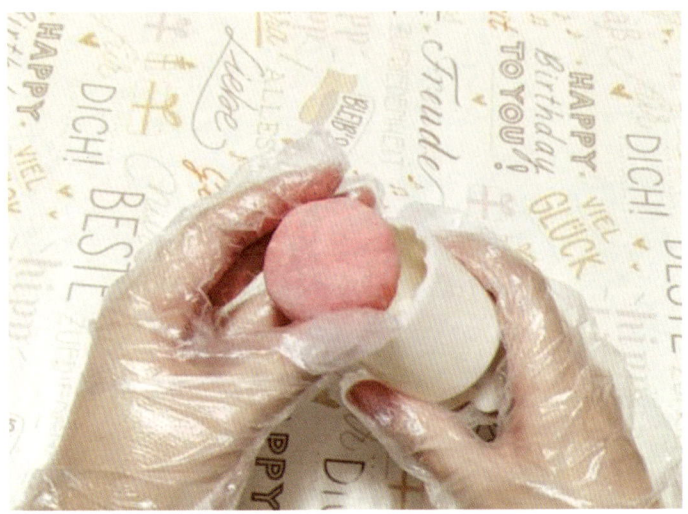

步骤（9）装模（乔龙妍 摄）
Step（9）Place into the Mold（By Qiao Longyan）

（10）按压下去再脱模。
（10）Press down and then demold.

步骤（10）①按压（乔龙妍 摄）
Step（10）①Press down（By Qiao Longyan）

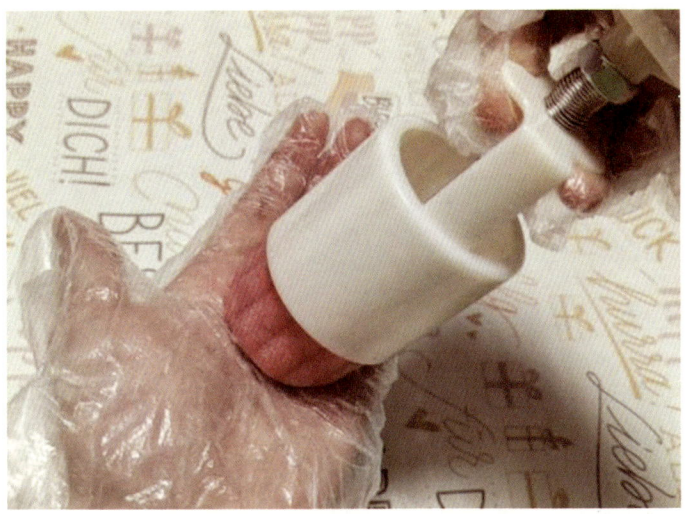

步骤（10）②脱模（乔龙妍 摄）
Step（10）②Demold（By Qiao Longyan）

（11）放入冰箱冷藏后风味更佳。

（11）The flavor is better after the moon cakes being refrigerated.

步骤（11）冷藏（乔龙妍 摄）
Step（11）Refrigerate Moon Cakes（By Qiao Longyan）

第四节　中秋节文化双语教案

一、教学对象

对中华文化感兴趣的外国学生。

二、教学内容

1. 中国传统节日中秋节的起源及风俗；
2. 中秋节在海内外的体现和表征；
3. 冰皮月饼的制作方法。

三、教学目标

1. 帮助外国学生熟悉中国传统节日之中秋节文化，并了解中秋节在海内外的体现和表征；
2. 帮助外国学生掌握中秋节传统美食冰皮月饼的制作方法；
3. 帮助外国学生理解中国传统节日中秋节的寓意：对五谷丰登的感恩、对阖家团圆的祈盼，对亲友安康的祝愿以及与此有关的传统价值观。

四、教学方法

1. 讲述法

通过教师的讲解来让学生了解中秋节的起源及各种风俗活动。

2. 演示法

通过教师现场演示，教授冰皮月饼的制作方法。

3. 课堂讨论法

通过教师提问、学生互相讨论的方式，请学生介绍各自国家中秋节文化的相关表征。

4. 启发诱导法

通过教师引导，启发学生总结对中秋节内涵的认识，并与本国相关传统文化内涵和价值观进行比较,揭示异同。

5. 练习法

通过练习提问的方式,检测学生是否掌握中秋节有关的重点知识。

五、课时安排

三课时完成,每课时40分钟。
第一课时介绍中秋节的起源及风俗;
第二课时介绍中秋节在海内外的体现和表征;
第三课时介绍冰皮月饼的制作方法。

六、教学过程(三课时)

第一课时(40分钟):中秋节的起源和风俗

设计意图: 以生动、精练的中华传统小故事开篇介绍中秋节的起源,力图通过"中国故事"吸引学生的注意力。利用图片、视频、实物等各种丰富手段展示中国人过中秋的习俗,帮助学生了解中秋节的表征,并揭示其中的深层含义:中国人民对和谐、幸福与团圆的祈盼。

(一)组织教学(约2分钟)

教师进入课堂,检查多媒体设备,将教学所用的教案、课件及手工材料准备放置妥当。师生互相问候,教师点名,准备上课。

> T: Good morning, everybody! How are you today? Let´s start the roll call first… Okay, everyone´s here. Class begins.

(二)进入新课,介绍中秋节的起源(约10分钟,内容详见双语讲稿导语)

1. 导入

教师展示视频,询问学生看见了什么,是否知道关于月亮的节日,引出主题"中秋节"。板书"中秋"二字及拼音,教师领读两遍。

> T: Now that we've finished watching the video, could you tell me what did you see in the video?

2. 介绍中秋节的起源:嫦娥奔月的故事

(1)教师结合图片讲述嫦娥奔月的故事。重点突出故事中后羿的善良勇敢、人们对嫦娥的敬意以及对美好生活和家人团聚的渴望。

> T: First, let's listen to the story of Chang'e Flying to the Moon.

(2)教师就中秋节起源故事中的小细节进行提问,考查学生对故事的理解并为后文介绍中秋节的风俗做准备。

问题:①嫦娥是谁的妻子?(答案:后羿)
　　　②谁要偷仙药?(答案:逢蒙)
　　　③嫦娥吃下仙药后飞升到哪里去了?(答案:月亮)

> T: Whose wife was Chang'e? Who wanted to steal the elixir? Where did Chang'e go after taking the elixit?

(三)介绍中秋节的主要风俗(27分钟,内容详见双语讲稿第一节)

1. 导入

(1)教师提问学生,知道哪些过中秋节的风俗。

> T: What are the customs of Chinese people celebrating the Mid-Autumn Festival?

(2)教师整理学生答案,帮助学生梳理与中秋节有关的记忆并整合学生知道的中秋节风俗。

2. 介绍中秋节主要风俗之二：饮桂花酒

（1）教师展示桂花图片，询问学生桂花什么时候开？桂花能够做什么？并公布答案。通过互动，引入桂花酒的话题。

（2）教师结合有关桂花的故事，帮助学生了解中国传统文化中好人好报、与人为善等相关价值观。

> T：Now, let's look at this picture. Guess what kind of flower this is? When does this flower bloom? What can these make?

3. 介绍中秋节主要风俗之一：赏月

（1）教师给出三张月亮的图片，让学生猜测哪一张是中秋节时的月亮，引出赏月习俗。

问题：你知道下面三个月亮，哪一个是中秋节时的月亮吗？（答案：第一个）

> T：Look at these three pictures of the moon, and can you guess which one is the moon at the Mid-Autumn Festival?

（2）教师帮助学生理解中国传统文化中借月亮表达相思和渴望团圆的文化意蕴。

（3）教师结合苏轼《水调歌头》和歌曲帮助学生感受中国诗歌之美，同时深化学生对赏月习俗的认知：赏月既能传递相思还能表达对未来的祝福与希望。

> T：Now, let's enjoy the song adapted from the poem *Prelude to Water Melody*.

4. 介绍中秋节主要风俗之三：吃月饼

（1）教师展示月饼的图片，询问学生月饼是什么形状？为什么月饼要做成圆形呢？

问题：你知道月饼是什么形状的吗？为什么要做成这种形状？（答案：圆形，象征团圆）

> T: What's the shape of the moon cakes? Do you know why moon cakes are round?

（2）教师说明原因，帮助学生理解中国传统文化中圆形表示团团圆圆、幸福美满的寓意。

（3）教师结合图片介绍月饼，帮助学生感受中秋文化的中外交融。

（四）小结（1分钟）

教师简单回顾中秋节的起源故事并梳理元宵节的风俗。

第二课时（40分钟）：世界各地的多元中秋

设计意图：通过对其他国家中秋节习俗的介绍，与我国中秋节习俗进行比较。引导学生了解中国传统文化节日——中秋节在国际舞台上的表征，帮助学生更好地体会中国中秋节文化对全球的影响。

（一）复习回顾（约5分钟）

1. 教师请学生复述嫦娥奔月的故事。
2. 教师展示图片，提问学生中秋节有哪些主要的风俗。

> T: Let us briefly review the origin of the Mid-Autumn Festival.
> T: Do you remember the main customs of the Mid-Autumn Festival? Yes! Drinking osmanthus wine, appreciating the moon and eating moon cakes.

（二）进入新课，介绍世界各地的多元中秋（约25分钟，内容详见双语讲稿第二节）

1. 导入

教师提问学生，还知道哪些国家过中秋节。

> T: Which other countries do you know celebrate the Mid-Autumn Festival?

2. 介绍世界各地的多元中秋节之一：越南

（1）教师结合图片，讲述越南中秋节的名称"望月节"以及舞狮表演等习俗。

（2）教师讲述有关阿贵和鲤鱼灯的故事，帮助学生理解该习俗背后祈求平安、鱼跃龙门的美好寓意。

3. 介绍世界各地的多元中秋节之二：泰国

（1）教师结合图片介绍泰国的中秋节，了解中国民间传说"八仙拜寿"在泰国的传播与影响。

（2）师生互动：教师让学生猜测泰国的特殊月饼并进行介绍。

> T: Can you guess what is special about moon cakes in Thailand?
> T: Yes! Durian! Does anyone like durian moon cakes?

（3）通过交流与互动，教师引导学生关注与思考传统节日背后传递出的文化记忆与温暖真情。

4. 介绍世界各地的多元中秋节之三：韩国

（1）教师展示韩国地图，帮助学生了解中秋节在其他国家的传播与影响。

（2）师生互动：教师结合韩国中秋节的照片，让学生猜一猜这是在做什么？

（3）教师结合图片介绍松饼。

> T: Why do you think the atmosphere of the Mid-Autumn Festival is still strong outside of China?
> T: Do you celebrate festivals in your own country when you are abroad? Why?

5. 介绍世界各地的多元中秋节之四：日本

（1）教师结合满月讲述日本与中国相同的中秋习俗：赏月。

（2）教师展示江米团子图片，引导学生联想江米团子的满月象征，感受中秋明月之美。

（3）师生互动：教师询问学生中秋节食物或者习俗，以及中外中秋节的异同。

（4）通过互动与交流，教师引导学生关注传统节日的变化与发展、价值与意义。

> T: So do you remember what are the features of the moon on this day?

（三）练习（10分钟，内容详见双语讲稿第四节）

1. 连一连

教师列出越南、泰国、韩国、日本等国中秋节的别名，请学生指出每个名称分别对应哪个国家。

2. 选一选

教师编写与中秋节起源和风俗相关的选择题若干，请学生根据教学内容进行选择并订正。

第三课时（40分钟）：学习制作冰皮月饼

设计意图：通过详细教授制作月饼的步骤，帮助学生更好地理解和体会中秋节文化的内涵和表征。同时鼓励学生制作月饼并分享，激发学生热爱中华文化的热情。

（一）导入（约2分钟）

教师展示自己制作的冰皮月饼，并向学生提问。

问题：你们想不想自己动手学做月饼？

> T: Do you want to learn how to make ice skin moon cakes?

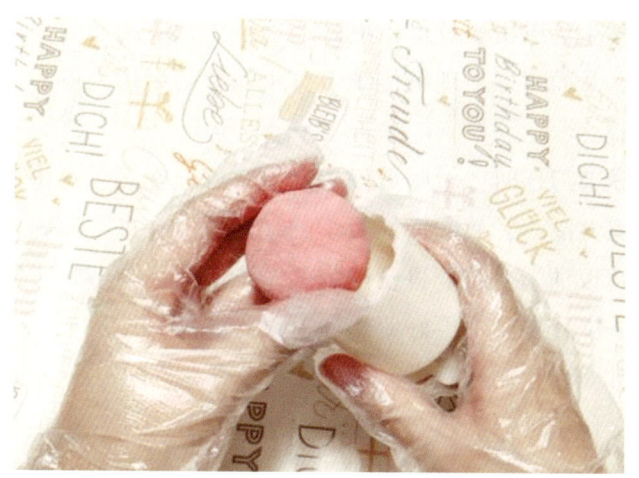

（二）文化体验：制作冰皮月饼（约 30 分钟，内容详见双语讲稿第三节）

1. 教师发放材料并注意加以介绍。
2. 教师现场演示并结合动图，教授学生如何制作冰皮月饼。
3. 教师请学生展示各自成品，并谈谈有什么感想。

（三）本课小结（约 7 分钟）

1. 教师总结中国中秋节的起源、习俗和其他国家人民庆祝中秋节的习俗。
2. 教师总结世界人民庆祝中秋节的美好愿望：对自然的欣赏与感恩，对团圆的期许与祝福，对家庭幸福、民族和谐、世界大同的热爱与追求。

（四）布置作业（1 分钟）

请学生课下试着做月饼并与同学和老师分享。

> T：Please try to make moon cakes after class and share them with our classmates and teachers! Class is over, see you next time!

七、教学反思

中秋节是中华民族负有盛名的传统节日，外国学生多有了解，通过本节课程的讲授，学生可以由表及里，更好地理解中秋节的起源传说以及各种风俗的深层含义，从而更好地理解传统节日中蕴含的中国人民对家庭幸福、美满的追求和渴望。

在讲授中秋节习俗时，教师可以提前准备好桂花酒、月饼等饮食，在课堂上请学生观察并品尝，从而增加教学的趣味性。在进行海内外中秋节文化习俗比较时，可以请学生结合自己国家的中秋节或类似节日进行介绍，从而帮助学生在中外文化比较中更好地理解中国文化和中国精神。

体验环节涉及动手制作月饼，可考虑在条件允许的情况下进行圆桌教学，从而方便学生分组学习。教授过程中，教师应把注意事项提前交代清楚，以帮助学生提升体验环节的成就感和满足感。

附：辅助教学资源

1. 月亮视频：https://m.baidu.com/video/page?pd=video_page&nid=7719812507786291537&sign=10942839481825650076&word=%E6%9C%88%E4%BA%AE%E7%9F%AD%E8%A7%86%E9%A2%91&oword=%E6%9C%88%E4%BA%AE%E7%9F%AD%E8%A7%86%E9%A2%91&atn=index&frsrcid=5377&ext=%7B%22jsy%22%3A1%7D&top=%7B%22sfhs%22%3A1%2C%22_hold%22%3A2%7D&sl=4&trace=11927914082891291234&isBdboxShare=1&isBdboxShare=1&_t=1628914334908。

2. 酷狗《水调歌头》王菲音频：https://t1.kugou.com/song.html?id=2CFHgb1y0V2。

讨论与练习
Discussion and Practice

1. 讨论

1. Discussion

（1）你们国家过不过中秋节？有没有类似的节日？又有哪些习俗？

（1）Do you celebrate the Mid-Autumn Festival in your countries? Is there any similar festivals? What are the customs?

（2）你们觉得为什么中国以外的其他国家的中秋节氛围仍然很浓厚？

（2）Why do you think the atmosphere of the Mid-Autumn Festival is still strong outside of China?

（3）你们在国外时会按照传统过自己国家的节日吗？为什么？

（3）Do you celebrate festivals of your own country when you are abroad? Why?

（4）对比中国的中秋节与你们国家的传统节日，你们觉得传统节日有什么共同之处？结合具体的节日，对比古今，你认为传统节日有什么发展与变化呢？

（4）Comparing the Mid-Autumn Festival in China with the traditional festivals in your country, what do you think the traditional festivals have in common? What do you think about the development and changes of traditional festivals?

2. 练习

2. Practice

（1）连一连

（1）Matching

泰国 Thailand	A. 望月节 Tết Trung Thu
越南 Vietnam	B. 秋夕 Chuseok
日本 Japan	C. 芋名月 Moon-viewing Festival
韩国 South Korea	D. 祈月节 Moon-Praying Festival

（2）选一选

（2）Choosing（Select the correct one from the four options）

- 泰国中秋节的特色水果是什么？（　　）

　What is the special fruit of Mid-Autumn Festival in Thailand?（　　）

　A. pear　　　　B. watermelon　　　C. apple　　　　D. grapefruit

- 越南的中秋节又是属于哪种人群的节日？（　　）

　What kind of people do Vietnam's Mid-Autumn Festival belong to?（　　）

　A. children　　B. women　　　　　C. teachers　　　D. workers

- 韩国的松饼是如何烹饪的？（　　）

　How are Republic of Korean Songpyeon cooked?（　　）

　A. boiled　　　B. steamed　　　　C. fried　　　　D. toasted

- 日本的江米团子象征着什么？（　　）

　What do Dango in Japan symbolize?（　　）

　A. harvest　　　　　　　　　　　B. the full moon

　C. happy　　　　　　　　　　　 D. Thanksgiving

答案
Answer

(1) D　　　　A　　　　C　　　　B

(2) D　　　　A　　　　B　　　　B

第六章 中国结文化双语教学设计
Chapter VI Bilingual Teaching Design of Chinese Knot Culture

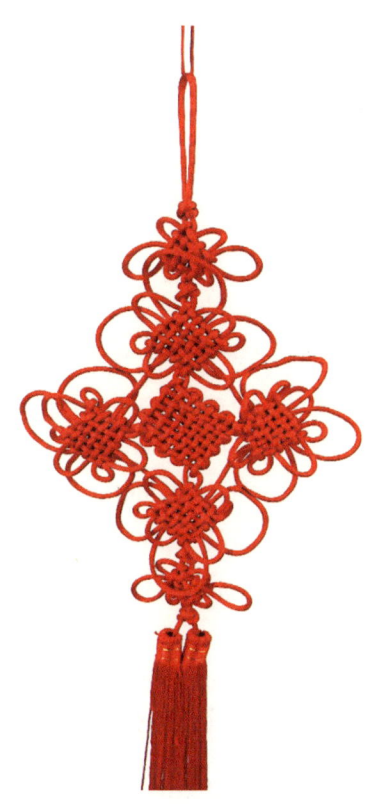

中国结（孙慧莉 摄）
Chinese Knot (By Sun Huili)

中国传统文化体验式双语教学设计

导语
Introduction

在中国古代，新婚夫妻进入洞房后有一套复杂的礼仪，其中一项就是一对新人沿床边而坐，男左女右。夫妻各自剪下一缕头发，再把两缕头发打结缠绕起来，以誓结发同心、永不分离。中国古人受"身体发肤，受之父母"传统孝道思想的约束，一生都不会轻易剪断头发。但在新婚之时夫妻则结发缠绕，足可见中国人对婚姻的重视以及与另一半荣辱与共、相携到老的美好期望。后来，人们就把第一次结婚的夫妻，称为"结发夫妻"。如今，夫妻不会在新婚之夜剪断头发并将其缠绕在一起，但是会在洞房里挂上一个"同心结"，古今这两种仪式都表达了紧密结合、结伴同行和恩爱白头的意思。

In ancient China, newlyweds had a complicated set of etiquette after entering the bridal chamber. One ceremony was a couple sitting along the bedside, male left and female right. The husband and the wife each cut a strand of hair, then tied the two strands into a knot to vow never be separated. The ancient Chinese were bounded by the traditional filial piety thought—We should take care of our body, hair and skin because our parents gave them. The couple cutting their hair to make a knot in the wedding shows that Chinese attach great importance to marriage and symbolizes good wishes of sharing weal and woe and loving each other forever. Later, people refer to couples who get married for the first time as "a couple with a hair knot". Nowadays, there are fewer rituals of cutting and tangling hair on the wedding night. People started to hang "concentric knot" in the bridal chamber, which also expresses the meanings of tight closeness, sweet companionship and ever-lasting love.

第一节　中国结的分类
Section 1　Classification of Chinese Knot

"结"与"吉"谐音，"吉"有着丰富多彩的内容，福、禄、寿、喜、财、安、康无一不属于吉的范畴。"吉"是人类永恒追求的主题,中国结这种具有生命力的民间技艺也就自然作为中国传统文化的精髓流传至今。2022年北京冬奥会闭幕式就用中国结向世界展示了美美与共、心心相连的美好愿景。冬奥会的中国结更是采用了先进的 AR 技术,融入了景泰蓝、青花瓷、丝绸、丝带等象征着吉祥、友谊的中国文化元素,不仅反映了团结的奥运精神,还传达了中国对世界的美好祝愿。并且,中国结中的每根丝带都可以独立成结,许多根这样的丝带又可以共同组成一个大大的中国结,代表着和谐合作的国际大家庭需要所有人共同建设。

　　中国结的种类非常多,以简单的基本结点构图变换出各种结,可以列出成百上千的不同图案。其中双联结十分常用也较有代表性的,因为"联"有连、合、持续不断等美好之意,悬挂双联结也寄托了人们期盼连年有余、连科及第的心愿。同时,它小巧牢固,也非常实用,常见于结饰的开端或结尾,有时也用来编项链或腰带中间的装饰结。双联结主要包括双钱结、龙形结和祥云结等几类。

　　"Jie"(knot)and "Ji"(auspicious)in Mandarin Chinese are homophones. The meaning of Ji (auspicious) includes prosperity, status, longevity, happiness, wealth, safety and health, which are our eternal pursuits. Therefore, the folk art of the Chinese knot, as the essence of Chinese traditional culture, has its vitality and is handed down until today. At the closing ceremony of the 2022 Beijing Winter Olympic Games, the Chinese knot was used to show the world a beautiful vision of sharing and caring. The Chinese knot integrated the most representative Chinese cultural elements such as cloisonne, blue and white porcelain, silk and ribbon via advanced AR technology. It symbolizes auspiciousness and friendship, the Olympic spirit of "unity" and China's good wishes to the world. Moreover, each ribbon of the Chinese knot was cleverly designed to not only form a knot by itself, but also form a large Chinese knot together, representing the harmonious and cooperative international family that needs everyone to build together.

　　There are many kinds of Chinese knots, and hundreds of different knots can be made by using a simple basic node composition. Among them, the double connection knot is very common and representative because the Chinese pronunciation of connection, "lian", has good meanings such as connection, unity and continuity, and the suspension of the double connection also places people's wish to have abundance and gain excellent rank in Imperial Examination in the years coming. The double connection knot is also more practical because its shape is small and it is not easy to loosen. This knot is often used to weave the beginning or end of the knot accessories, and is sometimes used in the middle of a necklace or a belt as decoration. There are mainly three kinds of double connection knots: double coin knot, dragon knot and auspicious cloud knot.

1. 双钱结

双钱结又名金钱结或双金线结,以其貌似两个古铜钱相连而得名,寓意"好事成双"。古时"钱"也称"泉",与"全"同音,因此"双钱"又象征着"双全"。双钱结有多种组合变换形式,数个双钱结组合可构成各式各样的美丽图案,如云彩、十全结,它们常被应用于项链、腰带等饰物。

1. Double Coin Knot

The double coin knot, also known as the money knot or double gold thread knot, is named after two ancient copper coins linked together. This knot is a symbol of "good things in pairs". In ancient China, money is also called "quan", which is a homophone of the word "quan" (whole). Therefore, "double coins" can embody "having the both". There are many combinations of double coin knot, combining a number of double coin knots can form more beautiful patterns, such as the cloud knot and the perfect knot. These knots are often applied to necklaces, belts and other ornaments.

2. 龙形结

龙是中国古代传说中的四灵之长,一向被中国人视为祈雨避邪的神。中国人崇拜龙,称自己为"龙的传人",古时皇帝更是以龙自喻。龙形结既能与其他结式相搭配,构成双龙抢珠、苍龙教子等吉祥而美丽的图案,也可以单独当胸针、摆饰等。

2. Dragon Knot

According to the legend, The dragon was the lead of the four spirits. The Dragon has been regarded as a god for praying for rain and warding off evil spirits in China. Chinese people respect and worship dragons and call themselves "descendants of dragons", In ancient times, the emperor referred to himself as the dragon. The dragon knot can be matched with other knots to form auspicious and beautiful patterns, such as two dragons playing with a pearl, a father dragon teaching his son and so on. This knot can also be used as a brooch and an ornament.

3. 祥云结

祥云结素以美观大方著称。云,不仅被认为是神仙的座乘,而且能造雨滋润万物。祥云作为吉祥纹样用途极为广泛,可寓意绵延不断。"云"与"运"谐音,如以蝙蝠飞舞于云中的模样寓意福运。在纽扣结(纽扣结由双钱结变化而来)编至最后时,将两线头分别向左右平抽,即可得祥云结。祥云结可用于编制吉祥图案中的云彩,也可以相互连接编成寓意吉祥的项链、腰带等装饰。

3. Auspicious Cloud Knot

Auspicious cloud knot is famous for its beauty and generosity. Clouds are the seat of the gods and make rain to nourish all creatures in the world. The auspicious clouds as an auspicious pattern have a meaning of continuous and are widely used. "clouds" (yún) and "fortune" (yùn) have similar pronunciations in Chinese. For example, "a bat flaying in the clouds" means good fortune. The auspicious cloud knot is made by pulling the two threads of a button knot to the left and right (the button knot is changed from a double coin knot). The auspicious cloud knot can be used to compile clouds in auspicious patterns, and be linked together into necklaces and belts, which imply auspiciousne.

4. 其他结样

除了上面介绍的双联结,桂花结、双鱼结、双喜结在中国人的生活中也十分常见,它们常用于馈赠亲友或室内装饰。在中国文化中,"桂"与"贵"

同音，桂花既代表崇高优雅，又是地位和财富的象征，桂花结代表富贵无疆，寄托了对受赠人蟾宫折桂、仕途顺达的美好祝愿。因为"鱼"谐音为"余""裕"，所以素有"年年有余""金玉满堂"的含义。双鱼结代表了人们对生活优裕、财富有余的期盼。双喜写作"囍"，中国人以偶数为佳，尤其喜欢成双，"囍"自然成为了中国老百姓喜闻乐见的文化符号，双喜结最常用于装扮喜庆场所，增添吉祥热闹的氛围，表达双方欢喜、双喜临门之意。

4. Other Knots

In addition to the double connections introduced above, Osmanthus knots, double fish knots and double happiness knots are also very common in Chinese life, and they are often used to give gifts to relatives and friends or interior decoration. In Chinese culture, "osmanthus" is synonymous with "wealth". Osmanthus knots not only represent lofty elegance, but also a symbol of status and wealth. Osmanthus knots represent boundless wealth and place the best wishes to the recipient for passing the exam smoothly and an outstanding official career. Because the homonym of "fish" is "surplus" and "affluence", it has the meaning of "have abundance every year" and "full of gold and jade". Double fish knots represent people's expectation of affluent life and more wealth. Two "Xi" (happiness) characters are written together as one on account of Chinese people prefer even numbers, especially things in pairs. "Xi" (happiness) has naturally become a cultural symbol that the Chinese people like to see and hear. Double happiness knots are most often used to dress up festive places, add auspicious and lively atmosphere and express each individual's joy and two happiness comes together.

"结"在漫长的演变过程中被人们赋予了各种情感愿望，不同的中国结有着不同的内涵，但都蕴含着华夏儿女的美好心愿。

"Knot" has been conveying a variety of wishes and connotations over time in China. Different Chinese knots have different connotations but all kinds of them show Chinese people yearning for a joyful life.

第二节　中国结的海外传播：托结寓美意

Section 2　The Chinese Knot Implies a Good Meaning

20世纪60年代，毕业于台北中兴大学的陈夏生在工作之余学会了中国传统的编结技艺。随着手艺日渐娴熟，陈夏生与中国结的缘分也越来越深。1978年，随着第一本关于"中国结"的书籍出版，此前按照国际惯例称谓的"中国结绳技艺"被正式命名为"中国结"。1981年，陈夏生将"中国结"带到美国纽约进行展览，《纽约时报》用了半个版面的篇幅来介绍这个让人沉醉的东方手工艺品。至此，在西方人眼中，"中国结"成为中国文化的象征之一，每年都有"中国结"展览在全世界举办。

Chen Xiasheng learned Chinese knotting in his spare time after graduating from National Chung Hsing University in Taipei in the 1960s. Her love for the knot deepened as her knotting skills developed. In 1978, the first book on "Chinese knot" was published and the "Chinese rope knot technique" was officially named "Chinese knot". In 1981, Chen Xiasheng brought the Chinese knot to New York for exhibition. The *New York Times* devoted a half page to introduce this enchanting oriental handicraft. Since then, the Chinese knot has become one of the symbols of Chinese culture, and the Chinese knot exhibitions are hosted all over the world every year.

"中国结"再度风靡全球始于2008年的北京奥运会。开幕式上出现了中国红配以黄色穗坠的巨大中国结，奥运场馆里随处可见中国结，中国奥运健儿也随身佩戴中国结。从用色到形式都十分喜庆的中国结在全世界人民心中留下了深刻的印象。

The Chinese knot became a hit again during the 2008 Beijing Olympic Games. There was a huge red Chinese knot with a yellow tassel at the opening ceremony and there were many Chinese knots in Olympic venues. Chinese Olympic athletes also wore the knots. The Chinese knot, which is very festive from color to form, has left a deep impression on people all over the world.

除此之外，坐落于湖南长沙梅溪湖上的中国结步行桥，也彰显了中国结在中国人心中跨越千古的美好象征。中国结步行桥结构设计融合了中国古老的民间艺术中国结和西方的莫比乌斯环，得到世界性的认可，和"梦露塔"、北京望京SOHO共同跻身于美国CNN评选的十大"世界最性感建筑"排行榜。红色的线条在波光粼粼的梅溪湖上交织缠绵而又蜿蜒盘旋，热烈浓郁的喜庆氛围包裹着东西方文化的智慧结晶。

In addition, the Chinese knot pedestrian bridge, located on Meixi Lake in Changsha, Hunan province, also demonstrates the beautiful meaning of the Chinese knot for Chinese people. The Chinese knot pedestrian bridge combines the ancient Chinese folk art with the Western Mobius ring. The bridge has gained worldwide recognition because of its mysterious aesthetics from the East. Along with Monroe Tower and Wangjing SOHO in Beijing, the Chinese knot pedestrian bridge was ranked the top 10 sexiest buildings globally by CNN. Red lines are intertwined and meandered on the sparkling Meixi Lake, and the warm and full-bodied festive atmosphere wraps the wisdom of Eastern and Western cultures.

时至今日，中国结早已成为代表中国内涵的文化符号，是中国传统文化的一张靓丽名片 2022 年北京冬奥会闭幕式上，中国结的多次亮相也让世界再次感受到中国传统文化的独特魅力。除此之外，中华传统服饰旗袍和唐装上的盘扣（也叫盘花扣），同样是古老中国结的一种。除了盘扣，在国际时尚界，中国结也越来越受到优秀设计师们的青睐。传统的中国结和潮流结合在一起，缔造了新的美，在国际时装秀的舞台上大放光彩。越来越多的外国友人爱上穿"中国风"的衣服。泰国王后访问泰国的中国城时，亦是穿上了一身带有盘扣元素的中国旗袍。中国结也成为赠送外国友人的上上之选。中国结和中国传统节日、汉语一样成为被外国人热爱的中国元素。

Today, the Chinese knot has become a cultural symbol of China and a beautiful business card of Chinese traditional culture. The Chinese knot appeared at the closing ceremony of the 2022 Beijing Winter Olympic Games for many times and demonstrated the charm of Chinese traditional culture to the world again. In addition, the frog fastener on cheongsam and the Tang costume is also a kind of Chinese knot. The

Chinese knot is also more and more favored by excellent designers in the international fashion industry. The combination of traditional Chinese knot and the nowadays fashion trend creates the new beauty in the international fashion show. More and more foreign friends have fallen in love with Chinese styleclothes, for example, the Queen of Thailand wore a cheongsam when she visited Chinatown in Thailand. Chinese knots have also become the best selection for gifts to foreign friends. The Chinese knot, like Chinese traditional festivals and Chinese language, has become a Chinese element loved by foreigners.

与此同时，编织中国结已成为外国人来中国必不可少的体验项目，是来华留学生的"必修课"。在课堂上，老师们一边向同学们讲解中国结的制作方法，一边向同学们解释中国结蕴含的文化渊源。寓教于乐的一堂手工课，让很多留学生对探索中华民族丰富的文化内涵产生兴趣，成为他们学习汉语、了解中国的无穷动力。

Meanwhile, weaving a Chinese knot is an essential experience and a "compulsory course" for foreign visitors and international students in China. In the class, teachers explain to students how to make a Chinese knot while introducing the cultural origin of Chinese knot. A handicraft class that combines teaching with fun has aroused many international students' interest in exploring rich Chinese culture and motivations to learn Chinese and understand China.

不仅是在华的外国人，没来过中国的外国人也通过网络了解到中国这一古老的传统手工工艺。跟着网络视频学习编制中国结并发布在自己的社交网站上已成为一种风潮。还有许多外国人喜欢在家里挂上各式各样的中国结作为装饰。国内的中国结工厂也收到越来越多的国外订单，"中国结""平安结""富贵结""同心结"等都很受海外市场的青睐。在世界各地的华人街，每逢春节，家家户户门口挂起中国结，处处洋溢着新年的味道。这种喜庆热闹的氛围也感染了外国友人，春节变得国际化，中国结也变得国际化。中华元素把世界像结绳一般联结起来，一同编织着浸润了中华文化的"中国结"。

Not only foreigners in China, but also People who have never been to China have also learned about this traditional Chinese handicraft. It has become a trend to learn how to make Chinese knots by following online videos and post them on social media. Many people from other countries also like to hang various kinds of Chinese knots as decorations at home. Chinese knot factories receive more and more orders from abroad, and some knots such as the Chinese knot, the peace knot, the wealth knot and the concentric knot are trendy in the overseas market. In the Chinesetown worldwide, the Chinese knots are hung on the doors during the Spring Festival. This festive and lively atmosphere has also attracted foreign friends, and was made the Spring Festival and the Chinese knot become international. Chinese elements tie the world tighter to weave the "Chinese knots" infiltrated with Chinese culture together.

小小绳结，丝丝环扣，看似简单，却蕴含着博大精深的中华文化。中国结在海外的风靡也让外国人感受到华夏儿女质朴、勤劳、积极向上的品格。作为一种符号，中国结具有象征性和隐喻性，体现了中华文化在表达时的委婉与含蓄。一根红绳，三缠两绕，手指翻飞间编织出来的不仅仅是一个火红的中国结，更是中国人乃至全世界人民对美好的共同向往。

The Chinese knot, small and simple, but contains rich Chinese culture, showing the unadorned, hard-working and positive characters while getting popular overseas. As a symbol, the Chinese knot is symbolic and metaphorical, showing the euphemism and implicit expression of Chinese culture. A red rope, twisted and wriapper, is not only a fiery red Chinese knot woven between the fingers, but also the common yearning of the Chinese people and the people of the world for better life.

第三节 "百年有结是同心"：同心结的制作
Section 3 "A Hundred Years of Knot is Concentric": the Production of Concentric Knot

1. 材料

红绳。

1. Materials

Red strings.

2. 注意事项

如果你有任何问题，请举手提问。

2. Attention

If you have any questions, please raise your hand to ask.

3. 步骤

3. Steps

（1）把红绳按照图片上的形状固定好。

（1）Secure the red string according to the shape in the picture.

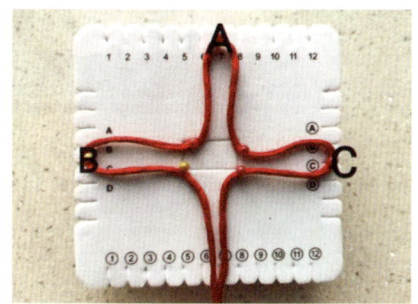

步骤（1）固定红绳（黄婧瑶 摄）

Step（1）Secure the Red String（By Huang Jingyao）

（2）把 A 点的绳子翻折到 D 点。

（2）Fold the string from point A to point D.

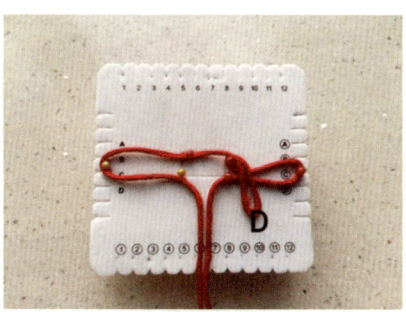

步骤（2）把 A 点的绳子翻折到 D 点（黄婧瑶 摄）

Step（2）Fold the String from Point A to Point D（By Huang Jingyao）

（3）把C点的绳子翻折到E点。

（3）Fold the string from point C to point E.

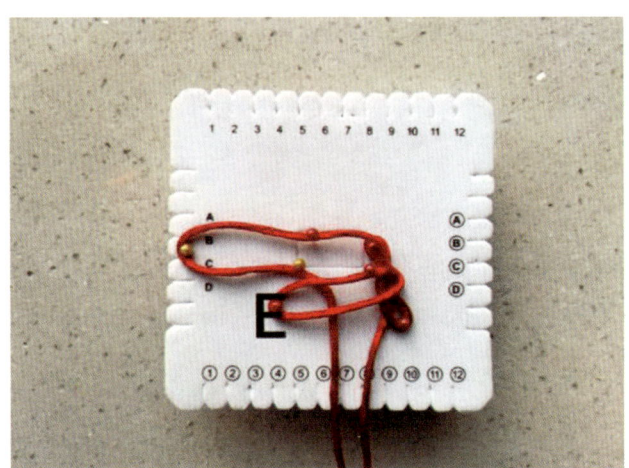

步骤（3）把C点的绳子翻折到E点（黄婧瑶 摄）
Step（3）Fold the String from Point C to Point E（By Huang Jingyao）

（4）把B点的绳子翻折到F点。

（4）Fold the string from point B to point F.

步骤（4）把B点的绳子翻折到F点（黄婧瑶 摄）
Step（4）Fold the String from Point B to Point F（By Huang Jingyao）

（5）拉紧四个方向的绳子，整理形状。

（5）Tighten the string in all four directions to tidy up the shape.

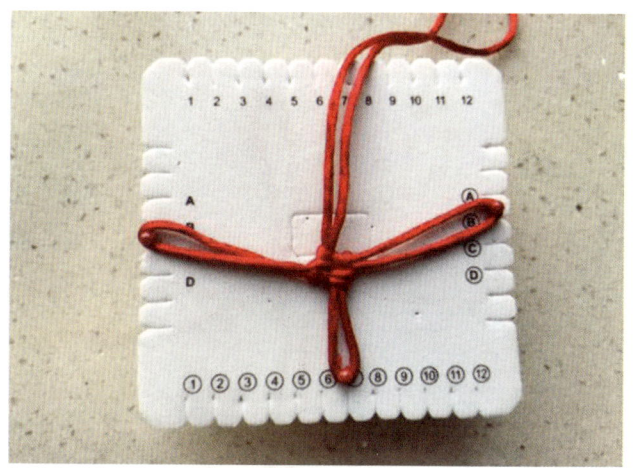

步骤（5）整理好绳子（黄婧瑶 摄）
Step（5）Tidy up the String（By Huang Jingyao）

（6）把四个方向的绳子按照图片的方式依次串在一起。

（6）Thread the string in four directions together in the same way as shown in the picture.

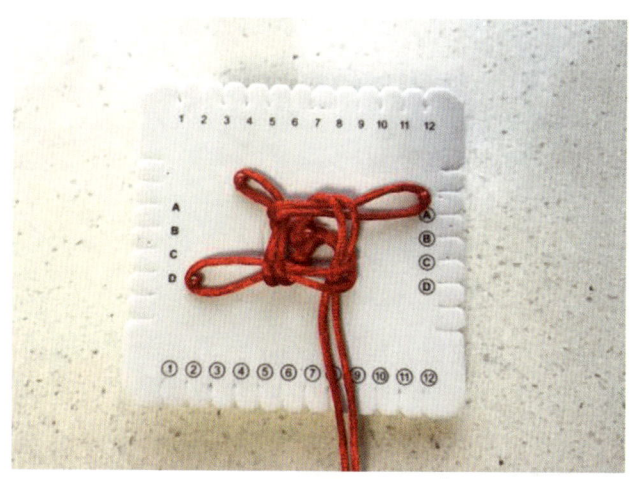

步骤（6）穿好的绳子（黄婧瑶 摄）
Step（6）Threaded String（By Huang Jingyao）

（7）拉紧四个方向的绳子，整理形状，得到同心结。

（7）Pull the string in four directions and arrange the shape to get the auspicious concentric knot.

步骤（7）同心结（黄婧瑶 摄）
Step（7）Concentric Knot（By Huang Jingyao）

第四节　中国结文化双语教案

一、教学对象

对中华文化感兴趣的外国学生。

二、教学内容

1. 中国结的起源及分类；
2. 中国结的国际性传播以及国际形象；
3. 同心结的编法。

三、教学目标

1. 帮助外国学生了解中国结的起源、分类及今天在国际舞台上的影响与传播；

2. 帮助外国学生掌握同心结的编织方法；

3. 帮助外国学生理解中国结中所蕴含的劳动人民的智慧和对生活的美好期盼以及中华传统手工艺与现代潮流的融合和创造性转化、创新性发展，从而感受中华民族劳动人民对"天下大同，美美与共"的追求。

四、教学方法

1. 直观法

利用实物、图片和视频直观地向学生展示中国结的形态、寓意和编织方法。

2. 演示法

通过演示法，教授中国结的编织方法。

3. 互动法

通过教师提问、学生回答的方式，请学生叙述对中国结的理解。

4. 启发诱导法

启发学生总结对中国结起源、中国结的国际性传播以及国际形象的认识，表达自己对所讲内容的看法和感受。

五、课时安排

三课时完成，每课时 40 分钟。

第一课时介绍中国结的起源及分类；

第二课时介绍中国结的国际性传播以及创新性发展；

第三课时介绍同心结的编织方法。

六、教学过程（三课时）

第一课时（40 分钟）：中国结的起源和分类

设计意图：将"结发夫妻"的故事娓娓道来，帮助学生理解中国结的深意。启发学生对比不同类型中国结和与其对应的各类实物,以揭示中国结所蕴含的情感和价值。

(一) 组织教学(约2分钟)

教师进入课堂,检查多媒体设备,将教学所用的教案、课件及手工材料准备放置妥当。师生互相问候,教师点名,准备上课。

> T: Good morning, everyone! How are you today? Let's start the roll call first... Okay, everyone's here. Class begins.

(二) 进入新课,介绍中国结的起源(10分钟,内容详见双语讲稿导语)

1. 导入

(1) 教师播放中国结宣传片,并请学生根据内容回答问题,从而引出中国结与"结发夫妻"的关系。

问题:①猜一猜,视频中的男子和女子是什么关系?(答案:夫妻)

②中国结和这对夫妻有什么关系?(答案:夫妻结发、永结同心)

> T: Guess, what is the relationship between the man and the woman in the video?
> T: What is the relationship between Chinese knot and this couple?

(2) 教师板书"中国结"三字及拼音,教师领读两遍。

2. 介绍中国结的起源:"结发夫妻"的故事

(1) 教师利用图片介绍古代男女的"结发",说明头发之于人们的重要性。

(2) 教师结合视频和图片说明何为"结发夫妻",并揭示其蕴含的深意。

问题:"结发夫妻"的意思是?(答案:夫妻二人把彼此的头发缠绕在一起)

T: What does "a couple with a hair knot" mean?

（三）介绍中国结的分类（约27分钟，内容详见双语讲稿第一节）

1. 导入

（1）教师先展示龙、古铜钱、祥云三张图片，并向学生说明其各自的含义。

2. 介绍双联结

（1）展示双联结中的龙形结、双钱结和祥云结，并请学生与上述三张图片进行连线。

问题：请大家看看下面几种中国结，你们觉得它们分别像上面哪幅图？

（2）教师整理学生答案，并分别介绍龙形结、双钱结和祥云结，同时说明双联结的含义。

T: Please take a look at the following Chinese knots. Which picture do you think they look like above?

3. 拓展介绍其他常见中国结

（1）教师分别展示桂花结、双鱼结和双喜结的图片，请学生进行描述。
（2）教师分别介绍桂花结、双鱼结和双喜结及其寓意。

（四）小结（1分钟）

教师简单回顾中国结的起源故事并梳理中国结的类型。

第二课时（40分钟）：中国结的传承与海外传播

设计意图：通过视频、图片等方式介绍中国结如何走出国门、走向世界。帮助学生了解中国结在今天日常生活中的表现形式，如建筑、服饰等，从而传递出人们追求美、共享美、传承美、创造美的不懈努力。

（一）复习回顾（约5分钟）

1. 教师请学生复述结发夫妻的故事。

2. 教师展示图片，提问学生双联结有哪些分类以及它们分别象征什么。

> T: Let us briefly review the origin of the couple with a hair knot.
> T: Look at these Chinese knots. Do you remember their names?

（二）进入新课，介绍中国结的海外传播（25分钟，内容详见双语讲稿第二节）

1. 导入

教师询问学生在自己国家是否见过中国结，以此引出中国结如何漂洋过海。

问题：①同学们，你们在自己的国家见过中国结吗？

②你在哪里见到的中国结？这些中国结是什么类型的？你知道这些中国结是如何传播过去的吗？（无固定答案）

> T: Have you seen Chinese knots in your own country?
> T: Where did you see the Chinese knot? What kind of Chinese knots are these? Do you know how these Chinese knots spread to your country?

2. 中国结的"传承者"：陈夏生

（1）教师通过图片，介绍陈夏生与中国结的故事。

（2）教师通过图片，介绍陈夏生出版第一本关于"中国结"的书籍并将中国结传播至海外的历程。

（3）教师总结陈夏生和中国结的故事：对中华传统文化的由衷热爱以及为中国结的普及和传播所做出的不懈努力。

3. 中国结与建筑：世界最性感建筑之"中国结步行桥"

（1）教师展示湖南长沙梅溪湖中国结步行桥的图片，请学生谈谈感受。

> T: Let's look at this bridge. How do you feel?

（2）教师介绍湖南长沙梅溪湖中国结步行桥的历史和特点，同时说明该桥曾被美国 CNN 评选为十大"世界最性感建筑"之一。

4. 中国结与奥运：2008 年北京奥运会和 2022 年北京冬奥会

（1）教师展示两届奥运会上的图片，并提问同学还注意到了奥运会上哪些中国结元素。

问题：大家觉得为什么奥运会中随处可见中国结元素，它代表了什么精神？

> T: Why do you think Chinese knot elements can be seen everywhere in the Olympic Games? What spirit does it represent?

5. 中国结与服饰：古老的中国结盘扣

（1）教师展示各国第一夫人的旗袍照图片，并请同学注意观察旗袍或唐装上的盘扣。

问题：大家觉得这些第一夫人穿的旗袍美不美？这些旗袍的扣子是不是很特别？像不像我们今天学习的中国结？

（2）教师播放视频，展示国际时装展上的中国结元素并请学生观看后交流感受。

（3）教师总结：含有中国结元素的"中国风"服饰被越来越多的外国友人所接受和喜爱，中国传统文化正在当代国际舞台上展示其独特魅力和风采。

> T: Do you think these first ladies' cheongsam beautiful? Are the buckles of these cheongsam very special, like the Chinese knot we learned today? In fact, this kind of buckle is a kind of ancient Chinese knot.

（三）练一练（10分钟，内容详见双语讲稿第四节）

1. 连一连

教师列出中国结代表的不同含义，请学生选出每种含义对应哪种中国结。

2. 选一选

教师编写与中国结的寓意、中国结的当代价值和海外传播相关的选择题，请学生根据教学内容进行选择并订正。

第三课时（40分钟）：学习制作同心结

设计意图：通过详细教授同心结的制作步骤，帮助学生更好地理解和体会中国结特别是同心结的寓意。同时鼓励学生制作同心结，激发学生热爱中华文化的热情。

（一）导入（2分钟）

教师展示自己制作的同心结，并向学生提问。

问题：这是什么？你们想不想自己学学做同心结？

> T: What is this? Do you want to learn to make the concentric knot by yourself?

（二）文化体验：教授同心结（30分钟，内容详见双语讲稿第三节）

1. 教师发放材料并逐一介绍。
2. 教师现场演示并结合动图，教授学生如何制作同心结。
3. 教师请学生展示各自成品，并谈谈有什么感想。

（三）本课小结（7分钟）

1. 教师总结中国结的起源、类型以及中国结在当代的表征和海外传播。

2. 教师总结中国结的寓意：中华儿女质朴、勤劳、积极向上的品格以及对美好生活坚韧的追求。

（四）布置作业（1分钟）

教师请学生课下试着制作中国结并与同学和老师分享。

> T: Please try to make Chinese knots after class and share them with our classmates and teachers! Class is over, see you next time!

七、教学反思

中国结是一种手工编织工艺品，蕴含了中华民族高雅的情致与千百年来积淀的智慧。因其外观对称精致，可以代表中华民族悠久的历史，符合中国传统装饰的习俗和审美观念，故命名为"中国结"。中国结的命名多利用自然形态、谐音，有丰富的祈福内涵，被作为民间祝祷的符号，成为世代相传的吉祥饰物。

本课教学过程中，应由中国结的不同外形深入至对其中所蕴含的美好愿景和感情的介绍，帮助学生在种类繁多的中国结名目中清晰地感受到中国人的美好情感寄托。

中国结的当代表征和海外传播是本节课程的教学重点，教师应在多列举案例的基础上帮助学生拓宽视野，更好地理解中国结在海内外的传承和传播；此外，这部分的教学可以多利用启发式，请学生就自己生活中常见的、熟悉的中国结形象进行交流互动，以此调动课堂气氛，增加趣味性。

文化体验环节选择同心结的制作，也是希望借由"同心"之意，倡导"和而不同"的基本理念，从而彰显中华民族与人为善、与人修好的博大胸襟。

附：辅助教学资源

1. B站Up主"可以吃饭了吗"的视频：https：//www.bilibili.com/video/BV1qt4y1z7CZ？from=search&seid=15839218663111632743。

2. B站Up主"秋夕的落雨"的视频：https：//www.bilibili.com/video/BV1yW411F7bz？from=search&seid=14242860740449821744。

3. 腾讯网视频：https：//new.qq.com/omn/SPO20210/SPO2021080800231300.html。

4. 优酷视频：https：//v.youku.com/v_show/id_XNjQ2MDE4NjAw.html。

5. 春晚节目之《中国喜事》视频：https：//www.bilibili.com/video/BV1w4411X7iW？share_source=copy_web。

讨论与练习
Discussion and Practice

1. 讨论

1. Discussion

（1）你在哪些地方见到过中国结？发挥你的想象力，你认为中国结还可以跟哪些元素相融合？

（1）Where have you seen the Chinese knot? What other elements do you think the Chinese knot can be combined with?

（2）你最喜欢哪种中国结？为什么？

（2）Which Chinese knot do you like most? Why?

（3）你认为中国结为什么能走向世界，受到各国人民的喜爱？

（3）Why do you think the Chinese knot can be loved by people all over the world?

（4）对比中国结和你们国家的传统手工艺，你认为它们之间有什么不同？

（4）Comparing the Chinese knot with traditional handicrafts in your country, what are the differences between them?

2. 练习

2. Practice

（1）连一连

(1) Matching

好事成双	A. 祥云结
Good things in pairs	Auspicious cloud knot
绵延不断	B. 双钱结
Continuous	Double coin knot
龙的传人	C. 龙形结
Descendants of dragons	Dragon knot
年年有余	D. 双鱼节
Have abundance every year	Double fish knots

（2）选一选

(2) Choosing（Select the correct one from the four options）

- 代表紧密结合、结伴而行和永不分离的中国结是？（　　）

Which Chinese knot has the meanings of tight closeness, sweet companionship and never being separated?

A. Peace knot B. Double Happiness knot

C. Concentric knot D. Osmanthus knot

- 下面不属于双联结寓意的是？（　　）

Which is not the meaning of the double connection knot?

A. Three goals B. Have abundance in the years to come

C. Tie the knot D. All the best

- 结合了古老的民间艺术中国结和西方的莫比乌斯环的建筑是？（　　）

Which architecture combines the Chinese knot with the Western Mobius Ring?

A. Monroe tower B. Chinese knot pedestrian bridge
C. The Great Wall D. Wangjing SOHO

答案
Answer

(1) B	A	C	D
(2) C	C	B	B

第七章 泥塑文化双语教学设计
Chapter VII Bilingual Teaching Design of Clay Sculpture Culture

泥塑（陈瑶 摄）
Clay Sculpture（By Chen Yao）

导语
Introduction

相传庞涓和孙膑都是战国时期著名的军事家。庞涓因嫉恨孙膑，而用计剜去了孙膑的双膝。孙膑逃亡至吴国惠山，并利用泥人、泥马以寻求庞涓"五雷阵"的破解之道。后来孙膑出任齐国军师，以"泥人兵阵"战法破解了庞涓的"五雷阵"，大败庞涓，而这一战法正是之前在惠山研究所得。从此惠山居民开始捏泥人，惠山泥人声名远扬。"泥人兵阵"就是泥塑的由来。

During the Warring States period, Pang Juan and Sun Bin were both well-known military strategists. Pang Juan was jealous of Sun Bin, so he devised a plan to cut off Sun Bin's knees. Sun Bin fled to Huishan of WuState and kneaded clay figures and clay horses to look for ways of attacking Pang Juan's "Five Thunder Array" strategy. Later, Sun Bin served as the military advisor for the Qi State, and defeated Pang Juan's "Five Thunder Array" strategy with the "Clay Figurine Array" strategy that Sun Bin developed in Huishan. Since then, Huishan residents began to knead clay figurines, and the reputation of Huishan clay figurines was widespread. This is the origin of clay sculpture.

第一节　泥塑的技法
Section 1　Clay Sculpture Technique

1. 泥塑的基本流程

泥塑在雕塑艺术中占据着重要的位置，可塑性极强。很多雕塑作品也会先以泥稿做模具。泥塑技法大致可分为四个步骤：制子儿、翻模、脱胎、着色。第一步制子儿即为制作原型，泥坯完成后再翻模，在泥塑制作完成并风干固定后再进行泥塑的脱胎，打磨均匀、涂上底粉、稍加修饰，最后着色。

1. The Basic Process of Making a Clay Sculpture

With a high degree of plasticity, clay sculptures play an important role in the art of sculpture. Clay sculptures are also used as moulds to make sculptures from other materials. The clay sculpting technique approximately includes four steps, creating the prototype, rolling over, removing, painting. The first step is creating the prototype. When the prototype is ready, clay is put on the prototype to make a mould. After that, the mould will be filled in clay and be removed when the clay is dry. The dry clay sculpture will be polished, underpainted and painted.

2. 泥塑的基本技法

泥塑的制作过程并不复杂,但需要制作者有耐心并掌握基本技法。简单来说,泥塑有四种基本塑型技法。

2. Basic Techniques of Clay Sculpture

Making clay sculptures is not complicated, but the producer needs to be patient and master fundamental techniques. Simply speaking, there are four basic sculpting techniques.

(1) 挖空法

挖空法的优点是材料俭省、制品重心稳定。取适量泥团,先做成实心泥坯,然后静置,待表面微硬,便可挖空。因不易变形且内部仍然湿润,故可使用工具,也可直接用手。挖至泥坯逐渐变成空心结构。现在,许多造型精美的花瓶、人物立像等,均由传统挖空法制作而成。

(1) Hollowing

This method has the advantage of saving materials and making sculptures more stable. The first step is taking an appropriate amount of mud, moulding clay into the desired shape and waiting until the surface of the sculpture slightly hardens, and the sculpture's interior is still wet. The second step is hollowing the clay sculpture using tools or hands. Nowadays, this method is used for sculpting beautiful vases, figures and so on.

(2) 泥板法

泥板法可在表面刻画更多细节,制作出精美纹理。根据制作需求,采用厚薄不同的泥板,并在泥板上切割所需图案。制作多纹理的泥塑作品时,泥板法是主要塑型方式。著名的陕西凤翔泥塑制作工艺极其复杂,主要采用的就是泥板法。国家邮政局连续两年选中凤翔泥塑作为生肖邮票主图，这不仅加快了泥塑文化的传播，也带动了当地的农村建设与经济发展。

（2）Clay Slab Method

Using a clay slab makes it easier to sculpt more details and exquisite texture effects. Clay slabs of different thicknesses are used for different requirements, and desired shapes are cut out of clay slabs to make sculptures. This method is the primary method of shaping a sculpture with many textures. For example, the famous Fengxiang clay figurines in Shaanxi Province are mainly made with clay slabs and through a complicated process. Fengxiang clay figurines were selected as the main picture of zodiac stamps for two consecutive years, which accelerated the promotion of traditional clay figurines and drove the rural construction and economic development of Fengxiang.

（3）泥条法

泥条法可用于制作立体形状。首先用手搓泥，形成长条状的泥条。其次把泥条两端相接成圆，再不断重复这一过程，把泥条一段段叠起来围住。最后得到泥条组成的器物或形状。在堆叠时，可适当按压使泥条粘连牢固。许多茶壶及装饰上的精美花纹都采用这一手法制作而成。

（3）Clay Stick Method

Three-dimensional shapes can be made by using clay stick method. This method starts with rolling clay into long sticks. Then, the ends of each stick are pinched together to shape the stick into a circle. Repeating this process continuously, stacking and surrounding the mud sticks, finally get the desired utensil or shape When stacking, pressing properly can make the clay firmly. Many teapots and exquisite patterns are all made by this method.

（4）手捏法

手捏法不借助工具，通过拉、捏、搓、卷、压、插、接、贴、扭、揉、抹、团等灵巧的手指动作直接塑型。用手掌心按压出体积较大的造型，然后由手指揉捏刻画细节部分。其中，"抹"这一手法可保证泥塑成品表面光滑。现在市面上栩栩如生的泥人娃娃、装饰品以及许多小物件的制作，都会使用这一技法。这不仅有助于泥塑文化的广泛传承，而且带动了社会经济的发展。

（4）Pinching and Kneading

Without using any tools, this method requires finger movements such as pulling, pinching, rubbing, rolling, pressing, inserting, connecting, sticking, twisting, kneading, wiping and balling to shape. Larger shapes and patterns are made by pressing with palms, and details are kneaded with fingers. The surface of the clay sculpture can be smoothed by wiping. Many clay sculptures in the market today, like clay dolls, decorations and small objects, are all made with these techniques. These clay sculpture products promote social and economic development while inheriting clay sculpture culture.

作为重要的艺术门类，中国泥塑从古至今不断发展。不仅宗教题材的大型泥塑继续繁荣，小型泥塑玩具也发展起来。有许多人专门从事泥人制作和设计。泥塑艺术具有强烈的视觉冲击效果，欣赏角度也极为丰富和多样化。在高科技迅猛发展的今天，它是人们追求返璞归真的具体写照，是真、善、美精神意蕴的充分体现，为越来越多的国家和人民所接受和喜爱。

As an important art species, Chinese clay sculpture has successively developed up to now. Not only did large clay sculptures with religious themes remain flourishing, but small clay sculpture toys also developed. Many people specialize in making and designing clay sculptures. Clay sculpture art with a strong visual impact can be appreciated from abundant and diverse angles. Today, with the rapid development of high technology, clay sculpture art illustrates people's pursuit of recovering original simplicity and embodies the spiritual meaning of truth, goodness and beauty. It has been accepted and loved by more and more countries and people.

第二节　泥塑与西方雕塑的"和而不同"
Section 2　Harmony and Uniformity between Chinese Clay Sculpture and Western Sculpture

泥塑与西方雕塑相比既有自己的独特之处，又呈现出雕塑发展的共性。

Chinese clay sculptures have their own uniqueness compared with western sculptures and present common features in the development of sculpture art.

1. 泥塑与西方雕塑之独特之处

1. Uniqueness of Chinese Clay Sculptures and Western Sculptures

（1）泥塑注重实用性，西方雕塑注重观赏性

发展早期，泥塑多为殉葬品，形式上既表现为泥牛、泥羊等牲畜，还表现为盘碗等器物。后来分化出宗教和民俗两类功能。供奉于佛堂、寺庙中的神像多为泥塑。除彩塑着色外，还常以金箔装饰来凸显佛像的神圣。而民俗功能则多表现为泥塑玩具和摆件，这些都是节日庙会期间不可或缺的商品。现代泥塑匠人不断创造出与时俱进的作品，广受年轻人青睐。而西方雕塑早期多用于建筑装饰，后来才逐渐发展为独立的艺术门类，并成为各种文化思潮转变的传播载体，如在文艺复兴时期，雕塑艺术就取得了辉煌成就。

（1）Chinese Clay Sculptures' Practicality and Western Sculptures' Ornamental Value

In the early stages of development, clay sculptures mainly were used as burial objects, including livestock such as mud cattle and sheep and utensils such as plates and bowls. Later the sculptures were differentiated into two types of functions, religion and folklore. Most of the clay Buddha statues made by artisans are enshrined in Buddhist halls and temples. In addition to the coloring of sculptures, gold foils will also be used to highlight the holiness of the Buddha. Clay sculptures of folklore were mainly toys and ornaments that were indispensable commodities during the festival temple fair. Modern clay sculpture artisans continue to create works that keep up with the fashion trend of the times, making clay sculpture crafts widely loved by young people. However, western sculptures were mostly architectural decoration in the early days and gradually developed into an independent art category. And it has also become a dissemination vehicle for the transformation of various cultural thoughts, such as the brilliant achievements of sculpture art during the Renaissance.

（2）千变万化的泥塑和专注于人像的西方雕塑

泥塑作品形态种类多样，除人和动物等常规造型外，还有龙、凤、麒麟等虚构生物，甚至是人与动物的合形，如人首蛇身的伏羲和女娲。泥塑还能够表现出山川树木、生活场景、历史故事以及神话传说等。其塑造"妙在似与不似之间"，注重写意和气韵，有时采用夸张手法来突出事物的特点。

另外，西方雕塑则在较长的时间内以人像为主要刻画主题。古希腊神与人同形同性的观念，奠定了以人体、人像为主的雕塑形式。与此同时，西方雕塑还追求写实风格，人物动作细腻丰富，通过肌肉、衣物纹理的处理，着力表现人体的优美。

(2) Chinese Clay Sculptures in Diverse Shapes and Western Sculptures Focusing on Portraits

The forms of Chinese clay sculptures are diverse. Apart from the regular styling such as figures and animals, there are fictional creatures such as dragons, phoenixes and Kylin, and even combinations of humans and animals, such as Fu'xi and Nu'wa with a human head and the body of a snake. Chinese clay sculptures can also show mountains and rivers, trees, life scenes, historical stories, myths and legends. The beauty of clay sculptures derives from their similarity and dissimilarity to the original items they embody. More attention is paid to freehand brushwork and rhythm of "Qi", and sometimes exaggeration techniques are used to highlight the characteristics of things.

On the other hand, western sculptures are dominated by portraits for a long period of time. This was influenced by the ancient Greek concept of homogeneity between gods and people. At the same time, western sculptures also pursue of realistic style and have delicate and various movements. The beauty of the human body is demonstrated through vivid muscles and clothing wrinkles on the sculptures.

2. 泥塑与西方雕塑之共性发展

2. Common Features of Chinese Clay Sculptures and Western Sculptures

（1）发展早期对孕育生命的共同崇拜

威伦道夫的维纳斯与红山文化的孕妇像和女神像都以夸张手法，凸显了女性在孕育生命时的身体特征，弱化甚至忽略了其他与生育无关的细节，寄托了原始先民对母性的崇拜和歌颂，以及祈求生育的愿望。

（1）Fertility Worshiping in the Early Stages of Development

Willendoff's Venus sculpture, the pregnant woman sculpture and the goddess sculpture of Hongshan Culture exaggerated and highlighted the physical characteristics of women when nurturing life, and weaken or even ignore other details unrelated to fertility. These sculptures indicate ancestors' worship and praise for motherhood and pray for fertility.

（2）宗教题材的表现

早期泥塑所塑造的神是各类本土神话传说中的角色。汉代佛教传入中国以后，泥塑所制作的佛像开始通行。举世闻名的敦煌彩塑就是以泥塑的技艺制作而成。泥塑在制作神佛塑像时多表现为站立姿势，脸型方正饱满、五官清秀，使佛像表现出庄重、慈悲的神态，凸显其神圣感。泥塑神佛塑像具有中国的写意特质，常对面部、肢体等部位进行变形和夸张表现。发展到后期，佛像的服饰也往往淡化其性别特征和肉体轮廓，着重刻画眼神、表情以及整体姿态。

西方雕塑所着重表现的多为神话人物，比如希腊神话中的宙斯、阿波罗、缪斯等。此外，人体的美感也是西方雕塑所着重表现的主题，因而雕塑的着装通常轻薄适体，或是以裸体形式展现人体肌肉和健美的体型。雕塑的比例也参照真实的人体比例。在创作题材方面常以战争、体育竞赛等为背景。发展到后期，西方雕塑则在基督教环境下，以圣经故事和教义为雕塑灵感来源。

（2）The Expression of Religious Themes

The gods shaped by early clay sculptures are the roles in various local myths and legends. After Buddhism was introduced into China in the Han Dynasty, Buddhist statues made of clay sculptures began to popularize. The world-famous Dunhuang colored sculptures are also made of clay sculpture. Clay sculptures mostly show a standing posture when making statues of gods and Buddhas, with a square and round face and beautiful facial features, so that the Buddha statues show a solemn and compassionate demeanor, highlighting their sense of sacredness. The clay statue of the Buddha has the characteristics of Chinese freehand, often deforming and exaggerated the face, limbs and other parts. In the later stages of development, the costumes of Buddha statues also tended to dilute their gender characteristics and flesh contours, focusing on depicting the eyes, expressions and overall posture.

Western sculpture focuses on mythological figures, such as Zeus, Apollo, and muses in Greek mythology. In addition, the beauty of the human body is also the theme of western sculpture, so the clothing of the sculpture is usually light and suitable, or it shows the muscles and toned body shape in the form of nude. The proportions of the sculpture also refer to the real human body. In terms of creative themes, it is often set against the background of war and sports competitions. Later in its development, western sculpture was inspired by biblical stories and doctrines in a Christian context.

（3） 现代泥塑与西方雕塑交融发展

在功能上，早先泥塑的实用性较强，而西方雕塑则侧重观赏性。但现在，日用品通常由金属、陶瓷和塑料制作而成，泥塑制品如盘、碗等则逐渐成为一种装饰和收藏物。传统工艺所作泥塑比较易碎，现代匠人不断吸收西方雕塑之铸模技艺，吸收其优势达到改良传统工艺的目的，使得泥塑更加坚固，满足了贸易运输需要，行销海外。"摔不烂"泥塑是泥塑工艺产业化的一大推动力，提升了泥塑产量，满足了市场需求。泥塑中独具特色的纹样也常应用于服饰、箱包、文具等产品上，在年轻人中掀起了一阵"国潮热"。

（3） The Blending and Development of Modern Chinese Clay Sculptures and Western Sculptures

Functionally, Chinese clay sculptures were more practical initially, while western sculptures focused on ornamental value. However, materials such as metal, ceramics and plastics take the place of clay to make daily necessities nowadays, so clay sculptures like clay plates and bowls are becoming more and more of a decoration and collection. Clay sculptures made by traditional techniques are fragile. Modern artisans learn the casting technique from western sculpture to improve the process, make the clay sculpture firmer, meet trade and transportation needs, and sell overseas.

"Not broken" is a major driving force for the industrialization of clay sculpture technology, which improves the output of clay sculpture and meets market demand. Besides, clay sculptures with unique artistic styles are often used in the design of clothing, bags, stationery and other supplies, which has set off a mania of national fashion among young people.

第三节 "活脱世间泥塑样":泥塑的体验
Section 3 "Living Clay Sculpture Record the World": Let's Try Clay Sculpting

1. 材料

黄泥、泥工板(或塑料画板)、湿布、喷壶、竹刀、切割绳、牙签、木棒(木槌)、各类小型木质泥塑刀、围裙。如需制作彩塑,则准备上色笔刷、毛笔、颜料、打磨砂纸等工具。

1. Materials

Yellow clay, carve pad (or plastic drawing board), wet cloth, watering can, bamboo knife, cutting rope, toothpick, wooden stick (mallet), various small wooden clay knives and aprons. If you need to make colored sculptures, coloring brushes, brushes, pigments and sanding paper are needed.

2. 注意事项

(1) 使用刻刀时要小心不要伤到自己。

(2) 如果你离开座位的话,把刀盖好。

(3) 如果你有任何问题,请举手提问。

2. Cautions

(1) Be careful and do not hurt yourself when using the knife.

(2) Keep the cap on the knife if you leave your seat.

(3) If you have any questions, please raise your hand to ask.

3. 步骤

(1) 设计草图

在白纸上绘制草图,并思考制作的时候使用何种起形方法。注意初学者尽量选择相对简单的目标,以免造成制作上的困难。

3. Steps

(1) Sketch design

Sketch on white paper, and think about what method should be used for sculpting. Beginners are suggested to choose simple goals for avoiding difficulties.

步骤(1) 设计草图(陈瑶 摄)
Step (1) Sketch Design (By Chen Yao)

(2) 制坯

运用挖空法、泥板法或泥条法等起形方法,用手或工具塑型,捏制出大概的形状。此后使用工具对作品进行不断的细化。如果耗时太长,泥土开始干燥,可使用喷壶喷湿泥坯表面,再用"抹"的手法来减少泥坯表面的细纹。

(2) Create the prototype

Use the shaping methods such as hollowing, using clay slabs or clay stick method to shape with hands or tools and knead clay into an approximate shape. After that, use tools to refine the sculpture. If the clay starts to dry as time past, use watering can to wet its surface and smooth the fine lines on the surface by wiping.

步骤（2）制坯（陈瑶 摄）
Step（2）Createthe Prototype（By Chen Yao）

（3）着色

静置阴干泥坯。待泥坯完全干燥后，先上一层底色，再刻画小的色块。大面积的铺底色能够让泥塑的表面更加光滑，便于颜料附着。通常使用米白色作为底色。铺完底色后，可以用砂纸打磨一遍。注意控制颜料的湿度和黏稠度。过湿的颜料上色效果不佳。

（3）Painting

Dry the clay embryo in the shade and after it is completely dry, paint the clay surface. It is usually necessary to apply a layer of background color first, and then depict small color blocks. A large area of ground color can make the surface smoother and easy for pigment adhesion. Usually beige white is the background color. After painting the background color, you can polish it with sandpaper. Pay attention to control the humidity and viscosity of the pigment. Pigment that is too wet will worsen the result of coloring.

步骤（3）着色（陈瑶 摄）
Step（3）Painting（By Chen Yao）

（4）干燥

再次静置阴干，直至泥坯表面颜料完全干燥。如有需要，可用细砂纸对泥坯表面颜料结块、粗糙的地方进行轻柔打磨。

（4）Dry

Leave the clay embryo in the shade until the pigment on the surface is completely dry. If necessary, fine sandpaper can be used to gently polish the caked and rough places on the surface.

步骤（4）阴干（蒋颖琪 摄）
Step（4）Dry（By Jiang Yingqi）

第四节 泥塑文化双语教案

一、教学对象

对中华文化感兴趣的外国学生。

二、教学内容

1. 中国传统手工艺品泥塑的起源、制作流程和基本技法；
2. 泥塑与西方雕塑在功能、表现对象和主题方面的和而不同；
3. 简单小型泥塑摆件的手工制作。

三、教学目标

1. 帮助外国学生了解泥塑这一中国传统工艺品，包括其起源、制作流程和基础技法；
2. 引导外国学生通过西方雕塑与中国泥塑的对比，逐步感受泥塑或夸张或写实的独特表现手法，以及泥塑所蕴含的美好愿景；
3. 帮助外国学生学习简单小型泥塑摆件的手工制作方法。

四、教学方法

1. 图片、视频法

利用图片、视频向学生展示泥塑的起源、制作流程、基础技法，并展示典型作品。

2. 演示法

通过演示法，展示泥塑的四种基本技法。

3. 启发诱导法

课堂展示泥塑成品，教师提问，引导学生自行观察泥塑，说出泥塑的特点。

五、课时安排

三课时完成,每课时 40 分钟。
第一课时介绍泥塑起源、流程、技法;
第二课时介绍泥塑与西方雕塑在功能、表现方式、主题上的和"和而不同";
第三课时介绍制作泥塑并上色。

六、教学过程(三课时)

第一课时(40 分钟):泥塑的起源及泥塑的基本制作过程

设计意图:以生动、精练的泥人兵阵小故事开篇介绍中国泥塑的起源,力图通过"中国故事"吸引学生的注意力。利用图片、视频、实物等各种丰富手段展示中国泥塑的制作过程和基本技法,并揭示其中的深层含义:既展现出了中华民族将黄土变为宝贝的智慧,也联结了中华民族与土地的不解之缘。

(一)组织教学(约 2 分钟)

教师进入课堂,检查多媒体设备,将教学所用的教案、课件及手工材料准备放置妥当。师生互相问候,教师点名,准备上课。

> T: Good morning, everyone! How are you today? Let's start the roll call first... Okay, everyone's here. Class begins.

(二)进入新课,介绍泥塑的起源(10 分钟,内容详见双语讲稿导语)

1. 导入

(1)教师展示多件泥塑实物,请学生回答问题。

问题：①请你们摸一下这些泥塑，有什么感觉？

②你觉得它们的样子如何？（无固定答案）

T：Please touch these clay sculptures, How do you feel?

T：What do you think of these clay sculptures?

（2）教师板书"泥塑"二字及拼音，教师领读两遍。

（3）教师介绍何为泥塑。

2. 介绍泥塑的起源：泥人兵阵的故事

（1）教师利用图片，以角色扮演的方式绘声绘色地向学生讲述孙膑和"泥人兵阵"的故事。

（2）教师就"泥人兵阵"故事中的小细节进行提问，考查学生对泥塑起源故事的理解程度。

问题：①孙膑的"泥人兵阵"里有什么？（答案：泥人和泥马）

②孙膑做"泥人兵阵"是为研究如何破解庞涓的_____。

（答案：五雷阵）

T：What are in Sun Bin's "Clay Figurine Array"?

T：Sun Bin made the "Clay Figurine Array" to study how to crack Pang Juan's _____.

（3）教师总结泥塑艺术的发展：具有强烈的视觉冲击效果，欣赏角度也极为丰富和多样化，更能贴近人们的生活；它是真、善、美精神意蕴的充分体现，为越来越多的国家和人民所接受和喜爱。

（三）简单介绍泥塑的制作过程：制坯、翻模、脱胎、着色（约15分钟，内容详见双语讲稿第一节）

1. 教师播放泥塑制作的视频，请学生观察泥塑制作的全过程。

2. 教师利用图片，分解泥塑制作过程，并简单讲授制坯、翻模、脱胎、着色各步骤的特点。

（四）介绍泥塑的基本技法：挖空法、泥板法、泥条法、手捏法（约12分钟，内容详见双语讲稿第一节）

1. 挖空法

教师准备几块泥塑用土，配合图片进行挖空法的展示。

2. 泥板法

教师准备几块泥塑用土，配合图片进行泥板法的展示。

3. 泥条法

教师准备几块泥塑用土，配合图片进行泥条法的展示。

4. 手捏法

教师准备几块泥塑用土，配合图片进行手捏法的展示。

（五）小结（1分钟）

教师简单回顾泥塑的起源故事并简单梳理泥塑的制作过程和基本技法。

第二课时（40分钟）：中国泥塑与西方雕塑的"和而不同"

设计意图：通过图片、视频，启发学生通过比较揭示中国泥塑与西方雕塑在功能、表现形式和主题方面的异同点，从而帮助学生更好地理解中国泥塑在功能上注重实用，在形态种类上丰富多样，在主题上从推崇生育到表现宗教的发展脉络。

（一）复习回顾（约5分钟）

1. 教师请学生简要复述泥塑起源的故事。
2. 教师展示图片，提问学生泥塑的制作过程和基本技法。

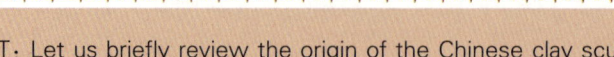

> T: Let us briefly review the origin of the Chinese clay sculpture.
> T: Look at these pictures, What are the manufacturing operation and basic techniques of Chinese clay sculpture?

（二）进入新课，介绍中国泥塑与西方雕塑的"和而不同"（30分钟，内容详见双语讲稿第二节）

1. 导入

教师利用图片展示具有代表性的中国泥塑作品和西方雕塑作品，引导学生观察两者的不同。

问题：请大家仔细观察中国泥塑和西方雕塑，比较一下它们有什么异同？（无固定答案）

> T: Please observe Chinese clay sculpture and western sculpture carefully and compare their similarities and differences?

2. 功能上的差异

（1）教师利用图片展示具有代表性的中国泥塑作品和西方雕塑作品，引导学生观察两者功能上的不同。

（2）教师介绍泥塑所制作的多为殉葬品，后来分化出宗教和民俗两类功能。匠人们制作的泥塑神像大多被供奉在佛堂、寺庙中；民俗功能则发展出了陈设品和儿童玩具两类。

（3）教师介绍西方雕塑早期多用于建筑装饰，逐渐发展成为一门独立的艺术门类。其不仅有装饰意义，还成为各种文化思潮转变的传播载体，如文艺复兴时期雕塑艺术取得的成就。

（4）通过比较，教师总结泥塑和西方雕塑的功能差异：泥塑的实用性比较强，与民众的生活也有着比较密切的关联；而西方雕塑则以观赏性为重点。

3. 表现形式上的差异

（1）教师利用图片展示具有代表性的中国泥塑作品和西方雕塑作品，引导学生观察两者表现形式上的不同。

（2）教师介绍泥塑作品的形态种类多样，包括人物造型，虎、兔、猪、牛、羊等动物，龙、凤、麒麟等虚构生物以及山川树木、生活场景、历史故事和神话传说。

（3）教师介绍西方雕塑以人体、人像为主的雕塑形式。

（4）通过比较，教师总结泥塑和西方雕塑在表现形式上的差异：泥塑注重写意和气韵，有时采用夸张的手法来突出事物的特点；而西方雕塑追求写实风格，人物动作细腻丰富，通过肌肉、衣物纹理的处理，着力于表现人体的优美。

4. 发展早期对孕育生命的共同崇拜

（1）教师请学生思考二者是否有共同点。

> T：Does clay sculpture have anything in common with western sculpture?

（2）教师展示图片，请学生观察比较，启发引导学生发现泥塑和雕塑都凸显了女性在孕育生命时的身体特征。

问题：请看这两幅作品，它们有什么共同之处？

> T：What do they have in common?

（3）教师总结，泥塑和雕塑都寄托了原始先民对母性的崇拜和歌颂，以及祈求生育的愿望。

5. 宗教题材的永恒主题

（1）教师展示图片，请学生观察比较，启发引导学生发现泥塑和雕塑都表现了宗教题材。

问题：请看这两幅作品，它们有什么共同之处？

> T: What do they have in common?

（2）教师总结，早期泥塑所塑造的神是各类本土神话传说中的角色，汉代佛教传入中国以后，泥塑所制作的佛像开始通行。西方宗教题材的雕塑最具有特点的是基督教雕塑艺术。

（三）练一练（5分钟，内容详见双语讲稿第四节）

1. 连一连

教师展示泥塑的技法与代表作品相关的连线题，请学生进行配对连线。

2. 选一选

教师编写与泥塑的起源、泥塑的制作过程和技法、泥塑和西方雕塑的异同点相关的选择题，请学生根据教学内容进行选择并订正。

第三课时（40分钟）：泥塑小摆件的手工制作

设计意图：通过详细教授泥塑小摆件的手工制作过程，帮助学生更好地理解和体会中国泥塑文化的内涵和表征，激发学生热爱中华文化的热情。

（一）导入（2分钟）

教师展示自己制作的泥塑作品，并向学生提问。

问题：这是什么？你们想不想自己学着做一个泥塑小摆件？

> T: What's this? Do you want to learn to make a Chinese clay sculpture?

（二）文化体验：教授泥塑小摆件的手工制作（30分钟，内容详见双语讲稿第三节）

1. 教师发放材料并说明注意事项。
2. 教师现场演示并结合动图，教授学生如何制作泥塑小摆件。

3. 教师请学生展示各自成品，并谈谈有什么感想。

（三）本课小结（7 分钟）

1. 教师总结中国泥塑的起源、制作过程和基本技法以及中国泥塑与西方雕塑在功能、表现形式、主题等方面的异同点。

2. 教师总结中国泥塑的寓意：既展现出了中华民族将黄土变为宝贝的智慧，也联结了中华民族与土地的不解之缘。

（四）布置作业（1 分钟）

教师请学生课下试着制作泥塑并与同学和老师分享。

> T: Please try to make Chinese clay sculpture after class and share them with our classmates and teachers! Class is over, see you next time!

七、教学反思

中华民族有着蓬勃的创造力和高超的智慧。作为中国的传统民间艺术之一，泥塑既展现出了中华民族的智慧，也联结起中华民族与土地之间的关联。泥塑的原料是混入少量棉花纤维或其他黏合剂的泥土，匠人用手或工具塑型捏制出不同形象的泥坯。阴干后的泥胚涂上底粉、施以彩绘，就成为了各式各样的工艺品，可做摆件、玩具，也可作为供人观瞻的人偶、佛像。

本课教学应通过大量丰富图片或实物的展示向学生介绍泥塑的基本技法，同时灵活运用启发式和观察法，帮助学生比较中国泥塑和西方雕塑的异同点，进而更好地帮助学生了解中国泥塑的特点。

体验环节为制作泥塑小摆件，对材料和工具的要求相对较高，教师应提前说明注意事项，特别是提醒学生安全使用各类泥塑工具。

附：辅助教学资源

1. B 站 Up 主 "可以吃饭了吗" 的视频：https://www.bilibili.com/video/BV1qt4y1z7CZ?from=search&seid=15839218663111632743。

2. B 站 Up 主"秋夕的落雨"的视频：https：//www.bilibili.com/video/BV1yW411F7bz?from = search&seid = 14242860740449821744。

3. 腾讯网视频：https：//new.qq.com/omn/SPO20210/SPO2021080800231300.html。

4. 优酷视频：https：//v.youku.com/v_show/id_XNjQ2MDE4NjAw.html。

讨论与练习
Discussion and Practice

1. 讨论

1. Discussion

（1）你觉得泥塑怎么样？泥塑通常有什么特征？在体验过程中，你觉得制作泥塑的最大困难是什么？

（1）What do you think of clay sculpture? What are the characteristics of clay sculpture? What do you think is the biggest difficulty in clay sculpting?

（2）如果你掌握了制作泥塑的所有技巧，你想要制作什么？为什么？

（2）If you have mastered all the skills of clay sculpting, what do you want to make? Why?

（3）你认为泥塑和西方雕塑的最大区别是什么？泥塑的独特之处在哪里？

（3）What do you think is the biggest difference between Chinese clay sculpture and western sculpture? Where is the uniqueness of Chinese clay sculpture?

（4）泥塑和西方雕塑有哪些共同点？

（4）What do Chinese clay sculpture and western sculpture have in common?

2. 练习

2. Practice

（1）连一连

（1）Matching

第七章　泥塑文化双语教学设计

泥人娃娃 　　　　　　　A. 挖空法
Clay dolls 　　　　　　　Hollowing

茶壶 　　　　　　　　　 B. 泥板法
Teapots 　　　　　　　　Clay slab method

凤翔泥塑 　　　　　　　 C. 泥条法
Fengxiang clay 　　　　　Clay stick method

花瓶 　　　　　　　　　 D. 手捏法
Vases 　　　　　　　　　Pinching and kneading

（2）选一选

(2) Choosing（Select the correct one from the four options）

- 制作泥塑的最后一个步骤是哪一个？（　　）

  Which is the last step in clay sculpting？（　　）

  A. Rolling over 　　　　　　B. Painting

  C. Removing 　　　　　　　D. Creating the prototype

- 凤翔地区的泥塑主要采用的是什么制作手法？（　　）

  What's the main technique of clay sculptures in Fengxiang region？（　　）

  A. Hollowing 　　　　　　　B. Clay Stick Method

  C. Clay Slab Method 　　　　D. Pinching and Kneading

- 哪个朝代后泥塑所制作的佛像开始通行？（　　）

  After which dynasty, the statues of Buddha made of clay became popular？（　　）

  A. Tang 　　　B. Song 　　　C. Han 　　　D. Qing

- 静置风干后的泥坯如果表面颜料结块、粗糙，用什么进行轻柔打磨？（　　）

  If the dry clay embryo has caked and rough places on the surface, what will you use to polish it？（　　）

  A. Wood board 　　B. Machine 　　C. Fine Sandpaper 　　D. File

答案
Answer

(1) D　　　　C　　　　B　　　　A

(2) B　　　　C　　　　C　　　　C

第八章　刺绣文化双语教学设计
Chapter VIII　Bilingual Teaching Design of Embroidery Culture

刺绣（俞梦涵 摄）
Embroidery（By Yu Menghan）

中国传统文化体验式双语教学设计

导语
Introduction

周朝时期，周王之子仲雍为了他的弟弟能够顺利继位，迫于继承制度只好出走到当时的苏州一带。苏州居民有纹身的习俗，仲雍入乡随俗，也刺上了纹身。但是，仲雍认为纹身是一种文化糟粕，理应被废除。于是，他召集当地德高望重的人到家里一起商议废除纹身的事宜。此时，仲雍的孙女女红正坐在屋内缝制衣服，一不小心，针刺破了手指，落下的血滴在衣服上晕染成一朵花，女红便想：能不能用绣在衣服上的图案代替纹身呢？受此启发，她便尝试参照当地纹身的图案在衣服上进行装扮。经过女红不懈的努力，她终于做成了一件五彩缤纷的绣衣。最后，仲雍号召改穿有刺绣图案的衣服，废除了纹身这一习俗。

During the Zhou Dynasty, Zhongyong, the son of the King of Zhou, had to leave for Suzhou so that his brother could succeed to the throne. The inhabitants of Suzhou had a custom of tattooing their bodies, so Zhongyong had his body tattooed as well. However, Zhongyong believed that tattooing was bad and should be abolished, so he called a group of respected local people to his home to discuss the abolition of tattoos. At that moment, Zhongyong's granddaughter Nv Gong was sitting in the house sewing clothes. She accidentally pricked her finger, which left the blood stain on her clothes that looked like a flower. Inspired by this, she then tried to decorate her clothes by referring to local tattoo patterns, and finally made a colourful embroidered garment after tireless efforts. Eventually, Zhongyong called for a switch to embroidered clothes and the abolition of tattoos.

第一节　四大名绣
Section 1　Four Famous Embroideries

中国的四大名绣是苏绣、湘绣、蜀绣和粤绣。四大名绣风格迥异，是中国不同地域文化的艺术结晶,充分体现了中华文化的丰富性和包容性。

The four famous embroideries of China are Su Embroidery, Xiang Embroidery, Shu Embroidery and Yue Embroidery. These embroideries have very different styles and are the artistic essence of different regions in China, showing the richness and inclusiveness of Chinese culture.

1. 苏绣

苏绣是苏州地区刺绣产品的总称。受江苏一带风土人情的影响,苏绣以精细淡雅的风格闻名,其绣品样式清秀,色彩清雅,绣工精致。

若绣山水,则山水远近成趣,意境雅致;若绣楼阁,则楼阁深邃,错落有致;若绣人物,则明眸皓齿,神采奕奕;若绣花鸟,则花鸟亲昵,姿色绰约。双面绣是苏绣当中最特殊的技法,即在同一块底料上的正反两面同时绣出不同的图案,但是轮廓一致。

苏绣作品充分体现出苏州人民灵巧细致的手艺,还有衍生于江南地区的文化鉴赏力及创造力。

1. Suzhou Embroidery

Suzhou embroidery also referred to as "Su embroidery". It is the general name for the embroidery products of the Suzhou region. Influenced by the local customs of Jiangsu, Suzhou embroidery is known for its delicate and elegant style, with clear and elegant colors and exquisite artistry.

If embroidered a landscape, the landscape is interesting and elegant; if embroidered a pavilion, the pavilion is deep and staggered; if embroidered a figure, the eyes and teeth are bright and glowing; if embroidered flowers and birds, the flowers and birds are intimate and graceful. Double-sided embroidery is the most unusual technique in Suzhou embroidery, different designs are embroidered on both sides of the same piece of material but with the same outline.

The work of Suzhou embroidery fully reflects the deft and meticulous craftsmanship of the Suzhou people, as well as the cultural appreciation and creativity derived from the Jiangnan region.

2. 湘绣

湘绣是带有鲜明湘楚文化特色的湖南刺绣产品的总称,既可作为名贵的艺术欣赏品,又可以运用到日常生活中。

湘绣的特点在于以针代笔,层次丰富。狮虎是湘绣的代表性题材,与苏绣有"苏猫湘虎"之称。湘绣绣品中的狮虎,兽毛直竖,眼睛炯炯有神,体现了绣工们炉火纯青的湘绣技艺。

湘绣用途广泛,绣品蕴含着深厚的湘楚文化。不仅展示了湘楚人民对艺术还原和再创造的深厚造诣,还体现了湘楚人民文化生活的丰富多彩。

2. Hunan Embroidery

Hunan embroidery also referred to as "Xiang embroidery", is a generic term for Hunan embroidery products with distinctive Xiangchu cultural characteristics, which can not only be appreciated as a valuable art object, but also be used in daily life.

Hunan Embroidery is characterized by the use of needles as a substitute for pen and the richness of its layers. The lion and the tiger are the representative subjects of Hunan embroidery. It is called "Su cat and Xiang tiger" with Suzhou embroidery. The lions and tigers in Hunan embroidery are shown with their upright hair and piercing eyes, reflecting the proficient skill of the embroiderers.

Hunan embroidery has a wide range of uses, and the embroidery is embedded in the profound culture of Xiangchu. It not only demonstrates the profound attainment of the Xiangchu people in restoring and re-creating their art, but also reflects the richness of their cultural life.

3. 蜀绣

蜀绣是四川地区在丝绸或其他织物上采用蚕丝绣线的刺绣产品的总称,题材多为花鸟虫鱼、湖光山色、人物走兽等。

蜀绣常用晕针来表现绣品的质感,绣品灵动多姿、惟妙惟肖;又与西蜀绘画相辅相成,独树一帜。作为传承时间最长的绣种之一,蜀绣色彩鲜艳夺目、针法精致细腻,工艺复杂程度居四大名绣之首。经过长期发展,蜀绣逐渐形成了针脚细腻、针面平整、构图疏朗、色彩明快的独特风格。

蜀绣的传承与发展，体现了四川人民善于从周围环境中发掘灵感并进行再创造的艺术能力。

3. Sichuan Embroidery

Sichuan embroidery is a generic term for embroidery made in Sichuan, also referred to as "Shu embroidery". It uses silk threads on silk or other fabrics, and embroidery patterns mainly are flowers, birds, insects and fish, landscapes, figures and animals.

It is used to express the embroidery texture through faint stitches. The embroidery is very dynamic and delicate; it is also unique that it complements the paintings of Western Shu. As one of the longest-established embroideries, it has vibrant colors and delicate stitches, its richness ranks first among the four famous embroidery. Over a long period of time, Sichuan embroidery has developed a unique style of delicate stitches, flat surfaces, sparse composition and bright colors.

The inheritance and development of Sichuan embroidery reflects the artistic ability of the Sichuan people to find inspiration in their surroundings and recreate it.

4. 粤绣

粤绣包括广绣和潮绣。广绣是以广州为中心的珠江三角洲民间刺绣工艺的总称。潮绣发源并流行于今潮汕地区。

粤绣以布局满、画面热烈、配色大胆而著称，并凭借着地理优势享誉中外。绣品多用金线绣花纹的轮廓，内塞织物以增加立体感，如同浮雕。其中，潮绣大部分是由男性——俗称"绣郎"所绣。粤绣题材多为寓意吉祥的事物，体现了广州、潮汕地区人民对于生活和艺术创作极高的热情。

粤绣作品远销海内外，享誉中外，不仅为我们带来了极大的经济效益，还增强了中华文化的传播力。

4. Guangdong Embroidery

Guangdong embroidery, also known as "Yue embroidery", includes both Guang embroidery and Chao embroidery. Guang embroidery is the general term for the folk embroidery craft of the Pearl River Delta, with Guangzhou as the center. Chao embroidery originated and became popular in the Chaoshan region.

Guangdong embroidery is known for its full layout, warm images and bold colors, and is renowned for its geographical advantage. Most of the embroidery is done with gold threads to embroider the outline of the pattern, stuffed with fabric to add a sense of three-dimensionality, like a relief carving. Most of the embroidery is done by men, commonly known as "embroiderers". The subjects of Guangdong embroidery are mostly auspicious, reflecting the enthusiasm of the people in Guangzhou and Chaoshan for life and artistic creation.

The works of Guangdong embroidery are sold at home and abroad, renowend Chinese and foreign, not only bringing us great economic benefits but also enhancing cultural transmission capacity of Chinese culture.

四大名绣是中华民族的伟大艺术创造和文化瑰宝，既为世界人民留下了无数珍贵的绣品，又为带动我国的经济发展和提高中华文化的国际影响力做出了突出贡献。

The four famous embroideries are great artistic creations and cultural treasures of the Chinese nation. Countless precious embroideries are appreciated by people around the world, making outstanding contributions to driving China's economic development and increasing the international influence of Chinese culture.

第二节 刺绣的国际性传播与融合
Section 2　The International Spread and Fusion of Embroidery

作为中华文化中最为夺目的宝藏之一，刺绣在中华文化的国际传播与融合中占据着一席之地。

As one of the most eye-catching treasures of Chinese culture, embroidery occupies a place in the international dissemination and integration of Chinese culture.

1. 刺绣的国际性传播

刺绣为对外输送中华优秀传统文化做出了巨大贡献，而粤绣在这方面的贡献尤为突出，它被誉为"中国给西方的礼物"。

在中国明朝时期，广东海外贸易兴盛，粤绣作品大量行销欧洲各国。1600年，英国贵族阶层创立了与刺绣相关的组织，为粤绣艺术在英国的传播奠定了坚实的基础。18世纪，英国开始了"粤绣热"，粤绣艺术风靡英国上层阶级乃至全社会，推动了粤绣出口贸易的进一步发展。

众所周知，粤绣作品常以中华文化中寓意吉祥的元素作为题材，极具中国特色。这类题材的作品深受海外友人的喜爱，也帮助海外友人了解了中华文化。粤绣作品吸收了外国油画的特点，兼具实用性和观赏性，从而更便于融入海外文化环境之中。

1. The International Spread of Embroidery

Embroidery has made a significant contribution to the global dissemination of traditional Chinese culture, among them, Guangdong embroidery is the prominent, it has been well known as "China's gift to the West".

During the Ming Dynasty, Guangdong's exporting trade flourished, so Guangdong embroidery was sold in large quantities to European countries. In 1600, the British aristocracy founded an organization related to embroidery, which laid the solid foundations for spreading embroidery art in Britain. In the 18th century, the "Guangdong embroidery craze" began in Britain, making embroidery art popular with the British upper classes and society. This led to the further development of the export trade in Guangdong embroidery.

It is well known that Guangdong embroidery works are riched in Chinese features because they are often based on auspicious elements from Chinese culture. These works are deeply loved by overseas friends and have helped them understand Chinese culture. Guangdong embroidery incorporates the characteristics of foreign oil paintings and is both practical and ornamental, thus making it easier to integrate into the overseas cultural environment.

2. 刺绣的现代性融合

除了近代史上的贸易活动外，刺绣在现代的跨文化交际过程中也发挥了重要作用。

在2017年的春夏季米兰时装周上，中国的刺绣艺术大放异彩。例如，在花鸟虫兽等极具中国特色的刺绣元素的搭配下，GUCCI的宫廷风手提包更显细腻。并且，无论是平铺手法还是点缀形式，刺绣的加入皆使得GUCCI的绣品更加立体、丰满，给人耳目一新之感。著名的服装品牌盖娅传说也多次在衣物上运用刺绣元素，使得带有刺绣艺术的华服登上了国际时尚舞台。

刺绣的外传不仅展现了刺绣无与伦比的魅力，还有助于弘扬源远流长的中华文化，讲述丰富多彩的中国故事。

2. The Integration of Modernity in Embroidery

In addition to trade activities in recent history, embroidery has also played an important role in modern cross-cultural communication processes.

At the Spring/Summer 2017 Milan Fashion Week, the art of Chinese embroidery shone through. For example, GUCCI's courtly handbag was enhanced by using Chinese embroidery elements such as flowers, birds, insects and animals. The addition of embroidery, in both flat and embellished forms, made GUCCI's show more three-dimensional and full-bodied, giving a refreshing twist to monotonous pieces. The famous clothing brand Gaia Legend has also used embroidery on many of its garments, bringing the art of embroidery to the international fashion stage.

The outreach of embroidery not only demonstrates its unparalleled charm, but also helps to promote the long-standing Chinese culture and tell colorful Chinese steries.

近年来，越来越多的服装品牌将刺绣元素作为必不可少的装饰形式，这充分体现了刺绣在海内外经久不衰的魅力。刺绣是中华民族创造的文化瑰宝，也逐渐成为我国进行对外文化交流的名片。

More and more clothing brands have adopted embroidery as an essential form of decoration in recent years, reflecting the enduring charm of embroidery at home and abroad. Embroidery is a cultural treasure created by the Chinese people and has gradually become a business card for cultural exchanges with foreign countries.

第三节 "古壁丹青色，新花绮绣纹"：苏绣体验
Section 3 "The color of the ancient walls, the color of the new flowers, the pattern of the beautiful embroidery": Learn the Suzhou embroidery

1. 材料

绣针、绣绷、绣线、绣布。

1. Materials

Embroidery needle, embroidery bandage, thread, embroidery cloth.

2. 基础绣法

2. Basic embroidery methods

（1）缎面绣：一段式的绣线绘制图案的绣法。

(1) Satin Stitch: A pattern drawn through a section of embroidery lines.

首先，找到所绣图案的位置，绣针从这个位置的背面穿出，再根据图案的轮廓穿入。在进行缎面绣时，绣线一定要互相紧贴，把图案排满，这样绣品才会饱满。

First, find the position where the pattern will be embroidered, thread the needle from the back of this position, and thread the needle according to the outline of the pattern. When doing the satin stitch, the thread must be tightly stitched together to fill the pattern, so that the embrlidery will appear fully.

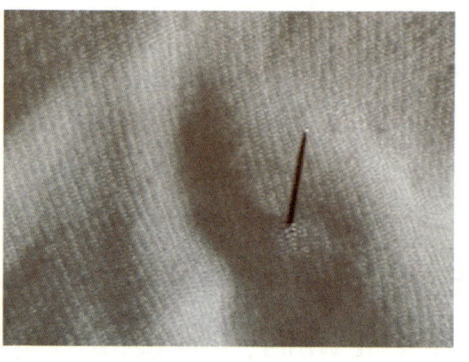

绣针从背面穿出（占丽雯 摄）
The Needle Goes Through the Back
(By Zhan Liwen)

根据图案的轮廓穿入（占丽雯 摄）
Insert the Needle into the Cloth According to the Outline of the Pattern
(By Zhan Liwen)

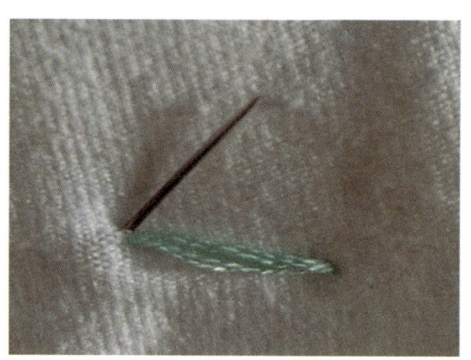

绣针从背面穿出（占丽雯 摄）
The Needle Goes Through the Back
(By Zhan Liwen)

根据图案的轮廓穿入（占丽雯 摄）
Insert the Needle into the Cloth According to the Outline of the Pattern
(By Zhan Liwen)

（2）结粒绣：通常用于点缀或者是花心的装饰。

(2) Grain Stitch：Usually used to ornament or decorate the center of the flower.

绣针从绣布的背面穿出后，把绣针固定在绣布上并在绣针上顺时针绕两圈绣线，把绣针按在绕圈绣线所在的位置穿出，形成一个结，再从结中穿入，一针结粒绣就完成了。注意在打结的时候不要把结拉得非常紧，这样方便绣针从结中穿入。

After threading the needle through the back of the cloth, fix the needle on the cloth and wrap the thread around the needle clockwise for two circles, threading at the place where the circle embroidery thread is, and form a knot. Then, thread through the knot, and a grain stitch embroidery is completed. Please do not pull the knot very tight when tying the knot, to make it easier to thread the knot.

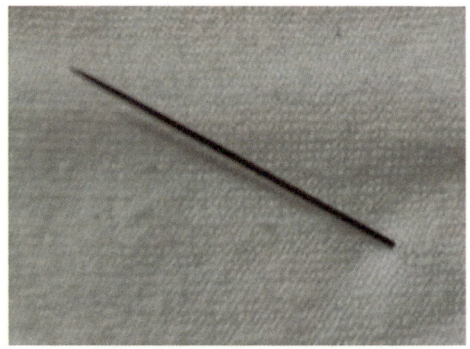

绣针从背面穿出（占丽雯 摄）
The Needle Goes Through the Back
(By Zhan Liwen)

在绣针上顺时针绕两圈绣线（占丽雯 摄）
Wrapping the Thread Around the Needle Clockwise for Two Circles
(By Zhan Liwen)

绣针按在绕圈绣线所在的
位置穿出（占丽雯 摄）
Threading at the Place Where the Circle Embroidery Thread Is (By Zhan Liwen)

结粒绣（占丽雯 摄）
Grain Stitch (By Zhan Liwen)

（3）回针绣：常用于绣制长线条。

(3) Back Stitch: commonly used to embroider long lines.

绣针从 A 点穿出 B 点穿入，留出一部分绣线，从 AB 的中间点 C 穿出并将绣线拉紧，再从 D 点穿入，留出一部分绣线，从 A 点穿出，循环重复该步骤即可。

Thread out from A and into B, leaving aside part of the thread. Thread through C, the middle point of AB and tighten the thread, then tread into D, leaving a part of the embroidery thread, pass through A, and repeat above steps.

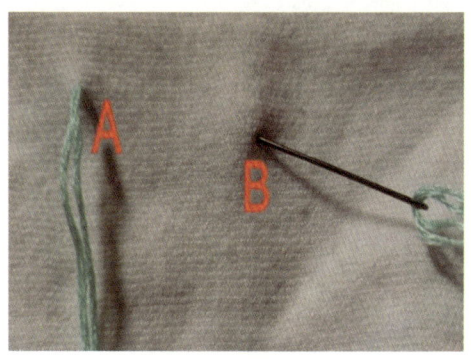

绣针从 A 点穿出 B 点穿入（占丽雯 摄）
Thread Through A and into B
（By Zhan Liwen）

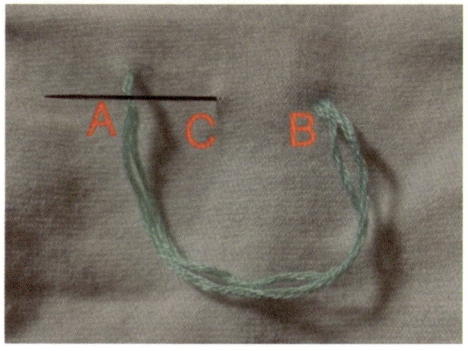

绣线从 AB 的中间点 C 穿出（占丽雯 摄）
Thread Through the Middle Point C of AB
（By Zhan Liwen）

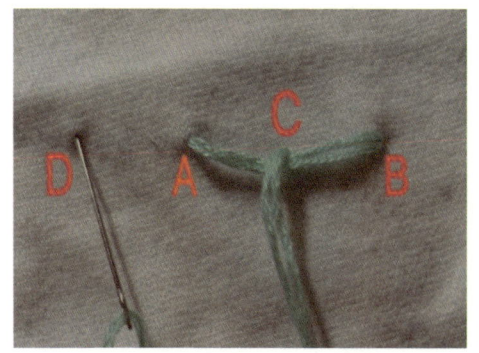

绣线从 D 点穿入（占丽雯 摄）
Thread into D（By Zhan Liwen）

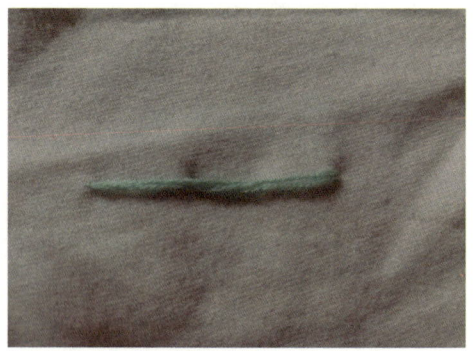

回针绣（占丽雯 摄）
Back Stitch（By Zhan Liwen）

4."月下玉兔"绣制步骤

4."Jade Rabbit under the Moon" Embroidery Steps.

(1) 固定绣绷。

(1) Fix the embroidery bandage.

将绣布固定在绣绷上是为了使刺绣图案变得平整。将绣绷中的圈放在绣布的下方,再将另一部分放在绣布的上方并拧紧螺丝固定绣布。

Attach the embroidery cloth to the embroidery bandage to make the embroidery patterns flat. Place the circle part in the embroidery bandage under the embroidery cloth, and then put another part above the embroidery cloth and tighten the screws to fix the embroidery cloth.

步骤(1) 固定绣绷(占丽雯 摄)
Step (1) Fix the Embroidery Bandage (By Zhan Liwen)

(2) 绣前打结。

(2) Tie a knot before embroidery.

将绣线穿入绣针中。再将绣线在手指上绕一圈,然后把线的尾部穿过在手指上绕出的圈,最后剪去结后多余的线。

Thread the embroidery through embroidery needle. Then wrap the embroidery thread around the finger and put the tail of the thread through the circle out on the finger, and cut off the excess thread after the knot.

 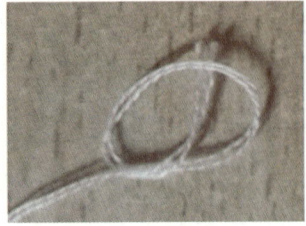 

步骤（2）绣线打结（占丽雯 摄）
Step（2）Tie a Knot of Embroidery Thread（By Zhan Liwen）

（3）用缎面绣针法绣兔子身体和耳朵。在绣兔耳朵时可以斜着绣，兔子更加生动。

（3）Embroider the rabbit's body and ears with satin stitch. When embroidering the rabbit's ears, you can embroider them sideways to make the rabbit more vivid.

 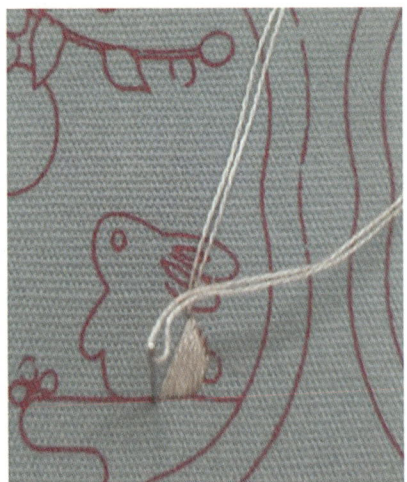

步骤（3）绣兔子身体（占丽雯 摄）
Step（3）Embroider The Rabbit's Body（By Zhan Liwen）

（4）用结粒绣针法绣"兔眼"。

（4）Embroider "rabbit eyes" with grain stitch.

·第八章 刺绣文化双语教学设计·

步骤（4）绣兔眼（占丽雯 摄）
Step（4）Embroider Rabbit Eyes（By Zhan Liwen）

（5）用缎面绣的针法绣"花、叶、月"。在绣"花"的时候，遵循"从中间向四周散开"的原则，更加自然。

步骤（5）绣"花、叶、月"（占丽雯 摄）
Step（5）Embroider "Flowers, Leaves and Moon"（By Zhan Liwen）

（5）Embroidering "flowers, leaves, moon" using satin sitch. When you embroidering the "flowers", follow the principle of "spreading out from the middle", making the "flowers" more natural.

（6）用结粒绣的针法来点缀"花心"。

（6）Use grain sitch for ornamenting "flower center".

步骤（6）绣花心（占丽雯 摄）

Step（6）Embroidered Flower Center（By Zhan Liwen）

（7）用回针绣的针法绣"枝条"。

（7）Embroidering "branches" with back sitch.

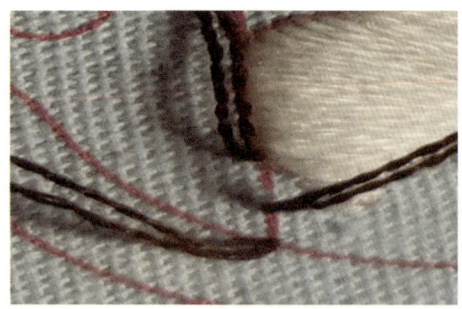 

步骤（7）绣枝条（占丽雯 摄）

Step（7）Embroidered Branches（By Zhan Liwen）

通过以上步骤，便可以绣出一幅美丽的作品了。

Through the above steps, you can embroider a pretty work.

第四节　刺绣文化双语教案

一、教学对象

对中华文化感兴趣的外国学生。

二、教学内容

1. 中国传统手工艺刺绣的起源及四大名绣；
2. 刺绣的国际性传播与融合；
3. 简易图案的刺绣针法。

三、教学目标

1. 帮助外国学生了解中国传统手工艺之刺绣文化，并对四大名绣有简单的了解。
2. 帮助外国学生通过刺绣这一手工艺的国际性传播，了解中华传统文化的创造性转化、创新性发展，感受中华民族劳动人民对美好事物的向往。
3. 帮助外国学生学会绣制简易图案的针法。

四、教学方法

1. 图片、视频法

利用图片、视频向学生展示刺绣的起源、四大名绣以及刺绣的国际性传播与融合。

2. 演示法

通过演示法，教授简易图案的刺绣针法。

3. 互动法

通过教师提问、学生回答的方式，请学生叙述其对各省的了解程度。

4. 启发诱导法

启发学生总结对刺绣起源、刺绣的国际性传播与融合的认识，表达自己的看法。

五、课时安排

三课时完成，每课时 40 分钟。
第一课时介绍刺绣的起源及四大名绣；
第二课时介绍刺绣的国际性传播与融合；
第三课时介绍简易图案的刺绣针法。

六、教学过程（三课时）

第一课时（40分钟）：刺绣的起源及四大名绣

设计意图：以生动、精练的绣衣代纹小故事开篇介绍刺绣的起源，力图通过"中国故事"吸引学生的注意力。利用图片、视频、实物等各种丰富手段展示四大名绣的特点，同时揭示刺绣的深层含义：是中华民族智慧的结晶，凝结着劳动人民对美好事物的向往。

（一）组织教学（约2分钟）

教师进入课堂，检查多媒体设备，将教学所用的教案、课件及手工材料准备放置妥当。师生互相问候，教师点名，准备上课。

> T: Good morning, everyone! How are you today? Let's start the roll call first... Okay, everyone's here. Class begins.

（二）进入新课，介绍剪纸的起源（10分钟，内容详见双语讲稿导语）

1. 导入

（1）教师播放电视剧《因为遇见你》中果果为外国友人补袖口的片段，

带领学生初步领略中国刺绣的精湛工艺。

问题：①果果为什么要为外国友人补袖口？（答案：果果弄破了他的袖口）

②果果在袖口上绣了什么？（答案：百合花）

③果果绣的这朵花有什么含义？（答案：友谊、祝福）

> T: Why does Guoguo mend the cuffs for the foreign friend?
> T: What does Guoguo embroider on his cuff?
> T: What is the meaning of this flower embroidered by Guoguo?

（2）教师板书"刺绣"二字及拼音，教师领读两遍。

2. 介绍刺绣的起源：绣衣代纹的故事

（1）教师利用图片，以角色扮演的方式绘声绘色地向学生讲述"绣衣代纹"的故事。

（2）教师就"绣衣代纹"故事中的小细节进行提问，考查学生对刺绣起源故事的理解程度。

问题：①周朝时期的苏州一带，人们有什么样的习俗？（答案：纹身）

②谁发明了在衣服上缝上装饰图案来替代纹身？（答案：女红）

> T: What customs did people have in Suzhou during the Zhou Dynasty?
> T: Who invented sewing decorative patterns on clothes instead of tattoos?

（3）教师总结刺绣起源故事内涵：体现了中华民族勤劳创新的性格特点，以及对美好生活的不懈追求。

（三）介绍四大名绣：苏绣、湘绣、蜀绣和粤绣（约27分钟，内容详见双语讲稿第一节）

1. 导入

教师展示四大名绣作品，请学生仔细观察并进行比较。

> T: Today I will introduce the four famous embroideries in China: Suzhou embroidery, Hunan embroidery, Sichuan embroidery and Guangdong embroidery. The four pictures above are four famous embroideries. Please take a closer look at the differences between them.

2. 四大名绣之苏绣

（1）教师利用地图，向学生展示苏绣的产地并介绍当地自然条件和盛产苏绣的原因。

（2）教师利用图片展示苏绣作品，详细说明苏绣的特点。

3. 四大名绣之湘绣

（1）教师利用地图，向学生展示湘绣的产地并介绍当地自然条件和盛产湘绣的原因。

（2）教师利用图片展示湘绣作品，详细说明湘绣的特点。

4. 四大名绣之蜀绣

（1）教师利用地图，向学生展示蜀绣的产地并介绍当地自然条件和盛产蜀绣的原因。

（2）教师利用图片展示蜀绣作品，详细说明蜀绣的特点。

5. 四大名绣之粤绣

（1）教师利用地图，向学生展示粤绣的产地并介绍当地自然条件和盛产粤绣的原因。

（2）教师利用图片展示粤绣作品，详细说明粤绣的特点。

6. 练一练

教师展示四大名绣作品，请学生分辨是哪一类刺绣，以考查学生对四大名绣特点的理解程度。

> T: Please look at these embroidery works. According to the teacher´s explanation just now, tell us which of the four famous embroidery works they are.

（四）小结（1分钟）

教师简单回顾刺绣的起源故事并梳理四大名绣的产地和特点。

第二课时（40分钟）：刺绣的国际性传播与融合

设计意图：通过利用图片、视频，介绍刺绣的出口贸易，并展示刺绣在"引进来"和"走出去"过程中的表征，凸显中国传统工艺在当代的创新和融合发展之路。

（一）复习回顾（约5分钟）

1. 教师请学生复述绣衣代纹的故事。
2. 教师展示图片，提问学生四大名绣的名称、产地和特点。

（二）进入新课，介绍粤绣的出口贸易（10分钟，内容详见双语讲稿第二节）

1. 导入

教师展示中国地图，介绍广东省的地理位置，并提问。

问题：你去过广东吗？你了解那里吗？

> T: Have you ever been to Guangdong Province? What do you know about Guangdong?

2. 粤绣的出口贸易

教师介绍粤绣在英国被誉为"中国给西方的礼物"的原因，使学生了解粤绣在国际上的地位，进而帮助学生理解中国刺绣所体现出的中国刺绣匠人对工艺的重视和在艺术创作方面的热情与新意。

（三）介绍刺绣与国际时尚的融合（15分钟，内容详见双语讲稿第二节）

1. 国际性元素的"引进来"

教师展示盖娅传说代表服饰的图片并介绍盖娅传说的创作理念，帮助学

生理解中国品牌盖娅传说融合典雅与现代,不断用服饰来展现东方文化魅力的创新理念。

问题:这些服装与你平时穿的有什么不一样?

> T: How are these clothes different from what you usually wear?

2. 刺绣元素的"走出去"

教师展示 GUCCI 秀品,帮助学生感受刺绣艺术与国际时尚的融合。

问题:看了 GUCCI 的这些服饰,你感觉怎么样?

> T: How do you feel after seeing Gucci's clothes and accessories?

3. 教师总结

教师就传统刺绣的国际化之路进行总结,帮助学生更好地理解刺绣元素在国际舞台上大放异彩的原因:充分展现了中华民族劳动人民对传统文化元素的创造性转化、创新性发展。

(四)练一练(10分钟,内容详见双语讲稿第四节)

1. 连一连

教师展示四大名绣及四种刺绣风格,请学生进行配对连线。

2. 选一选

教师编写与刺绣的起源、四大名绣、刺绣的国际性传播与融合相关的选择题,请学生根据教学内容进行选择并订正。

第三课时(40分钟):绣制简易图案

设计意图:通过详细教授绣制简易图案的步骤,帮助学生更好地理解和体会刺绣的技法和意蕴。同时鼓励学生自己设计、绣制作品,激发学生热爱中华文化的热情。

（一）导入（2分钟）

教师展示自己绣制的玉兔，并向学生提问。

问题：这是什么？你们想不想自己学着绣一个？

> T: What's this? Do you want to learn to embroider by yourself?

（二）文化体验：教授刺绣（30分钟，内容详见双语讲稿第三节）

1. 教师发放材料并说明注意事项。
2. 教师现场演示并结合动图，教授学生如何绣制玉兔。
3. 教师请学生展示各自成品，并谈谈有什么感想。

（三）本课小结（7分钟）

1. 教师总结刺绣的起源、四大名绣以及中国刺绣的国际性传播与融合。
2. 教师总结中国刺绣的寓意，其是中华民族创造的艺术，也是中国劳动人民的丰硕成果。刺绣不仅是中华民族的智慧结晶，还蕴含着劳动人民对美好生活的向往。

（四）布置作业（1分钟）

教师请学生课下试着绣一个图案并与同学和老师分享。

> T: Please try to embroider after class and share them with our classmates and teachers! Class is over, see you next time!

七、教学反思

刺绣是用针线在织物上绣制出的各种装饰图案的总称。它是中华民族优秀的民间传统手工艺，已有两三千年的悠久历史。刺绣的图案是人民群众从社会实践中总结创造出的意象，也是当地人民生活的写照。刺绣不仅可以用于日用品和欣赏品的装饰，为我们的生活增添美感，它还是艺术创造的重要物质载体，能为我们的文化生活增添乐趣。因此，刺绣在国内外广受好评。

  本课的教学重在刺绣作品的赏析，在赏析中了解四大名绣的特点并激发学生对刺绣作品的热爱。此外，刺绣的现代性创新发展也是本课教学过程中应重点提出的部分，并将之与刺绣的起源进行关联，从而说明无论是起源还是今天的发展，刺绣都离不开劳动人民的智慧。

  体验环节是绣制图案"月下玉兔"，教师应提前强调注意事项。由于刺绣相较于其他文化体验更加复杂且难度较大，教师可提前教授基本绣法并安排学生进行操练，在基本绣法掌握熟练之后进行"月下玉兔"的课堂教学。与此同时，穿插对苏绣产地、特点的介绍，帮助学生更好地认识苏绣。此外，还应向学生说明，由于丝线较细，不宜在初学时进行操作，因此选择较粗的棉线加以替代，等学生手法纯熟后，可对丝线的颜色、品种、质地进行自由选择。

附：辅助教学资源

  1. B 站 Up 主 "coldseleno" 的视频：https：//www.bilibili.com/video/BV1Mt411q77Q?p=6&share_source=copy_web。

  2. B 站 Up 主 "SXXXXXYM" 的视频：https：//www.bilibili.com/video/BV1vs411t7Xa?share_source=copy_web。

  3. B 站 Up 主 "风尚君" 的视频：https：//www.bilibili.com/video/BV1EU4y1s7sK?share_source=copy_web。

  4. B 站 Up 主 "烟消雾散—春暖花开" 的视频：https：//www.bilibili.com/video/BV1gJ411w7YC?share_source=copy_web。

  5. B 站 Up 主 "李宇春—音乐厨房" 的视频：https：//www.bilibili.com/video/BV1JE411d7p3?share_source=copy_web。

  6. B 站 Up 主 "中国广州国际纪录片节" 的视频：https：//www.bilibili.com/video/BV1KC4y1s7DT?share_source=copy_web。

讨论与练习
Discussion and Practice

1. 讨论

1. Discussion

（1）你在哪些地方见到过刺绣？发挥你的想象力，你认为刺绣还可以跟哪些元素相融合？

（1）Where have you seen embroidery before? Using your imagination, what other elements do you think embroidery could be combined with?

（2）你认为刺绣为什么能走向世界，受到各国人民的喜爱？

（2）Why do you think embroidery has gone global and is loved by people everywhere?

（3）对比刺绣和你们国家的传统装饰或者艺术，你认为它们之间有什么不同？

（3）Comparing embroidery with the traditional decoration or art of your country, what do you think are the differences between them?

2. 练习

2. Practice

（1）连一连

（1）Matching

湘绣 Hunan embroidery	A. 精细淡雅 Delicate and elegan
粤绣 Guangdong embroidery	B. 层次丰富 Richness of its layers
苏绣	C. 灵动多姿

Suzhou embroidery   Dynamic

蜀绣   D. 画面热烈
Sichuan embroidery   Warm images

（2）选一选

（2）Choosing（Select the correct one from the four options）

- 苏绣的发源地是哪里？（   ）

Where is the origin of Suzhou embroidery?（   ）

   A. Taizhou   B. Nanjing   C. Shanghai   D. Suzhou

- 狮虎是哪种绣品的代表性题材？（   ）

What kind of embroidery has the representative theme of lion and tiger?（   ）

   A. Suzhou Embroidery   B. Hunan Embroidery

   C. Guangdong Embroidery   D. Sichuan Embroidery

- 大熊猫是哪种刺绣的主要题材？（   ）

Which kind of embroidery theme is the panda?（   ）

   A. Suzhou Embroidery   B. Hunan Embroidery

   C. Sichuan Embroidery   D. Guangdong Embroidery

- 哪种刺绣被称为"中国给西方的礼物"？（   ）

What kind of embroidery is called a gift from China to the West?（   ）

   A. Guangdong Embroidery   B. Sichuan Embroidery

   C. Hunan Embroidery   D. Suzhou Embroidery

答案
Answer

（1）B   D   A   C

（2）D   B   C   A

第九章　篆刻文化双语教学设计
Chapter IX　Bilingual Teaching Design of Seal Engraving Culture

篆刻（谢梦璇 绘）
Seal Engraving (By Xie Mengxuan)

中国传统文化体验式双语教学设计

导语
Introduction

相传，皇帝尧和大臣舜泛舟游赏时，忽然一只背上有画的凤凰从祥云之中飞出。待凤凰飞近，二人方看出画上是一个用赤玉打造的石章，石章的两端系有白玉绳子，并且刻着"天赤帝符玺"几个字。凤凰将这画中的章授给尧后便飞走了。得到此印的尧受宠若惊，觉得自己获得了上天的认可，也更有了将国家治理好的信心。这就是人们最早接触篆刻的情形之一。

According to legend, the emperor Yao and the minister Shun were enjoying a boat trip when suddenly a phoenix flew out from the auspicious clouds and came to them, with a painting on its back. As the phoenix flew closer, they saw that the painting was of a stone medallion made of red jade, with white ropes tied to the both ends of the medallion and inscribed with the words "Heaven Emperor's Seal". The phoenix left the seal to Yao and then flew away. Yao was so flattered by the seal that he felt he had gained the approval of the heavens, so Yao got more confidence in governing the country well. This is one of the earliest stories about seal engraving.

凤凰（谢梦璇 绘）
The Phoenix（By Xie Mengxuan）

第一节　篆刻的分类
Section 1　Classification of Seal Engraving

在古代，近则有对酒当歌、吟诗作对时的署名，远则有国家机密文件的签署，篆刻的应用遍布人们的生活。篆刻艺术是中华传统文化中书法与镌刻的完美结合。篆刻种类纷呈，从形式上看，篆刻可以分为阴刻、阳刻和阴阳刻；从印章的用途上看，篆刻可以分为官印和私印，其中私印多为艺术篆刻；从内容上看，篆刻包括姓名印、斋馆印、记时记事印、考定鉴藏印、闲文印、肖形图画印等，形状多样，内容丰富。

In ancient China, seal engraving was widely used in people's daily lives, from signing poems to signing confidential government documents. The art of seal engraving is a perfect combination of calligraphy and engraving in traditional Chinese culture. There are many different types of seal engraving, according to the forms, it can be divided into Yin engraving, Yang engraving and Yin-Yang engraving; in terms of the functions, it can be divided into official seals and private seals (most of which are artistic seal engravings); in terms of the contents, it can be divided into name seals, pavilion seals, time and event seals, collection and identification seals, leisurely writing seals and animated picture seals. These types of seal engraving have various shapes and contents.

1. 阴刻

阴刻是将图案或文字刻成凹形的刻法。在玉石雕刻的初创阶段，就已经出现了"阴刻"。阴刻最大的特征是其主要突出表现的内容在印面上是凹下去的。相比于其他重视立体感的雕刻，阴刻更倾向于刻画汉字的轮廓。通过汉字轮廓的突出，印章传达了理性的美感和单纯的意境。

1. Yin Engraving

Yin engraving is a carving method that the design or text is engraved into a concave shape, and was already used by people during the early stages of jade carving. The most distinctive feature of the Yin engraving is that the content to be highlighted is concave on the printing surface. Compared to other carving methods that emphasize the art of three-dimensionality, the Yin engraving tends to portray the hard skeleton of the Chinese characters. By highlighting the outline of Chinese characters, the Yin engraving conveys a sense of rational beauty and pure artistic conception.

阴刻"万事如意"（殷圣嬴 摄）
Yin Engraving *Best wishes* (By Yin Shengying)

2. 阳刻

阳刻是将笔画或图案刻出立体形状的刻法。在印面上，阳刻要表现出来的部分是实体，凸出的就是阳文。阳刻在章面上形成了浅浮雕，立体感较强。阳刻多为男性所用，充满骨感的线条让男性的阳刚之气尽显。活字印刷术上使用的就是阳刻，阳刻通常出现在较为正式的场合，如官印等。在古代，为显示身份人们大多使用阳刻技法雕刻印章，这些印章有着强烈的线条，凸显用印人的地位。而现在，人们为了方便，更多选择使用签名。

2. Yang Engraving

Yang engraving is a carving method that the strokes or designs are carved out of a raised shape. On the surface of the seal, the part of the Yang engraving to be shown is the entity, prominent is the Yang text. Yang engraving creates a bas-relief on the surface of the seal, with a strong sense of three-dimensionality. Seals of Yang engraving are used mainly by men, and the bony lines of stone bring out men's masculinity. Yang engraving was applied to the mechanism of typography and was more often used on formal occasions, such as official seals. In ancient times, people prefer to displayed their identity primarily through seals of Yang engraving that contain strong lines to imply the user's social status. However, nowadays, people use signatures which are more convenient.

阳刻"谢梦璇印"（谢梦璇 摄）
Yang Engraving *Xie Mengxuan Yin* (By Xie Mengxuan)

3. 官印

官印包括皇帝的玉玺、各级官员的官印、军官官印等。官员品级的高低主要以印章的尺寸和材料来区别。印章的材料越名贵，持有者的身份也就越高。皇帝的印章独称"玺"或"宝"，多由上好的和田玉制作而成，故称"玉玺"。官印采用篆体阳文篆刻，印文布局讲究对等对称，体现了中国人所钟情的"对称美"。

3. Official Seal

Official seals include the emperor's jade seal, official seals for officials at all levels and military officers. The rank of an official was distinguished mainly by the size and material of the seal. The more valuable the material used, the higher the owner's status was. In particular, the seal of the emperor was called a "Xi" or "Bao" and was made of excellent Hetian jade (called Yu in Chinese); hence the name is "Yu Xi" (Jade Imperial Seal). The seal is made with the Yang engraving method. The layout of the seal is symmetrical, reflecting the beauty of symmetry favored by Chinese people.

4. 私印

私印内容包括姓名、字号、馆斋、鉴藏、闲文、吉语等，每个朝代各有其特点：春秋战国时期私印被称为"私玺"；秦朝开始，只有皇帝所使用的印章可以被称为"玺"，官印与私印一并称为"印"；汉朝时私印所使用的材质十分广泛，在章法和字体上也和官印有着鲜明的对比；隋唐时期的私印开始变得更具艺术性；宋代的印章杂糅了前朝的特色，兼具古色与新意；明代的私印出现多种材料并现的情形，且开始注重装饰；清朝的私印多为坊间制作，颇具艺术气息。

4. Private Seal

Private seals include name seals, pavilion seals, collection and identification seals, leisurely writing seals and auspicious saying seals. Private seals in each dynasty have their characteristics. In the Spring and Autumn Period and Warring States Period, private seals were called "private Xi". However, since the Qin Dynasty, only the seals used by the emperor could be called "Xi", officers' seals and private seals were called "Yin". In the Han Dynasty, private seals were made of a wide range of materials and had a distinctive contrast with official seals in terms of style and script. The seals in the Sui and Tang Dynasties became more artistic, and then the seals in the Song Dynasty had the characteristics of seals in the previous dynasties and new features. Private seals of the Ming Dynasty were made in various materials, and people began to focus on decoration on seals. In the Qing Dynasty, the private seals were artistic and mainly made in workshops.

除了以上两种分类以外，还可以从印章的形制进行分类，有单面印、多面印和套印等；按印材的材质分类，有石章、玉章、角章、铜章等。当然，还可按典型性的朝代划分，如秦印、汉印、宋印。尽管印章的年代、材质、形状、内容不尽相同，但朱白相间的视觉和谐感与精妙写意的布局相得益彰，筋肉运动的创作状态又增添了个人的独特风格，篆刻技艺兼具视觉美和力量美。

In addition to the above two classifications, seals can also be classified by their form, such as single-sided seals, multi-sided seals and sets of seals. We can also tell from the materials, such as stoneseal, jadeseal, hornseal, bronzeseal, etc. Of course, they can also be divided according to dynasties when they were made, such as seals in Qin, Han and Song Dynasties. Although the age, material, shape and content of the seals vary, the visual harmony of the vermillion and white vacancy are complemented by the subtlety of the layout, the movement of the flesh and sinew also adds to the unique style of the individual, which makes the art of seal carving have both visual beauty and power beauty.

随着时代的发展，篆刻也顺利完成了转型，成为传播中华文化的特色载体。北京作为唯一一个"双奥之城"，在奥运会这个全球盛会上尽情地向世界讲述着中国故事，而篆刻也被巧妙地融入其中。2008年北京夏季奥运会会徽是一个以篆刻形式呈现的"京"字图案，开幕式上更是通过数百位演员的努力向世界展示了活字印刷术的魅力。不仅如此，在2022年冬季奥会中，体育项目的图标皆以中国汉字为灵感，并使用篆刻艺术作为其主要呈现形式，将运动元素和中华文化有机融合，充分体现了冬季奥运会挑战自我的澎湃激情与中华文化的独特色彩。

After years of development, seal engraving has successfully completed its transformation into a unique medium for promoting Chinese culture. For example, as the only city that held two Olympic Games, Beijing has portrayed evocative Chinese stories to the world in various ways, including seal engraving during the Olympic Games. The 2008 Beijing Summer Olympics emblem was a seal-engraved representation of the character "京" (jing). Its opening ceremony showcased the magic of movable type printing through the efforts of hundreds of performers. In addition, in the 2022 Winter Olympic Games, the icons of the sports are also inspired by Chinese characters, and the art of seal engraving is used as the main form of presentation, combining sports elements and Chinese culture, fully reflecting the passion of challenging oneself in the Winter Olympics and the uniqueness of Chinese culture.

中国传统文化体验式双语教学设计

第二节 "方寸之间,便是天地":
金石文化的传播与交流
Section 2 "The World between Inches": the Communication and Exchange of Epigraphy Culture

篆刻是一门历史悠久的传统艺术,随着金石文化的传播与发展,在今天仍然熠熠生辉。

这其中,被称为"中国金石第一人"的晚清著名收藏家陈介祺,对金石文化的传承和传播做出了卓越贡献,其故里山东省潍坊市也被誉为"金石之都"。每年潍坊市都会举办陈介祺艺术节和金石文化周,这些文化交流活动成为潍坊金石文化走向全国乃至世界的重要窗口。

Seal engraving is a traditional art with a long history, and we can still see it shining today with the spread and development of epigraphy culture.

Chen Jieqi, a famous collector in the late Qing Dynasty, known as "the first person of Chinese Epigraphy Culture", made outstanding contributions to the inheritance and dissemination of Epigraphy Culture. Therefore, his hometown, Weifang city in Shandong Province, is now known as the capital of epigraphy. Weifang will hold Chen Jieqi Art Festival and Epigraphy Culture Week every year. These cultural exchange activities offer a platform for epigraphy culture in Weifang to be known to the whole country and the world.

艺术节开展前夕负责人会向海内外篆刻家和艺术团体发出征稿启事,并对征稿作品进行评选,同时将选手作品和最新的篆刻艺术珍品分会场进行展览,最后再开展专业的金石学术交流会。这是一场艺术和学术的盛会。艺术节的重头戏落在精品捐赠环节,每年海内外多个团体和学者名家都会向陈介祺先生建造的"万印楼"捐赠上千件文物藏品,这些藏品将会在艺术节期间展出并被捐赠。与此同时,金石界的名家也会亲临现场进行交流和教学。

Invitations for entries will be sent to seal engraving artists and groups in China and abroad before the Chen Jieqi Art Festival each year. The submitted seal engraving artworks and the latest artworks from famous seal engraving artists will be displayed in different exhibition sections. There will also be academic seminars about epigraphy. This festival is a grand artistic and academic event. The festival's highlight is the donation of thousands of pieces of cultural relics to the Wan Yin Housebuilt by Mr. Chen Jieqi, which will be exhibited and donated during the festival. At the same time, Famous artists will also come to the festival to communicate and offer experience.

中国印章自带的凭信功能代表着一种与西方截然不同的签名文化。在古代，玉玺是皇帝身份的象征，古代下发的圣旨需有玉玺盖章后方可生效，文人墨客也常用自己的私印展示身份。中国把印章作为一种凭信方式，西方则与此不同。西方没有印章，而是靠签名作为识别标记：人们会在文书或信件中签上自己的姓名，宪法需要最高法官签名才能生效，交易协议条约亦是如此。在不同的社会活动中，签字者代表的是责任承担者而非整个单位或机构，这种明确的责任或利益归属正是签名的主要作用。政府下发文件以公章核准，签署公文的最终责任也由该部门承担，即使当时签发公文的官员调离，该部门也须承担相应责任。今天，中国的印章文化和西方的签名文化正在融合。在中国，签名作为个体责任归属的使用已经非常普遍，而公司、部门及集体组织则仍使用公章作为授权证明。

The credential function that comes with the seal represents a different signature culture from the West. In ancient China, stamping with seals was a way of prooving that the information was true. Jade Imperial Seal symbolized the emperor's authority, and ancient decrees required the seal to be issued before they took effect. Poets and other literati also use their private seals to show their identification. In the West, people use a signature as a mark of identification rather than seals. People sign their names on documents or letters, and the Constitution requires the Supreme Judge's signature to enter into force, so as the treaties and trade agreements. In different social activities, the signatory represents himself or herself rather than the whole institution, and this specific attribution of responsibility or interests is the main function of the signature. Documents issued by the government are approved with an official seal, and the ultimate responsibility for signing official documents rests with that department, even if the officer who issued the document was transferred at that time. China's seal culture and Western culture are merging. Today, the use of signatures as the attribution of individual responsibility has become very common in China, as governments, companies and organizations still use the seal as proof of authority.

签名"Avief"(殷圣赢 摄)
the Signature "Avief" (By Yin Shengying)

说到印章就不得不提到封缄技术。古代在传递竹简文书时，会将信件放在竹筒里，竹筒的两端用泥封口，再在泥上加盖印章，以保证传输过程中未被拆封。在古代欧洲，人们常使用火漆印章进行封缄。将火漆烧化在信件封口处，再用刻图案而非文字的印章盖戳。时至今日，火漆的封缄功能仍被保留。由于其独特的美感，火漆不再只运用于信件，更多的是被人们收藏。并且，随着人们审美的变化，发展出了五花八门的火漆蜡与火漆印章。

When it comes to seals, we have to mention sealing technology. In ancient times, when bamboo documents were transmitted, the letters were placed in bamboo tubes. The bamboo tubes were sealed with clay at both end sand sealed with a stamp to ensure that they were not opened during transmission. In ancient Europe, the wax was often used for sealing. The wax was molten into the surface and then stamped with a seal that was engraved with a design rather than words. The wax is still used for sealing today, but the wax, not only used for letters, is more often collected due to its unique beauty. The change of a esthetics lead to the development of a wide variety of waxes and seals.

火漆（陈瑶 摄）
The Wax（By Chen Yao）

第三节 "拈笔古心生篆刻"：篆刻体验

Section 3 "Engraving a seal comes from the heart": Trying seal engraving

1. 材料

刻刀，铅笔，雕刻橡皮，印台，转印纸，白色卡纸。

1. Materials

Knife, pencil, engraving eraser, printing pad, transfer paper, white card paper.

2. 注意事项

（1）使用刻刀时要小心不要造成伤害。

（2）如果你离开座位的话，把刀盖好。

（3）如果你有任何问题，请举手提问，更不要四处走动。

2. Attention

（1）Be careful! do not hurt yourself when using the carving knife.

（2）Put the cap back on the knife if you leave your seat.

（3）If you have any questions, please raise your hand instead of walking around.

（由于雕刻石头难度较大，所以以下步骤用橡皮章来代替。）

（We will use an eraser instead because carving a stone is too difficult.）

3. 步骤

3. Steps

（1）拿一张转印纸，在纸上写下想刻的字或者图案。

（1）Take a piece of transfer paper and write down the words or patterns you want to carve.

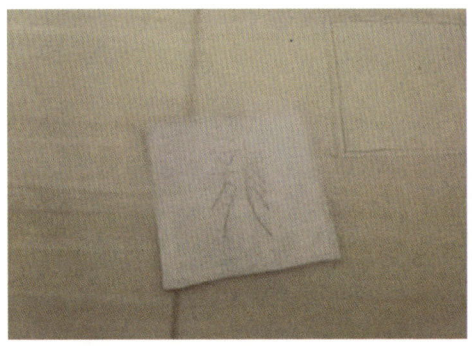

步骤（1）写字或图案（谢梦璇 摄）

Step（1）Write down the words or patterns（By Xie Mengxuan）

（2）将写有字的字条裁剪下。

（2）Cut out the paper with words.

步骤（2）裁下字条（谢梦璇 摄）

Step（2）Cut Out the Paper with Words（By Xie Mengxuan）

(3) 把有字的一面对准橡皮。

(3) Aim the side with the word at the eraser.

步骤（3）把字条对准橡皮（谢梦璇 摄）

Step（3）Aim the Side With the Word at the Eraser
（By Xie Mengxuan）

(4) 用卡片将纸上的字印在橡皮上。

(4) Use the card to transfer the words on the paper to the eraser.

步骤（4）转印（谢梦璇 摄）

Step（4）Transfer（By Xie Mengxuan）

（5）将不完整的部分补齐。

（5）Make up the incomplete part of the words with a pencil.

步骤（5）补字（谢梦璇 摄）
Step（5）Make up the Incomplete Part of the Words（By Xie Mengxuan）

（6）沿着字的形状用刻刀将橡皮切去。

（6）Cut off the eraser along with the shape of the word with a carving knife.

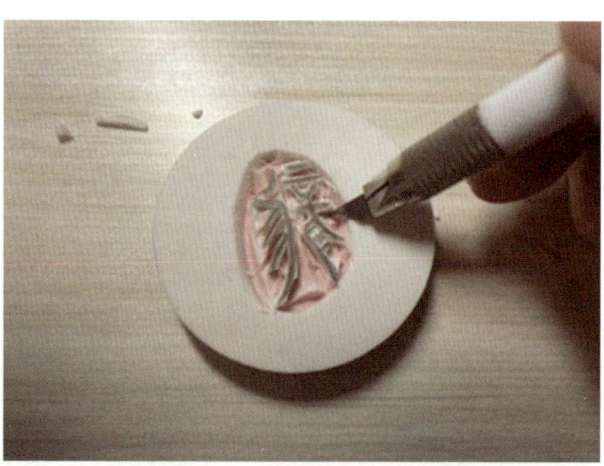

步骤（6）刻字（谢梦璇 摄）
Step（6）Carving the Word（By Xie Mengxuan）

（7）继续挖掉空白的部分。

（7）Dig out the blanks.

步骤（7）挖掉空白（谢梦璇 摄）
Step（7）**Dig Out the Blanks**（By Xie Mengxuan）

（8）将刻好的章盖在印台上。

（8）Put the seal on the ink pad.

步骤（8）将章盖在印台上（谢梦璇 摄）
Step（8）**Put Seal on the Ink Pad**（By Xie Mengxuan）

（9）把沾满墨水的章小心地放在白卡纸上。

（9）Stamp the seal filled with ink carefully on the white card paper.

步骤（9）把章放在白卡纸上（谢梦璇 摄）
Step (9) Stamp the Seal on the White Card Paper (By Xie Mengxuan)

(10) 拿开印章，得到成品。

(10) Take the seal off the paper.

步骤（10）篆刻成品（谢梦璇 摄）
Step (10) Take the Seal off the Paper (By Xie Mengxuan)

第四节　篆刻文化双语教案

一、教学对象

对中华文化感兴趣的外国学生。

二、教学内容

1. 篆刻的起源：凤凰授尧；
2. 篆刻的种类及当代价值体现；
3. 篆刻文化的传播与交流：贯穿古今，中西合璧；
4. 篆刻体验。

三、教学目标

1. 帮助外国学生了解篆刻的起源；
2. 帮助外国学生了解篆刻的种类及当代价值体现；
3. 帮助外国学生通过金石文化的传播及国际交流，了解从篆刻中展现出的传统高超的微雕技艺和刚柔并济的审美意境，感受中国人在方寸之中成就大事的精神；
4. 帮助外国学生学会利用橡皮章进行篆刻实践。

四、教学方法

1. 图片和视频法

利用图片和视频，结合实际与讲稿，帮助学生了解篆刻的起源、篆刻的分类和金石文化的传播；利用图片示范篆刻的动作。

2. 互动法

通过教师提问、学生回答的方式，了解学生对所教授知识的掌握程度。

3. 课堂讨论法

抛出问题，设置悬念，让学生产生思考并引导学生相互讨论，如：展示北京 2022 年冬季奥运会的图标让学生讨论各个项目的图标所代表的运动是什么。

4. 练习法

给学生布置课堂练习，通过问答、连线等题目，测试学生对篆刻文化的掌握程度。

5. 实践法

指导学生利用橡皮章体验篆刻技艺。

五、课时安排

三课时完成，每课时40分钟。

第一课时介绍篆刻的起源和种类；

第二课时介绍篆刻文化的传播、交流及古今中外对比；

第三课时介绍文化体验：学习篆刻。

六、教学过程（三课时）

第一课时（40分钟）：篆刻的起源和种类

设计意图：从凤凰授尧的故事开篇，介绍篆刻的起源和发展；同时利用图片、视频、实物等各种丰富手段介绍篆刻的不同分类，同时揭示篆刻的深刻内涵：方寸之印中，包含硬朗傲骨的书法线条、优美悦目的绘画构图、内敛细致的刀法神韵。

（一）组织教学（约2分钟）

教师进入课堂，检查多媒体设备，将教学所用的教案、课件及手工材料准备放置妥当。师生互相问候，教师点名，准备上课。

> T: Good morning, everyone! How are you today? Let's start the roll call first... Okay, everyone's here. Class begins.

（二）进入新课，介绍篆刻的起源（15分钟，内容详见双语讲稿导语）

1. 导入

（1）教师展示三幅篆刻图片，请学生欣赏并回答问题。

问题：你觉得这三幅图片好看吗？你觉得这些图案是用画笔画出来的吗？

为什么？

> T: Do you think these three designs look good? Do you think these patterns are drawn with a brush? Why?

（2）教师板书"篆刻"二字及拼音，教师领读两遍。

2. 介绍篆刻的起源：凤凰授尧的故事

（1）教师利用图片，分角色绘声绘色地介绍凤凰授尧的故事。

（2）教师就篆刻的起源进行提问，考察学生的理解程度。

问题：凤凰身上背的画作内容是什么？（答案：一只用赤玉打造的石章）

> T: What is the painting on the back of the Phoenix?

（3）教师总结篆刻起源故事内涵：其是书法、章法、刀法三者完美的结合，充满了时间的古朴和空间的浑厚。

（三）介绍篆刻的种类及当代价值体现（约22分钟，内容详见双语讲稿第一节）

1. 导入

教师展示篆刻的两组图片，请学生仔细观察这两组图片并进行比较。

问题：请大家从颜色和图案对篆刻的分类进行猜测。

> T: Please guess the classification of seal engraving from the color and pattern.

2. 介绍篆刻的种类：阴刻和阳刻、官印和私印

教师利用图片，逐一讲解阴刻和阳刻、官印和私印这两组篆刻的不同之处。

3. 篆刻与奥运

教师利用图片，请同学仔细观察并讲解篆刻和奥运的联系。

问题：大家熟悉这两张图片上的图案吗？说说它们和我们今天学习的知识有什么联系。

> T: Are you familiar with the patterns in these two pictures? Tell me how they relate to what we are learning today.

4. 练一练

教师展示篆刻相关的纪录片，请学生进行观赏和思考，以考查学生对篆刻种类的掌握和辨识。

> T: Please look at the video and guess the types of seal engraving.

（四）小结（1分钟）

教师简单回顾篆刻的起源与发展并梳理篆刻的不同分类。

第二课时（40分钟）：篆刻文化的传播、交流及古今中外对比

设计意图：利用地图和图片，介绍金石之都和艺术节；同时结合奥运图标，展示篆刻文化的创造性发展。最后从古今、中外进行对比，凸显篆刻文化的包容性和传承性。

（一）复习回顾（约5分钟）

1. 教师请学生简单复述篆刻的起源和发展。

2. 教师展示"阴刻与阳刻""官印与私印"等图片，提问学生篆刻的不同种类，并说出其显著特点。

> T: Let us briefly review the origin and development of seal engraving.
>
> T: What are the classifications of seal engraving? Can you describe their features?

（二）进入新课，介绍篆刻文化的古今传承（约 15 分钟，内容详见双语讲稿第二节）

1. 导入

教师展示中国地图，介绍潍坊市的地理位置，并提问。

问题： 大家还记得潍坊吗？它因为什么传统工艺品而闻名呢？

> T: Please look at this picture. Do you remember Weifang? What is it famous for?

2. 介绍陈介祺及潍坊陈介祺艺术节

（1）教师介绍"中国金石第一人"陈介祺其人其事。

（2）教师结合图片讲解陈介祺艺术节的流程和重要作用。

3. 练一练

教师带领学生回顾上节课所学的不同篆刻图案和奥运图标，请学生进行思考并回答，以考查学生对各类篆刻类型的掌握和辨识。

> T: Please look at these pictures and think about. What are the classifications of the seal engraving?

（三）篆刻文化的中西交流（10 分钟）

1. 教师结合图片比较中国印章和西方签名文化

2. 教师结合图片比较中西封缄技术

（四）练一练（10分钟，内容详见双语讲稿第四节）

1. 连一连
教授篆刻的不同分类方法及代表印章，请学生进行配对连线。

2. 选一选
教师编写与篆刻起源、篆刻类型以及篆刻方式相关的选择题，请学生根据教学内容进行选择并订正。

第三课时（40分钟）：学习篆刻

设计意图：通过详细教授用橡皮章进行篆刻实践的步骤，帮助学生更好地理解和体会篆刻文化。同时鼓励学生尝试创作不同的文化图案，激发学生热爱中华文化的热情。

（一）导入（2分钟）

教师展示自己制作的印章，并向学生提问。

问题：你们觉得这个印章图案好看吗？你们想不想自己学着制作一个？

> T: Do you think this seal engraving looks good? Do you want to learn to make one?

（二）文化体验：教授制作印章（30分钟，内容详见双语讲稿第三节）

1. 教师发放材料并说明注意事项。
2. 教师现场演示并结合动图，教授学生制作印章。
3. 教师请学生展示各自成品，并谈谈有什么感想。

（三）本课小结（7分钟）

1. 教师总结篆刻的起源、发展和篆刻的种类：阴刻与阳刻、官印与私印。
2. 教师总结潍坊的艺术节和奥运图标中蕴含的篆刻文化。
3. 教师总结篆刻的意义：篆刻和印章文化的现代性发展和中西交流展现了中华民族劳动人民对传统文化元素的创造性转化、创新性发展。

（四）布置作业（1分钟）

教师请学生课下试着描绘不同类型的印章并相互传递欣赏各自的印章作品。

> T: Please try to describe different types of seal engraving. And appreciate your seal works to each other.

七、教学反思

篆刻作为中国国粹之一，是书法、章法、刀法三者完美的结合，方寸之印中，包含硬朗傲骨的书法线条、优美悦目的绘画构图、内敛细致的刀法神韵，充满了时间的古朴和空间的浑厚，几经岁月更迭，却仍能以温润的光泽、古雅的韵趣，展现中国传统高超的微雕技艺和刚柔并济的审美意境。篆刻除了其本身的特色，它也体现了中国人在手工艺上持之以恒的工匠精神。因此，本课的教学应通过篆刻书法中的硬朗与温和向世界各地的人们展示中国智慧和中国精神。

潍坊不仅是风筝的故乡，还是"金石之都"。篆刻经过历史的沉淀在新时代展现出崭新的面貌。从古至今，从篆刻文化到签名文化，古老的艺术与时俱进。封缄技术的中西交流展现了劳动人民对传统文化元素的创造性转化、创新性发展。通过各类篆刻图案的展示，帮助学生认识篆刻的种类，加深学生对篆刻文化的理解；通过对当代篆刻艺术的案例呈现，帮助学生了解篆刻文化在新时代的创新发展面貌，帮助学生体悟中国的深厚文化底蕴和与时俱进的文化创新精神。

  体验环节是篆刻。在体验前，教师应说明因使用金石篆刻难度大，所以用橡皮章代替，并反复提醒学生安全使用刻刀。教师可以鼓励同学篆刻具有特色的印章，内容可以是姓名、国家、喜爱的图案等。篆刻体验能够更好地帮助学生辨识篆刻的种类，同时在方寸之间，于精雕细刻之中感受篆刻的视觉之美和力量之美。

附：辅助教学资源

  1.《中国印章》纪录片：https://v.youku.com/v_show/id_XMzE3MDQ3OTQwMA==.html。

  2.《匠心》之篆刻（优酷视频）：https://v.youku.com/v_show/id_XMTYxMzE4MTk4MA==.html。

讨论与练习
Discussion and Practice

1. 讨论
1. Discussion

（1）在你眼中，中国篆刻是什么样子的？在你的国家或者你的家乡有没有类似的？如果有，请简短描述它。

（1）In your eyes, what do you think of Chinese seal engraving? Does your country or hometown have the same kind of art? If so, please briefly introduce it.

（2）如果让你设计一枚印章，说说你的印章会是什么样子的？（材料、形制、内容、雕刻方式等）

（2）If you are going to design a seal, what does it look like?（Describe the material, shape, content, engraving method, etc.）

（3）如果你拥有了自己的印章，你会在什么场合使用它？

（3）If you have your own seal, in which situation would you like to use it?

（4）对比篆刻和普通的雕刻，它们之间有什么相同的地方？又有什么不同的地方？

（4）Comparing the seal engraving and other carving art, what are the similarities and differences between them?

2. 练习

2. Practice

（1）连一连

（1）Matching

| 形式
Form | A. 阴刻、阳刻和阴阳刻
Yin engraving, Yang engraving and Yin-Yang engraving |

| 用途
functions | B. 秦印、汉印、宋印
Qin, Han and Song Dynasties |

| 材质
Materials | C 官印和私印
Official seals and Private seals |

| 朝代
Dynasties | D. 石章和玉章
Stoneseal and jadeseal |

（2）选一选

（2）Choosing (Select the correct one from the four options)

• 皇帝专用的印章叫什么？（　　）

What do we call the emperor's seal？（　　）

A. jade seal　　　　　　　　B. bronze seal

C. imperor's jade seal　　　　　　D. stone seal

- 私印不包括以下哪一种？（　　）

Which of the following is not belong to private seals？（　　）

A. name seals　　　　　　B. pavilion seals

C. leisurely writing seals　　　　　　D. military officer seals

- 刻印凸起的刀法叫什么？（　　）

Which kind of engraving method can make a raised shape？（　　）

A. Yang engraving　　　　　　B. Yan engraving

C. Yin engraving　　　　　　D. Ying engraving

- 中国的"金石之都"在哪一座城市？（　　）

Which city in China is the capital of epigraph？（　　）

A. Dalian　　B. Weifang　　C. Chengdu　　D. Zhengzhou

答案
Answer

(1)　A　　　　C　　　　D　　　　B

(2)　C　　　　D　　　　A　　　　B

第十章 中医推拿文化双语教学设计
Chapter X Bilingual Teaching Design of Chinese Massage Culture

中医推拿（王萱 摄）
Chinese Massage (By Wang Xuan)

导语
Introduction

上古时期，我们的祖先过着十分艰苦的生活，只能依靠双手解决衣食住行等各类问题。因当时器具非常落后，人们经常在劳动中受伤。受伤后，则下意识按住伤口来止血。如遇肿胀和疼痛的情况，便通过摩擦自己手掌的方式以减轻伤情。久而久之，有人注意到这一现象，开始收集并整理相关资料，形成了原始推拿方法。中国殷商时期文献中有记载，当时的巫吏通过一些民间疗法的效果来印证自己有神力，其中就包括按摩推拿。发展到隋唐时期，推拿疗法在治疗儿童疾病时开始系统地发挥作用，人们就通过观察儿童生理结构总结出一套推拿方法，并将其命名为"子术按摩"。这就是推拿的由来，也称小儿推拿。"推拿"这一名称第一次出现在明代。清朝以后"按摩"与"推拿"在医籍中开始混用，通常在南方叫"按摩"，在北方叫"推拿"。

In ancient times, our ancestors lived a tough life. They could only rely on their hands to solve various problems such as food, clothing, housing and transportation. As a result, people often get injured while working with outdated tools. Once injured, they would subconsciously press on the wound to stop the bleeding. Also, if swelling or pain occurs, they rubbed their palms to ease the pain. Over time, some people noticed this phenomenon, then began to collect and organize relevant information, forming the oringinal massage method. According to Chinese literature from the Yin and Shang Dynasties, sorcerers used the effects of some folk remedies, including massage, to prove their divine power. In the Sui and Tang Dynasties, massage therapy played a role in the treatment of children systematically. A set of massage methods were gradually summarized by observing the physiological structure of children and named "Zi Shu Tui Na". It is the origin of massage, also known as pediatric massage. The name "Tui Na" first appeared in the Ming Dynasty. After the Qing Dynasty, "Tui Na" and "An Mo" began to be mixed in medical books. It is usually called "An Mo" in the south and "Tui Na" in the north.

第一节　推拿的手法及穴位
Section 1　Techniques and Acupoints of Massage

中医推拿向我们展示了中国古代劳动人民高超的医学水平，同时也反映了中国人民心地仁慈的道德观念。推拿正在逐步走向世界，努力发挥着更大的作用，让全世界人们都能够从中获得更多益处。中医推拿包含多种手法，并且针对不同穴位有不同疗效。

Chinese massage shows the superb medical level of ancient Chinese people and reflects Chinese people's benevolent moral concept. At the same time, the massage is gradually accepted by other countries and benefits everyone in the world. Tui Na massage involves a variety of techniques and has different effects on specific acupoints.

1. 推拿手法

推拿手法在传统中医治疗手段中十分重要。针对不同的疾病，在临床上会使用不同的推拿手法，一类是理筋类手法，一般用于缓解肩颈腰腿等软组织的疼痛；另一类是正骨类手法，主要治疗关节问题。

同时，不同的推拿流派在手法上也各有特点，主要有四种。第一种是摩擦类手法，主要用掌、指或肘贴附在体表做直线或环旋移动，包括摩法、擦法、推法、搓法等。第二种是挤压类手法，是用指、掌或肢体其他部位按压或对称挤压体表，包括按、点、压、拿、提、挤、捻等。第三种是叩击类手法，指用手掌、拳背、手指、掌侧面或桑枝棒叩打体表，包括拍法、击法、弹法等。第四种是运动关节类手法，是使关节被动活动的一类手法，包括摇法、扳法、拉法等。

1. Massage Techniques

The techniques of massage is a very important treatment of traditional Chinese medicine. For different diseases, different massage techniques will be used in clinical practice. One is the technique for treating tendon injuries, generally used to ease the pain of the soft tissue as neck, shoulder, waist and leg; the other is the bone-setting technique which mainly treats joint problems.

At the same time, different styles of massage have their own characteristics, including four main kinds of techniques. The first is the friction technique, mainly usingthe palm, fingers or elbow to rub the body surface in straight or circular lines. It includes many methods: rubbing, patting, pushing and pressing, etc.

The second is the squeezing technique, which refers to pressing or symmetrically squeezing the body surface with fingers, palms or other parts of the limbs, including pressing, tapping, holding, lifting, squeezing, twisting, etc.

The third is the percussion technique, which refers to percussion on the body surface with the palm, back of the fist, fingers, the palm's side and the mulberry stick, including slapping, beating, and bouncing.

The fourth is the technique of exercising joints. The kind of technique that makes the joint move passively. It includes methods of shaking, bending, and pulling, etc.

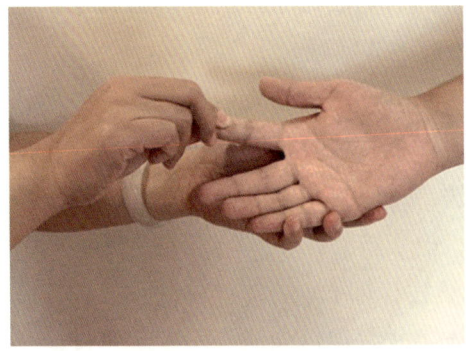

搓法（王子悦 摄）
Rubbing（By Wang Ziyue）

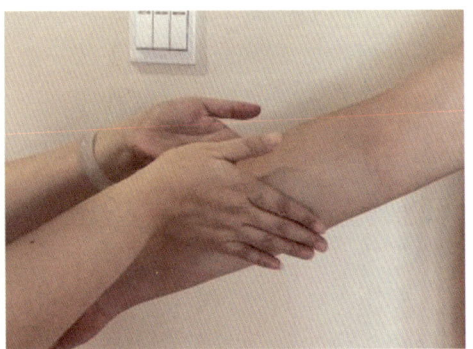

捻法（王子悦 摄）
Twisting（By Wang Ziyue）

· 第十章　中医推拿文化双语教学设计 ·

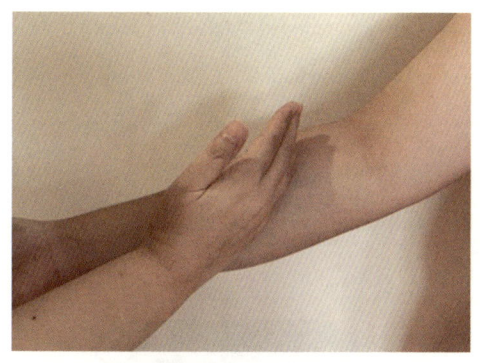

击法（王子悦 摄）
Beating（By Wang Ziyue）

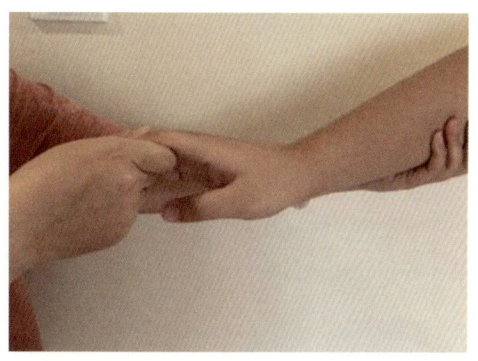

拉法（王子悦 摄）
Pulling（By Wang Ziyue）

2. 穴位

穴位，又称腧穴，是人体内各脏腑经络之气输出体表的部位。中医推拿通过推拿手法作用于人体腧穴或部位来疏通经气，恢复调节人体脏腑气血，从而达到治病的目的。一个推拿师需要掌握的穴位在 100 个左右，如腕骨、大椎、耳门、耳尖、脊中等。

其中常见穴位有迎香、大椎、足三里。迎香位于鼻翼旁 0.5 寸，鼻子和唇中间的沟中，即鼻翼外缘沟中央。这一穴位主治鼻塞、蛔虫症等。大椎位于第一颈椎与第一胸椎凸起的正中间。这一穴位主治咳嗽、气喘、头痛、癫痫。足三里位于外膝眼下三寸，胫骨外侧约一个手指头处。如出现胃痛、呕吐、噎膈、腹胀、泄泻、痢疾、便秘等症状，按摩足三里可有效缓解。

2. Acupoint

Acupoints are the parts of the human body which is the output of the Qi from the internal organs and meridians. Massage techniques are used on acupoints to regulate the Qi and blood, so as to achieve the purpose of curing diseases. A massage therapist needs to master about 100 acupoints, such as Carpal point, Dazhui, Auricular point, Erjian, Jizhong and so on.

There are some common acupoints: Yingxiang point, Dazhui and Zusanli. Yingxiang point is located 0.5 inch near the alar nose, in between the nose and the lip, and mainly used to treat nasal congestion and ascariasis. Dazhui is located the first cervical vertebra in the middle of the first thoracic protrusion. This acupoint can treat cough, asthma, headache and epilepsy. Zusanli is located three inches below the external knee and about one finger on the lateral tibia. Massaging the acupoint of Zusanli can effectively relieve symptoms like stomach pain, vomiting, diaphragm, abdominal distension, diarrhea and constipation.

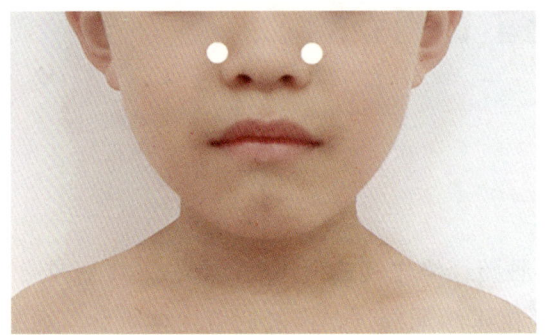

迎香穴（孙慧莉 摄）
Yingxiang Point（By Sun Huili）

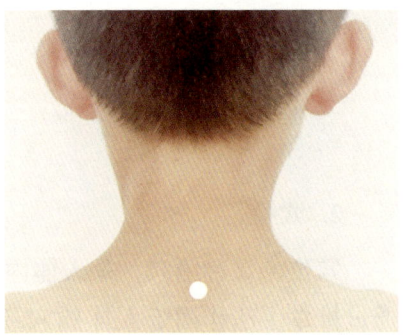

大椎穴（孙慧莉 摄）
Dazhui Point（By Sun Huili）

推拿可帮助人们恢复健康、调理身体。在中医药学中，推拿更是有着调和阴阳、补虚泻实、活血化瘀、疏经通络、理筋整络等作用。调和阴阳指让人体处于一种平衡的状态，以免出现湿气太重或阳气太旺的情况。补虚泻实则是补充人体正气、排除有余邪气。活血化瘀起到的是综合调理的作用，可以调整脏腑功能，疏通血管。

Massage can help people keep healthy and nourish their bodies. In traditional Chinese medicine, the role of massage is adjusting Yin and Yang, which can keep the body in a balanced state; treating deficiency and excess of Qi; promoting blood circulation and removing blood stasis, which can adjust the function of viscera organs and dredge blood vessels; dredging channels and collaterals, and strengthening and rectifying collaterals.

第二节　奥运会上神秘的东方力量：推拿走向世界

Section 2　The Mysterious Oriental Power at the Olympics：Massage is Going to the World

在 2020 东京奥运会和 2022 北京冬奥会上，各国运动健儿在奥运赛场上奋勇拼搏，为祖国赢得荣誉。在这些荣誉的背后，除了运动员自身的努力，更离不开背后团队的共同付出，尤其是队医和医疗保障人员，而推拿正是他们必备的"绝活"。

In the 2020 Tokyo Olympic and 2022 Beijing Winter Olympics Games, athletes from all over the world countries did their best to win the honors of their motherlands. In addition to the athlete's efforts, These honors couldn't have been achieved without the joint efforts of the support team behind the scene, especially the team doctors and medical personnel. Massage is their necessary skills.

在 2020 东京奥运会上，中国运动员苏炳添在田径百米半决赛中跑出了 9.83s 的成绩，成为首个进入百米决赛的亚洲选手，这一成绩也创造了新的亚洲纪录。苏炳添身边的按摩师朱志伟功不可没，无论是在赛场还是在酒店，他总是随时携带一张折叠按摩椅，时刻准备为苏炳添进行推拿放松。正因如此，苏炳添才能保持良好状态参加比赛。

推拿的身影在 2020 东京奥运会处处可见，50 米步枪三姿冠军张常鸿、获得七金一银的中国举重队队员等在赛前都接受了队医的推拿按摩，一枚枚来之不易的奖牌背后凝聚着队医的辛苦汗水。来自东方的神秘力量再次于奥运会上展现风采。

Su Bingtian from China set a new Asian record of 9.83s in the semifinals of the 100 meters in the 2020 Tokyo Olympic Games. Undeniably, his masseur Zhu Zhiwei played an important role. No matter in the stadium or in the hotel, Zhu Zhiwei always carried a foldable massage chair and was ready to give Su Bingtian a massage at any time. Therefore, Su Bingtian could keep in good condition to participate in the competition.

Massage can be seen everywhere in the 2020 Tokyo Olympic Games. Zhang Changhong, the Champion of the 50m Rifle Three Positions, and the Chinese weightlifting team which won seven gold medals and one silver medal, were both received the massage from the medical staff before the game. The Olympic medals are supported by the hard work of the team doctors. The mysterious power of the Chinese traditional massage has once again demonstrated its charm in the Olympic Games.

推拿不仅在国内广受欢迎,在海外也被越来越多的人所接受。2016年的里约奥运会上,31岁的美国老将菲尔普斯第五次走进奥运游泳赛场,并在当届奥运会中斩获了三金一银,同时也成为奥运会历史上获得最多金牌和奖牌的游泳运动员。除了引人瞩目的成绩,菲尔普斯身上的红印更受到西方记者的关注和热议,这一红印正是拔火罐和推拿留下的印记。菲尔普斯作为一名享誉世界的奥运冠军,平时享受着全球最前沿、最先进的运动医学护理,然而他却对推拿这一中国式治疗和恢复手段"情有独钟"。菲尔普斯在媒体采访中表示自己过去两三年一直在拔火罐和推拿,并认为推拿很有效果,因为这可以使他酸痛的肌肉得到放松。对他来说,拔火罐和推拿是最适合自己的恢复方式。随后,在菲尔普斯的《*Rule Yourself*》宣传片中也出现了拔火罐和推拿的镜头。

在菲尔普斯的带动下,美国游泳队员甚至是一些影视明星都开始尝试推拿。种种迹象都表明推拿已经开始走向世界,正向世人展现它独一无二的魅力。在2020东京奥运会上,不难发现越来越多的外国运动员用中国的推拿进行放松,如澳大利亚游泳名将查尔莫斯、日本运动员南场昭。比赛时他们身上的印记无疑再次验证了中医推拿的魅力。

Massage is not only popular in China but also accepted by more and more people overseas. At the 2016 Rio Olympics Game, it was the fifth time that Michael Phelps, the 31-year-old veteran, entered the Olympic swimming competition. He won three gold medals and one silver medal in this Olympics Game and became the one who won the most gold medals and the most medalsin the history of Olympic Games. In addition to the remarkable achievements, the red marks on Phelps's body attracted the attention of western journalists. The red mark on Phelps'body was left by the cupping and massage. As a world-renowned Olympic champion, Phelps usually enjoys the most cutting-edge and advanced sports medicine care in the world. However, he shows a special preference for Namassage, the Chinese-style treatment and recovery method. In an interview, Phelps said that he had been having cupping and massage for two or three years. He believed that massage was very effective because it could relax his sore muscles. Cupping and massage were the most suitable recovery methods for him. Phelps's "Rule Yourself" promotional film also showed cupping and massage.

Because of him, the United States Swimming team and even some film and television stars have begun to try Namassage. All the signs show that massage has begun to go to the world and is showing its unique charm to the world. In the 2020 Tokyo Olympic Games, it is not difficult to find more foreign athletes using Chinese massage to relax, like the Australian swimmer Chalmers and the Japanese athlete Akira Minamiba. The marks on their bodies during the competition undoubtedly confirmed the charm of massage once again.

推拿是中医学下的一个重要分支，而中医是中国传统文化的重要组成部分，中国古代的"天人合一"观念，直接铸就了中医学的基本框架，中医侧重增强人体自身对抗疾病的能力，其治疗原则处处都体现了中国古代的哲学思想。如今，越来越多的外国人愿意去了解推拿，并用推拿进行治疗。这有利于推动中医文化走向世界、走向现代化，中华文化得到了进一步传播，其影响力也在扩大。

Massage is one of the significant branches of traditional Chinese medicine, and traditional Chinese medicine is an important part of traditional Chinese culture. The ancient Chinese view of the "unity of man and nature" directly decides the basic framework of traditional Chinese medicine. Traditional Chinese medicine tends to strengthen people's ability to fight disease. Its treating principles reflect the ancient Chinese philosophy everywhere. Nowadays, more and more people from other countries are willing to learn about massage and use it to treat diseases. This is conducive to promote traditional Chinese medicine culture to the world and become more modernized. Chinese culture has been further disseminated and its influence expanded.

第三节　推拿的体验
Section 3　Let's Try Massage

1. 步骤

1. Steps

（1）捣小天心

小天心穴位位于手掌根部手掌外侧肌肉和内侧肌肉相接的地方。用捣或者掐的手法按摩。

（1）Pounding the acupoint of Xiaotianxin

The acupoint of Xiaotianxin is located at the bottom of the palm and is the join of palm lateral muscle and internal muscle. Use the finger pounding or pinching this acupoint.

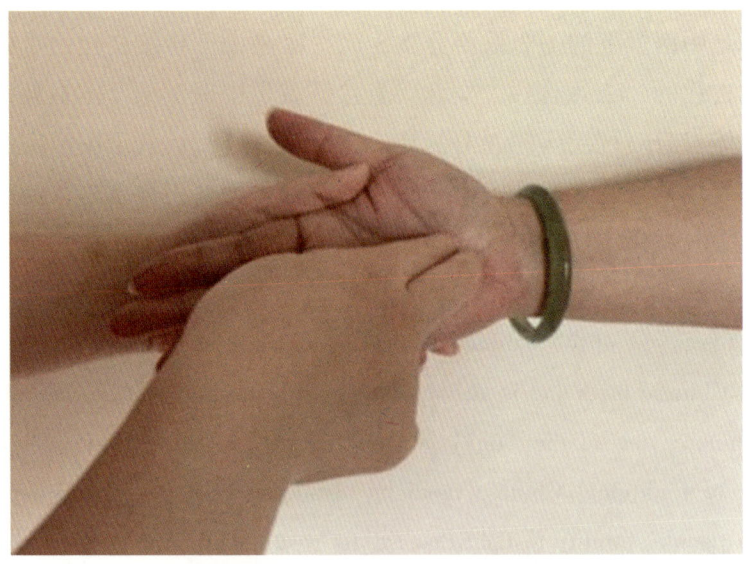

步骤（1）捣小天心（王子悦 摄）

Step（1）Pounding the Acupoint of Xiaotianxin（By Wang Ziyue）

（2）揉足三里

足三里位于外膝眼下三寸，胫骨外侧约一横指处。用揉或敲的手法按摩。

(2) Rubbing the acupoint of Zusanli

The acupoint of Zusanli is located three inches below the external knee. It's about one finger long below the knee on the outer side of the leg. You can use your fingers rubbing or tapping this acupoint.

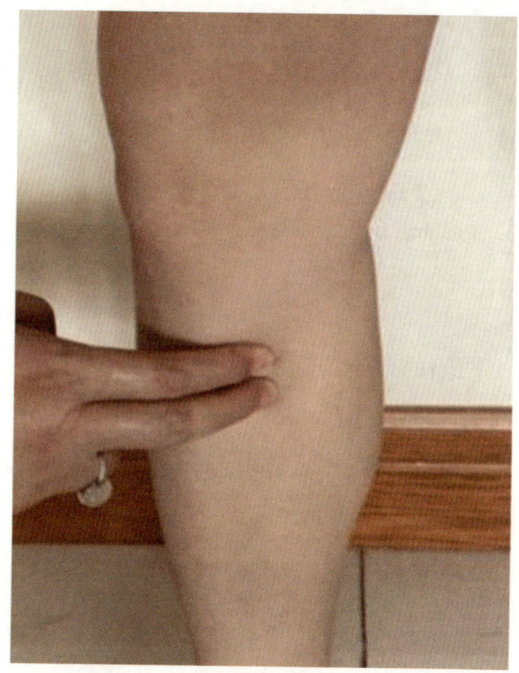

步骤（2）揉足三里（王子悦 摄）
Step (2) Rubbing the Acupoint of Zusanli (By Wang Ziyue)

（3）清大肠

食指内侧是大肠穴，从指根推向指尖就是清大肠。用推的手法按摩。

(3) Pushing the acupoint of Dachang

The inner side of the index finger is the acupoint of Dachang. Pushing Dachang means pushing from the root of the finger to the fingertips.

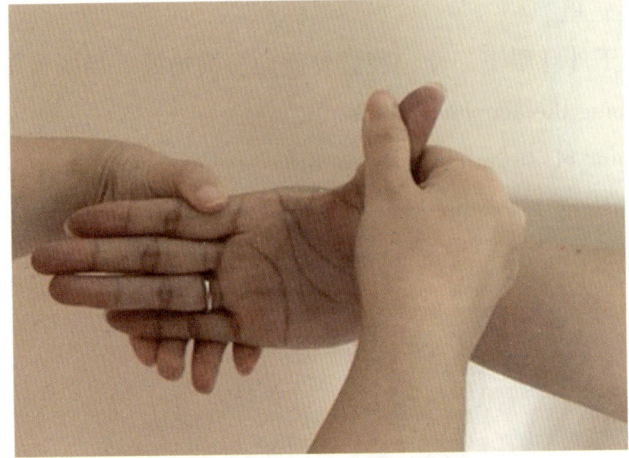

步骤（3）清大肠（王子悦 摄）

Step（3）Pushing the Acupoint of Dachang（By Wang Ziyue）

（4）拿肩井

拿肩井位于肩上凹陷的地方。用拿的手法按摩。

（4）Holding the acupoint of Jianjing

The acupoint of Jianjing（shoulder well）is located in the dent of the shoulder. Use your fingers holding this acupoint.

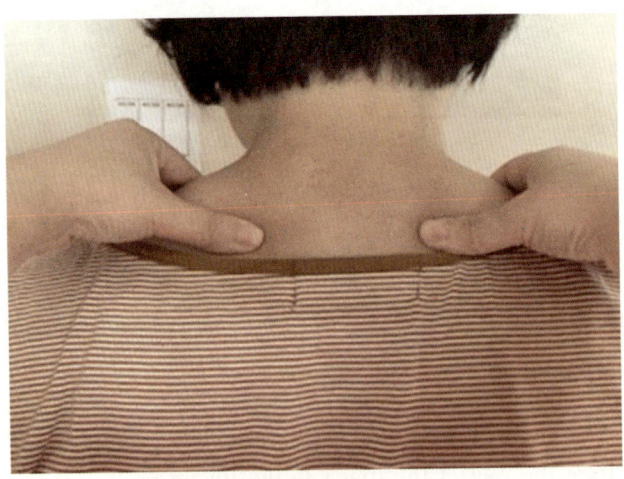

步骤（4）拿肩井（王子悦 摄）

Step（4）Holding the Acupoint of the Shoulder Well（By Wang Ziyue）

第十章　中医推拿文化双语教学设计

（5）捏挤大椎

大椎穴位于第一颈椎与第一胸椎棘突间正中处。用捏的手法按摩。

(5) Kneading the acupoint of Dazhui

The acupoint of Dazhui is located in the middle of the first cervical vertebra and the first thoracic vertebra. Use your fingers kneading this acupoint.

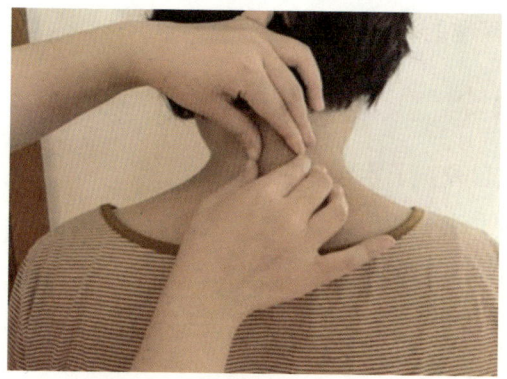

步骤（5）捏挤大椎（王子悦 摄）

Step（5）Kneading the Acupoint of Dazhui（By Wang Ziyue）

（6）拿风池

风池穴位于头后面与耳垂平行的两个地方。用拿的手法按摩。

(6) Holding the acupoint of Fengchi

The acupoint of Fengchi is behind the head andat two places parallel to the earlobes. Use your fingers holding this acupoint.

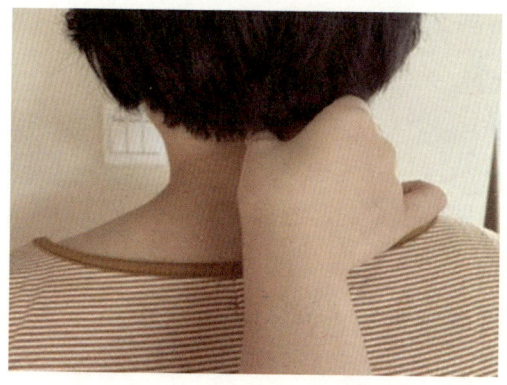

步骤（6）拿风池（王子悦 摄）

Step（6）Holding the acupoint of Fengchi（By Wang Ziyue）

第四节　中医推拿文化双语教案

一、教学对象

对中华文化感兴趣的外国学生。

二、教学内容

1. 中医推拿的起源：子术按摩；
2. 中医推拿的手法和穴位；
3. 推拿在奥运会上的运用；
4. 体验推拿。

三、教学目标

1. 帮助外国学生了解中医推拿的起源；
2. 帮助外国学生了解并体验中医推拿的穴位和手法；
3. 帮助外国学生理解中国人民自古以来的医学智慧以及美好心愿：对幸福安宁生活的向往，对和谐美满家庭的期盼，对健康强健身体的追求以及与此有关的温情、崇尚、健康与和谐的传统价值观；
4. 帮助外国学生体会到中医里的阴阳调和观，尊重自然热爱自然的美好品质。

四、教学方法

1. 图片法

利用图片向学生展示推拿的起源以及穴位、手法。

2. 演示法

通过演示法，指导学生找到穴位。

3. 互动法

通过教师提问、学生回答的方式，请学生根据课堂内容回答推拿治疗疾病的相关问题。

4. 启发诱导法

启发学生总结对推拿内涵的认识，展现推拿的中国精神。

五、课时安排

三课时完成，每课时 40 分钟。
第一课时介绍推拿的起源、手法和穴位。
第二课时介绍推拿在海内外的运用与传播。
第三课时介绍推拿的体验。

六、教学过程（三课时）

第一课时（40 分钟）：推拿的起源、手法和穴位

设计意图：从子术按摩的故事开篇，介绍推拿的起源；同时利用图片和视频介绍推拿的手法和穴位，揭示推拿的深刻内涵；不仅向我们展示了中国古代劳动人民高超的医学水平，也反映了中国人民心地仁慈的道德观念。

（一）组织教学（约 2 分钟）

教师进入课堂，检查多媒体设备，将教学所用的教案、课件及手工材料准备放置妥当。师生互相问候，教师点名，准备上课。

> T: Good morning, everyone! How are you today? Let's start the roll call first... Okay, everyone's here. Class begins.

（二）进入新课，介绍中医推拿的起源（15 分钟，内容详见双语讲稿导语）

1. 导入

（1）教师展示推拿相关图片，请学生观察并回答问题。

问题：你知道图片中的人在干什么吗？你是否有过类似的经历呢？

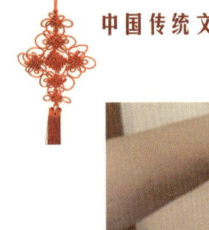

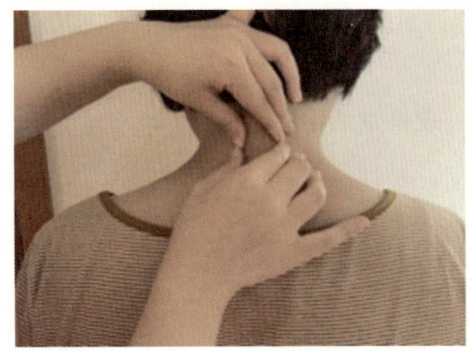 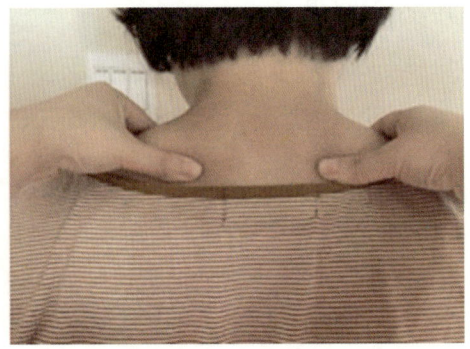

> T: Do you know what the person in the picture is doing? Have you ever had a similar experience?

（2）教师板书"推拿"二字及拼音，教师领读两遍。

2. 介绍推拿的起源：子术按摩的故事

（1）教师利用图片，分角色绘声绘色地介绍子术按摩的故事。

（2）教师就推拿的起源进行提问，考察学生的理解程度。

问题：子术按摩在古代又被称为什么？（答案：小儿按摩）

> T: What was Zi Shu Tui Na called in ancient times?

（3）教师总结推拿起源故事内涵：不仅展示了中国古代劳动人民高超的医学水平，同时也反映了中国人民心地仁慈的道德观念。推拿正在慢慢地走向世界，它努力地发挥着更大的作用，让全世界的人们都能够从中获得更多的益处。

（三）介绍推拿的手法：摩擦类、挤压类、叩击类和运动关节类（约12分钟，内容详见双语讲稿第一节）

1. 导入

教师展示四幅图片，请学生仔细观察并进行比较。

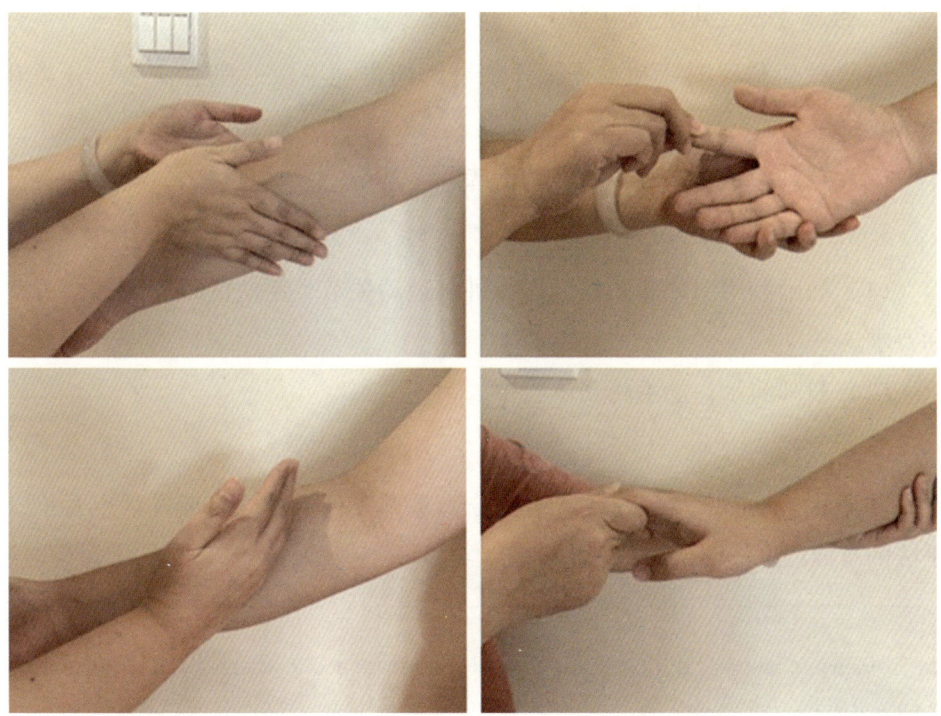

T: Please observe the four pictures above carefully. Who can learn the techniques on the pictures? What are differences?

2. 推拿手法之摩擦类手法

（1）教师利用图片和动作，详细讲解摩擦类手法的概念命名、分类和要求。

（2）教师演示，学生相互体验搓法。

3. 推拿手法之挤压类手法

（1）教师利用图片和动作，详细讲解挤压类手法的概念命名、分类和要求。

（2）教师演示，学生相互体验捻法。

4. 推拿手法之叩击类手法

(1) 教师利用图片和动作,详细讲解叩击类手法的概念命名、分类和要求。

(2) 教师演示,学生相互体验击法。

5. 推拿手法之运动关节类手法

(1) 教师利用图片和动作,详细讲解运动关节类手法的概念命名、分类和要求。

(2) 教师演示,学生相互体验拉法。

6. 练一练

教师演示四个推拿手法,请学生分辨是哪一种手法,以考查学生对推拿手法的掌握程度。

> T: Please observe the movement carefully and think about what kind of technique it is?

(四)介绍推拿的穴位:迎香、大椎、足三里(约10分钟,内容详见双语讲稿第一节)

1. 导入

教师展示拔火罐的照片,请学生思考拔火罐与穴位的联系。

> T: When you cupping, can you just put it on your back? Are there any strict acupoint requirements? What acupoints do you know?

2. 推拿穴位之迎香

教师利用图片和视频,详细讲解迎香的位置和疗效。

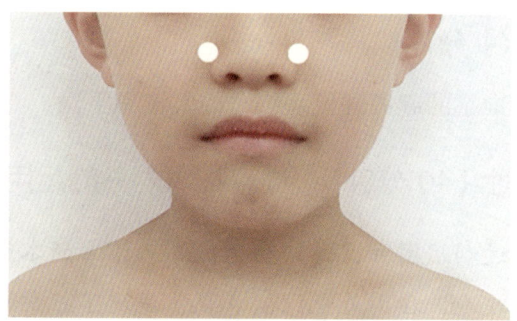

3. 推拿穴位之大椎

教师利用图片和视频,详细讲解大椎的位置和疗效。

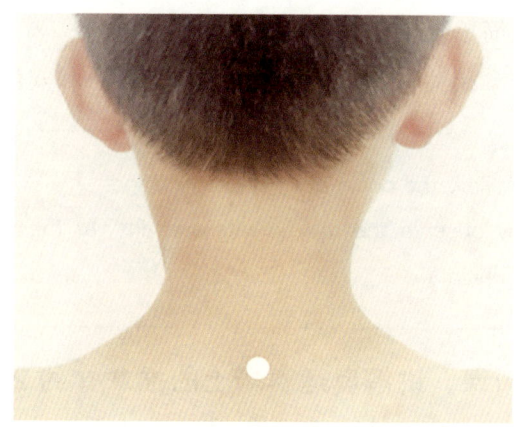

4. 推拿穴位之足三里

教师利用图片和视频,详细讲解足三里的位置和疗效。

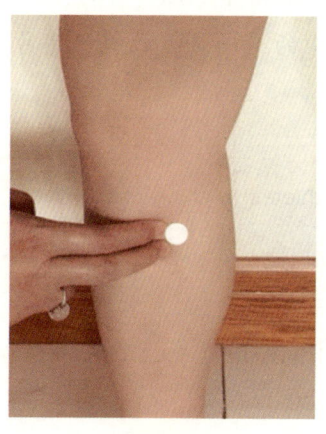

中国传统文化体验式双语教学设计

（五）小结（1分钟）

教师简单回顾推拿的起源并梳理推拿的穴位和手法。

第二课时（40分钟）：推拿在海内外的运用与传播

设计意图：通过利用图片，介绍奥运健儿和推拿的不解之缘；重点突出推拿不仅在国内受欢迎，在国外也深受喜爱，体现了推拿文化凭借自己的魅力走出国门、走向世界，凸显如今世界各地的人民对健康体魄的重视。

（一）复习回顾（约5分钟）

1. 教师请学生简单复述中医推拿的起源故事。
2. 教师演示推拿相关动作，提问学生推拿的手法和穴位。

> T: Let us briefly review the origin of Chinese massage.
> T: Please carefully observe the movements and answer the specific massage techniques and acupoints.

（二）进入新课，讲解奥运赛场上的推拿（约25分钟，内容详见双语讲稿第三节）

1. 导入

教师展示两张运动员体验推拿的照片，并提问。

问题：大家知道图片中的运动员是谁吗？图片中的他们正在或曾经体验过什么吗？

> T: Do you know these athletes in the picture? What are they experiencing or have experienced?

2. 介绍奥运运动员和推拿的不解之缘

（1）中国运动员和推拿

教师结合图片介绍中国运动员对推拿的热爱。

（2）外国运动员和推拿

教师结合图片介绍外国运动员对推拿的热爱。

问题：大家仔细看一看想一想。这三幅图有什么共同之处呢？

> T：Let's take a closer look and think about it. What do the three pictures have in common?

3. 教师总结

教师就推拿逐渐走向世界进行总结，帮助学生更好地理解中医的重要性：推拿是中医学下的一个重要分支，而中医是中国传统文化的重要组成部分。中国古人"天人合一"的观念，直接铸就了中医学的基本框架，中医偏向于增强人自身对抗疾病的能力，其治疗原则处处都体现了中国古代的哲学思想。

（三）练一练（10分钟，内容详见双语讲稿第四节）

1. 抢答题

教师展示与推拿起源、手法、类型有关的问题，请学生进行抢答。

2. 判断题

教师编写与推拿起源、推拿穴位以及推拿手法相关的判断题，请学生根据教学内容判断正误。

第三课时（40分钟）：体验推拿

设计意图：通过详细教授各种穴位的位置，帮助学生更好地理解和体会推拿文化。在了解基础穴位的基础之上，能够独自或合作完成一系列的按摩动作，激发学生对中医推拿文化的浓厚兴趣。

（一）导入（2分钟）

教师展示人体穴位图，并向学生提问。

问题：你们是否想自己也学习一些按摩手法，帮助自己缓解不舒适的感觉呢？

> T: Do you want to learn some massage techniques to help you relieve uncomfortable feelings?

（二）文化体验：推拿穴位体验（30分钟，内容详见双语讲稿第三节）

1. 教师现场演示并结合动图，教授学生具体推拿穴位。
2. 教师请学生互相按摩，并谈谈有什么感受。

（三）本课小结（7分钟）

1. 教师总结推拿的起源和推拿的手法和穴位。
2. 教师总结推拿在奥运赛场的重要作用。
3. 教师总结推拿的意义：推拿作为中医治疗方式的代表，凭借自身蕴含着的智慧逐渐被全世界的人民喜爱和追求，并且推拿也展示了人们对健康、和平、美好生活的祝愿。

（四）布置作业（1分钟）

教师请学生课下试着给自己的好朋友进行一次推拿体验。

> T: Please try to massage your good friend after class!

七、教学反思

中医是中国传统文化的重要组成部分，推拿则是中医学下的一个重要分支，它通过刺激体表或体表的穴位来达到增强体质、防病养生等目的。如今，中医和推拿不仅在国内被广泛应用，在国际上的影响也渐盛。有很多海外国家都派人来中国学习推拿，用推拿手法来治疗疾病的方式正逐渐被世界认可并加以重视。

本课教学应通过大量丰富图片或视频的展示向学生介绍推拿的手法和穴位，同时灵活运用互动法，帮助学生更好地参与课堂，更好地掌握推拿的各种知识。在学习中外健儿与推拿的联系时，应帮助学生准确把握推拿在体育赛事中的重要性，从而体现中医传承和交流的时代需要。

体验环节是体验推拿，体验过程中需合作完成，教师应组织好课堂秩序，保证教学有条不紊地进行。

附：辅助教学资源

1. 大椎穴：https：//haokan. baidu. com/v？pd＝wisenatural&vid＝7429277341828780749。

2. 足三里：https：//v. qq. com/x/page/j0500b79f5b. html。

3. 迎香：https：//haokan. baidu. com/v？pd＝wisenatural&vid＝8458399515636220774（定位第10秒开始）。

讨论与练习
Discussion and Practice

1. 讨论
1. Discussion

（1）你们接触过或者看过别人推拿吗？你们觉得它是什么样的？你们家乡或者国家也有推拿吗？又是什么样的？

（1）Have you ever had or seen massage? How was it? Does your country or hometown have massage? What's that like?

（2）你觉得中医推拿为什么能够走出中国，走向世界？

（2）Why do you think Tui Na massage can go beyond China to the world?

（3）针对摩擦类、挤压类、叩击类、运动关节类推拿手法，你对哪种推拿方式的印象更深刻，为什么？你喜欢哪种推拿方式呢？

（3）Among friction, squeezing, percussion and joint exercising techniques, which kind of massage techniques impresses you most? Why? Which kind do you like most?

（4）如果让你接受按摩，说说你想重点按摩什么身体部位呢？为什么？

(4) If you can receive one kind of massage, which body parts do you want to be massaged? Why?

2. 练习

2. Practice

（1）抢答题

(1) Quick Response Questions

①子术按摩是通过观察哪类人群的身体结构总结出的一套推拿方法？

①Whose body structure was observed for developing Zi Shu massage (pediatric massage)?

②奥运会期间苏炳添进行的哪种推拿？

②What kind of massage did Su Bingtian receive during the Olympic Games?

③老师最近觉得疲劳，腰很酸痛，应该进行哪种推拿？

③ Recently the teacher feels tired and the waist is very sore. What kind of massage should receive?

④如果一个老人常年腰椎间盘突出，应该进行哪种推拿？

④If an old man has lumbar disc protrusion, which massage should be carried out?

（2）判断题（正确为 T，错误为 F）

(2) True or False Questions

①不是所有的人群都适合进行推拿。

①Not all the people are suitable for massage.

②风池穴用推的手法按摩。

②Massage Fengchi acupoint by pushing.

③李文把胳膊摔伤了，他想用医疗推拿来治疗。

③Li Wen hurt his arm and he wanted to treat it by massage.

④图片上是捻法推拿。

④This is a picture of the twisting technique.

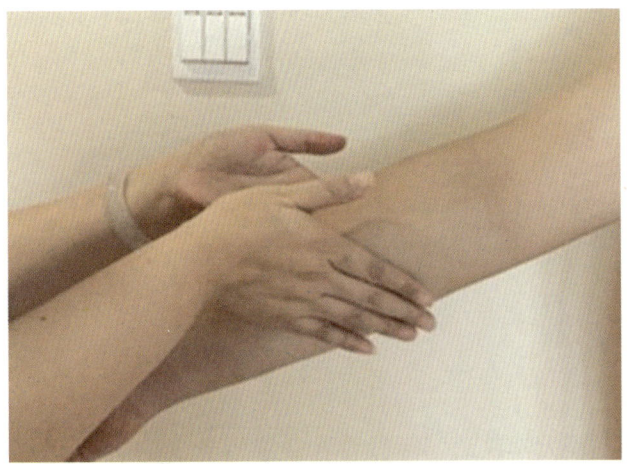

答案
Answer

(1)

①小儿　　　　　The child
②运动推拿　　　Sports Massage
③保健按摩　　　Healthcare Massage
④医疗按摩　　　Medical Massage

(2)

①T　　　　②F　　　　③F　　　　④F

后 记

南京信息工程大学汉语国际教育专业肇始于 2007 年，是江苏省较早开设汉语国际教育专业的高等院校之一。2013 年专业大纲修订，"双语教学理论与实践"写入汉语国际教育专业教学运行计划，后更名为"传统文化体验与双语传播实践"。自此，我们用近十年的时间不懈探索和打磨该课程的教学内容和教学模式。

打造精品课程、培养优秀人才、服务国家需求，是我们为之奋斗的初心；使汉语国际教育专业学生成为中华文化的传播者、中国故事的讲述者和践行者是我们勇于登攀的目标，为此，我们对课程内容进行反复凝练、对教学方法和模式不断探讨，最终将《中国传统文化体验式双语教学设计》集结成册。

《中国传统文化体验式双语教学设计》凝结着师生的共同心血：王萱、黄婧瑶、贺艳珠、葛瑞彤、游艺涵、曾可欣、方霖菲、赵银莹、张嘉好、乔龙妍、陈静、蒋颖琪、陈瑶、占丽雯、赵美琪、殷圣赢、谢梦璇、王子悦、薛瑞、俞梦涵、区凯欣、陈文慧、张琪琦、季彦等同学为本书的体验设计提供了丰富多彩的原创图片和文字；新西兰坎特伯雷大学的程梦娉博士受邀对教材的英文部分进行了校订。

我们希望这本教材能为汉语国际教育专业"传统文化体验与双语传播实践"课程的建设和改革提供思路，也希望该教材能够抛砖引玉，为汉语国际教育专业师生探索如何更好地传播中华优秀文化提供有益尝试。

编者

2022 年 6 月

于南京信息工程大学